Reimagining democratic societies

A new era of personal and social responsibility

Sjur Bergan, Ira Harkavy
and Hilligje van't Land (eds)

Council of Europe Publishing

Cover design: Documents and Publications Production Department (SPDP), Council of Europe
Layout: Jouve, Paris

Council of Europe Publishing
F-67075 Strasbourg Cedex
http://book.coe.int

ISBN 978-92-871-7537-3
© Council of Europe, January 2013
Printed at the Council of Europe

Contents

Introduction

1. A word from the Council of Europe's Director General for Democracy

As the Council of Europe's Director General for Democracy, I am proud to invite you to read this collection of essays on reimagining democratic societies.

The subtitle "A new era of personal and social responsibility" emphasises that we all have a democratic duty as individuals and that we also carry responsibility together as societies. This is very much in line with the Council of Europe's political priorities of democracy, human rights and the rule of law, as well as our emphasis on the need for intercultural dialogue.

The double focus on individuals and institutions is also that of higher education, which is the topic of this book. Higher education prepares a large proportion of our citizens of tomorrow and even of today. Few will dispute that preparation for citizenship is an important purpose of education and this is reflected in many education laws. However, the public discourse on education is – at least in Europe – very strongly focused on another of its purposes: preparation for the labour market. Another fairly commonly held view – again, at least in many European countries – is that general education stops at age 17 or 18, with graduation from secondary school, hence the idea that students in higher education should focus on "their subject". Put these two attitudes together and defining the role that higher education could and should play in reimagining our democratic future becomes something of a challenge.

This is one reason why this book is important. Higher education is essential not only in developing our economy but in shaping our society. Higher education must fulfil all its major purposes as defined by the Council of Europe:

- preparation for sustainable employment;
- preparation for life as active citizens in democratic societies;
- personal development;
- development and maintenance, through research, teaching and learning, of a broad, advanced knowledge base. [1]

Higher education institutions must fulfil these purposes through teaching and research as well as through their role as societal actors. The book makes the case why higher education needs to engage in favour of democracy and provides many innovative examples of how this can be done.

Our democratic institutions were developed through a long and sometimes painful process. They are essential to our democracies, but they will continue to serve us

---

1. Recommendation Rec(2007)6 of the Committee of Ministers to member states on the public responsibility for higher education and research.

well only on two conditions. Firstly, institutions and structures must be underpinned by the set of attitudes and behaviours that the Council of Europe has labelled "democratic culture". Secondly, structures and institutions must evolve as society evolves or they will risk becoming less and less relevant. Modern societies are characterised by a multitude of actors, with different and often highly specific agendas, and a multitude of arenas in which influence is exercised, ranging from elections to social media. Democracy can only thrive if, as societies, we are able to take a coherent view of the way we should develop and if we can combine a view of what needs to be done in the short term with a vision of where we need to go in the longer term.

Thought of in this way, the case for democratic innovation is easy to make. We need not only to imagine but – as the title of this book says – to reimagine. That is perhaps more difficult: imagining on a blank sheet of paper is difficult enough, but reimagining and adapting what already exists and is part of our democratic identity is infinitely more difficult. Who could be better placed to engage in an exercise in democratic innovation and reimagination than the university community?

I would like to thank all the authors who share with us their experiences and ideas – and indeed their imagination – through this book. I would like to thank our friends and colleagues in the US Steering Committee of the International Consortium for Higher Education, Civic Responsibility and Democracy for their close co-operation over more than a decade, which has helped the US and European experiences to meet. I would like to thank the International Association of Universities (IAU) for helping us look beyond Europe and North America towards a global perspective and for a shared commitment to the proposition that higher education is about developing society and individuals as well as the economy. The European Wergeland Centre, the University of Oslo and the Norwegian authorities were key partners in the conference that gave inspiration for this book and I would like to extend my sincere gratitude to all of them. I am grateful and proud that this result of a co-operation between several partners is published in the Council of Europe higher education series. As the 18th volume in the series, this book confirms the position of our series as a forum for thinking seriously and innovatively about higher education in modern societies.

It gives me particular pleasure to thank the editors – Ira Harkavy of the International Consortium, Hilligje van't Land of the IAU and my Council of Europe colleague Sjur Bergan – who have not only brought the authors and their essays together but turned them into a coherent argument for democratic culture and innovation, and the role of higher education in shaping it.

I hope reading this book will not only be an enjoyable experience but also will stimulate the imagination of readers and encourage them to contribute to reimagining democratic societies.

Snežana Samardžić-Marković
Director General for Democracy
Council of Europe

2. A word from the Executive Director of the European Wergeland Centre

According to the Council of Europe, one of the key tasks of higher education is to prepare students for life as active citizens in democratic society. In order to become active citizens, students need to acquire competences that include not only skills and knowledge but also attitudes, dispositions and values. These competences need to be taught and learnt throughout life.

However, in recent years, higher education institutions have been under pressure to act as production centres, delivering skilled graduates able to adapt to the quickly changing needs of the economy. One could argue that less emphasis has been put on preparing future citizens for quickly changing social and political realities. In order to prepare students for life as active citizens in democratic society, higher education institutions need democratic development within their own walls and a systematic involvement outside, in other words, interaction between the institutions and the societies in which they function. Interaction means, for example, the way transfer of theoretical and empirical knowledge can be enriched when teacher training institutions listen carefully to educational professionals and learn from their practice at grassroots level. Furthermore, specific structures that encourage community focus and education for democracy should be developed to improve the opportunities for students to work in their local communities. Along the same lines, schemes for participation in international mobility programmes increase students' general competences, raise awareness and understanding of different cultures and encourage students to reflect on their own background, experiences and context.

Within the education system, higher education institutions have a special responsibility. To quote Ira Harkavy, from Chapter 6 in this book: "[higher education institutions] play a pre-eminent role in shaping the schooling system, notably through the education of teachers". Accordingly, teacher training institutions should pay particular attention to: 1. the role of teachers in promoting an increased sense of civic responsibility; 2. their own responsibility in equipping these teachers with the necessary skills, attitudes and knowledge to fulfil this role; and 3. exploring and implementing types of partnership across educational institutions and local communities that might promote change and reinforce democratic culture.

In a culturally diverse Europe faced by rapidly changing economic, social and political realities, education professionals, especially teachers, are confronted every day by the big questions of a changing society: the frustration of the present economic crisis and its consequences in students' homes and families; heated debate about immigration, rights and responsibilities and social exclusion; issues of diversity, identity and equal opportunities, and much more. The role of education professionals is paramount: they are entrusted with preparing children and other young persons to live and participate in a diverse society, supporting their individual, social and civic development.

Participation in democratic society is closely connected to education at all levels, including higher education. When looking to the civic participation of young people in Europe, we can observe a general disenchantment with politics and democratic institutions, with many refraining from traditional political participation. In parallel, there is a rising number of new ways of involvement in politics and society (such as the use of new media, as witnessed in Russia or the Arab Spring, and every day in most countries), which broaden the concept of participation. Political opinions are developed through new as well as traditional media, and opinion leaders are no longer only a relatively limited group of people in well-established positions. Research shows that political involvement is highly dependent on access to education (in its widest sense). Young people with little access to education remain partly excluded from political processes and thus from active participation. Access to quality education is a key to democracy.

These aspects were closely scrutinised at the conference Reimagining Democratic Societies: A New Era of Personal and Social Responsibility?, which took place in June 2011 in Oslo. Within the framework of the University of Oslo's 200th anniversary celebrations, the European Wergeland Centre had the pleasure of hosting the conference, together with the university, the Council of Europe and the US Steering Committee of the International Consortium for Higher Education, Civic Responsibility and Democracy. The conference aimed to provide a forum specifically to reflect on a new and strengthened democratic agenda for higher education, focusing on its strategic role in building sustainable democratic development. This book arises from the conference and some chapters build on presentations made in Oslo. Some chapters, however, have been written especially for this book, so what you are about to read is not a repeat of what was heard in Oslo but rather an important step beyond the conference.

It was fitting that this event took place in Norway, which, as one of the founding members of the Council of Europe, has always been committed to developing the key role of education in the promotion of democratic citizenship and human rights. As a result of this commitment, and as an innovative joint initiative by the Council of Europe and Norway, the European Wergeland Centre (EWC) was established in 2008. It encourages capacity-building activities and research and development in the whole field of education for intercultural understanding, human rights and democratic citizenship.

With its core target group being teacher trainers, teachers and other educational practitioners (in formal and informal learning), the EWC's activities have from the beginning been informed by the idea of creating links between higher education institutions and the communities in which they are located. With its twin focus on capacity-building for educators and on research and development, the EWC deeply shares the vision that higher education institutions can play a vital role in building tomorrow's sustainable democracies by educating tomorrow's responsible citizens.

I am therefore proud to introduce this book on *Reimagining democratic societies* and I hope and trust that readers will find it both enriching and inspiring.

Ana Perona-Fjeldstad
Executive Director
The European Wergeland Centre

3. A word from the editors

Sjur Bergan, Ira Harkavy and Hilligje van 't Land

You are about to read a collection of essays on the role of higher education in reimagining democratic societies. This seemingly simple sentence raises several issues that will be explored in the book.

The question that immediately comes to mind is perhaps why we would need to "reimagine" democracy. Does not democracy work well as it is? And – as the saying goes – "if it ain't broke, don't fix it".

At one level, democracy does work well in Europe and North America, the places where most contributors to this book come from. Almost without exception, governments in Europe and North America are elected and, even though there are always margins for improvement, elections are for the most part open and fair. The one obvious exception – Belarus – is the subject of attention and concern from other governments as well as from civil society inside and outside the country. Not least, the academic community has played and continues to play an important role in the democracy movement in Belarus, often under very difficult circumstances.

In Europe, in particular, the status and practice of democracy have improved dramatically since the 1980s. The fall of the Berlin Wall in 1989-90 symbolises the broad changes in central and eastern Europe that ultimately enabled the Council of Europe to move from being the Council of half of Europe to being the Council of all of Europe. That in turn made true pan-European co-operation in education and culture possible, making it much easier for academics and higher education institutions all over Europe to co-operate with partners not only in North America – represented in this book by the US Steering Committee of the International Consortium for Higher Education, Civic Responsibility and Democracy – but also on a global scale, represented here by the International Association of Universities (IAU). Democracy is progressing not only in Europe: the end of apartheid in South Africa and the replacement of military dictatorship by elected governments in many countries of Latin America are examples which come to mind. More recently, the dream of democracy has been a potent element of the Arab Spring and of the move towards greater participation in the governance of Burma/Myanmar, even if it is still too early to say whether these dreams will come at least partly true. On the face of it then, democracy needs not so much imagination as determination.

While there is reason to be optimistic about the development of democracy, there are also reasons for this optimism to be cautious. In Europe as well as North America, commitment to the public sphere is suffering at the expense of a focus on our individual private spheres. Whether expressed as often-unfocused complaints about "big government" or political programmes to scale back public funding, reduce taxes, privatise a number of public services or, more broadly, the by now not-so-"new public management", there is widespread scepticism that public authorities and their elected leaders are well suited to finding solutions to many of our most pressing problems. The financial crisis that the world – but in particular Europe – is undergoing as we write these lines would at first sight seem to underpin this view. However, even if Europe's elected leaders have hardly excelled in displaying democratic imagination to solve the financial crisis – perhaps with exceptions like Iceland – the same must be said of financial and business leaders, many of whom are deeply attached to the primacy of the private sphere.

Both North America and Europe have welcomed high numbers of immigrants from other countries on the same continent and from further afield. However, using the term "welcome" in conjunction with immigrants – or indeed most kinds of foreign visitors, whatever their intended stay – seems less and less appropriate. In both Europe and North America, populist politicians often "blame it on the foreigner", making reasoned discussion about the rightful place of foreigners in our societies (and the advantages and the challenges of immigration) difficult. In both continents, politicians vowing to be tough on immigrants can be assured of votes.

Some countries have official slogans like "with law the land shall be built (and not by unlaw destroyed)" (Denmark, Iceland), "the law is equal for all" (Italy) or "Justice the Guardian of Liberty" (the United States). Unless the legal system is seen as saddled by corruption, citizens often look to courts for arbitration and protection – sometimes to the extent that the functioning of the courts is threatened by the number of cases brought before them. At the same time, however, there is legitimate doubt whether the legal system is quite the dependable arbiter it was a generation or two ago. The reason is not necessarily doubt about the democratic or fair nature of the law but rather about its reach. The nation state came into being at a time when legal, political and economic space largely overlapped. Today, economic space is very largely global, political space is largely national – as is voting – but with a significant international dimension, and legal space is – with the exception of binding treaties like the European Convention on Human Rights and European Union legislation – national in scope and jurisdiction.

Some protests against higher education policies – in Europe, typically against the Bologna Process – mix dissatisfaction with the state of higher education with dissatisfaction of a broader political nature, one part of which is protest against globalisation. While we believe a general protest against globalisation to be misguided – globalisation has both positive and negative features – it often translates into a feeling of impotence in the face of forces over which many feel they have no control. If political decisions are seen as being made at global level, the individual is understandably seen as disappearing. At the same time that the international and transnational dimension of the economy and of the political arena –as well as of higher education itself – are gaining in prominence, there is, however, also something of an opposing trend. Several of the essays in this book, and in particular those by US authors, underline the importance of locality. In an age where many businesses and institutions cross borders, higher education institutions stand out by their physical location – as shown in the US term "anchor institutions" – and engage strongly with their local community. All politics may not be local[2] but democratic culture is built locally as well as nationally, regionally and globally and higher education must engage at all levels.

The role of the political arena is also changing. Whereas classic civics teaching underlines the primacy of elected assemblies, reality is somewhat more complicated. Elected assemblies at local, regional and national levels of course play an essential role and remain crucial to democratic societies. However, many actors play a role in modern societies and only some of them are elected. Non-elected does not necessarily mean non-representative, at least of considerable segments of society. Organisations like trade unions, employers' federations, environmental organisations, parents' associations or human rights organisations are representative of significant groups, and their representatives are normally elected through democratic procedures within the organisations. Nevertheless, they are representative of specific groups and not – like elected assemblies – of all voters. Other groups may act without an elective mandate altogether: the frustrations emerging because of the financial crisis are in part due to a widespread feeling that economic power is in the hands of smaller groups with agendas of their own and that these overrule democratic processes. At least some forms of populism, left or right, may be seen as frustration on the part of often unorganised individuals with developments in society which they see as going against their own vital interests. Whatever the reality, there does seem to be a perception that the relationship between different societal actors is shifting and that, also from this point of view, democracy needs to be reimagined.

This list of challenges is nowhere near complete but it is more than sufficient to make the case why we need to reimagine democracy. In this, we face challenges of a similar nature to, yet very different from, those faced by past generations.

The challenge outlined in this book is, however, not to reimagine "democracy" but to reimagine "democratic societies". This hints at how our understanding of democracy is evolving. The traditional civics course would emphasise institutions and elections. These remain important and no society can be democratic without fair elections and representative institutions. At the same time, however, an emphasis on institutions and elections runs the risk of downplaying the role of active citizenship. The word itself may seem strange to some, since they would associate it with the kind of citizenship confirmed by a passport and the right to vote in national elections – and sometimes by the duty to do military service. "Citizenship" as used here, however, indicates that the members of a society need to play an active role in developing it and in making the major decisions about what kind of society they want and how to become it. Citizen participation is a cornerstone of democracy and it needs to

---

2. "All politics is local" is an assertion whose origin is much disputed. It is usually ascribed to former Speaker of the US House of Representatives "Tip" O'Neill.

go beyond citizen mobilisation on just a few issues. Single issues may mobilise, and legitimately so, but cohesive and consistent policies cannot be developed through an accumulation of single-issue politics. Politics needs a comprehensive view of where the *polis* should go and how it should get there.

That brings us to the role of education, and specifically higher education. Why should higher education be concerned with reimagining democratic societies? Is that not a luxury that higher education can ill afford at a time of economic crisis and high unemployment? Should not higher education focus on teaching "facts" as transmitted through academic disciplines and "stay away from politics"?

There is certainly more than a trace of such an attitude in our societies. Public debate on education is very much focused on its contribution to the labour market, and criticism of education is often cast in terms of it not providing the skills the labour market needs. A similar yet opposite approach is quite widespread in the academic community, where many faculty members consider their duty to be to their academic discipline and anything beyond that is "background noise". This came out clearly in a survey of 15 US and 13 European institutions on the role of the university as a site of citizenship (Plantan 2004); many readers will have their own experience of the phenomenon. One of the editors had a particularly poignant reminder of it when, as a student representative many years ago, he asked a professor for permission to make a brief presentation on student government at the beginning of a lecture series and was told that the professor had five centuries of French literature to cover, two hours in which to do it and not a minute to lose.

The role of higher education in preparing for the labour market is essential, but it is not the only role for higher education in our societies. The Council of Europe has identified four main purposes of higher education:

- preparation for sustainable employment;
- preparation for life as active citizens in democratic societies;
- personal development;
- development and maintenance, through teaching, learning and research, of a broad, advanced knowledge base (Council of Europe 2007; Bergan 2005).

The multiple purposes of higher education are also now being recognised in the context of the European Higher Education Area by statements such as "We will support our institutions in the education of creative, innovative, critically thinking and responsible graduates needed for economic growth and the sustainable development of our democracies" (Bologna Process 2012) and "The aim is to ensure that higher education institutions have the necessary resources to continue to fulfil their full range of purposes, such as preparing students for life as active citizens in a democratic society; preparing students for their future careers and enabling their personal development; creating and maintaining a broad, advanced knowledge base; and stimulating research and innovation" (Bologna Process 2009).

Nevertheless, US higher education is overall more emphatic in its insistence on the democratic, citizenship and societal mission of higher education. The concept of liberal education strongly emphasises the role of education in preparing for life, of which work is a part but not the entire part, and in developing a strong sense of civic and societal responsibility. The commitment of US higher education to a broad societal agenda is expressed in many ways and interesting examples are the 2008-09 financial report by the University of Pennsylvania (University of Pennsylvania 2010: 3-9), in which – under the heading "Engaging locally" – its president chose to include the university's work in its local community of West Philadelphia as the main featured article, and work by the Association of American Colleges and Universities on "Liberal Education and America's Promise". [3]

At a global level, the International Association of Universities is engaged in developing a higher education of competences, values and citizenship, as witnessed among other things by the fact that recent IAU conferences have focused on topics like The Wealth of Diversity: The Role of Universities in Promoting Dialogue and Development (São Paulo 2004), The Role of Universities in Fostering the Culture of Dialogue and Understanding (Lebanon 2009), Ethics and Values in the Age of Globalisation (Vilnius 2010) and Strategies for Securing Equity in Access and Success in Higher Education (Nairobi 2011). [4] The IAU's 14th general conference, on Higher Education and the Global Agenda – Alternative Paths into the Future, will take the discussions that took place in Oslo and are developed in this book a step further by devoting a session to the issues raised here. Besides furthering debate through conferences and seminars, the IAU has adopted a series of statements to support its engagement in values-based higher education [5] and in continued dialogue on better co-operation and understanding between higher education leaders, institutions and systems.

Together, these examples and many more make a strong case that higher education should not only be concerned by, but also play a key role in, reimagining democratic societies. The contributions in this book strengthen the case further.

The book is organised in four main parts. The first section – called "Overview and context" – provides just that. Tora Aasland, who was the Norwegian Minister of Higher Education and Research from 2007 to 2012, points out that freedom of expression and thought are fundamental to democratic societies and these principles are fundamental to higher education. She makes her point by referring to a recent case in which these freedoms were denied – the repression against politically active faculty

---

3. See www.aacu.org/leap/index.cfm (accessed on 29 June 2012).
4. Further information on all events is available at www.iau-aiu.net/content/events (accessed on 29 June 2012).
5. The list of IAU statements of interest to the discussions in this publication is available online at www.iau-aiu.net/content/complete-list. It is also worth drawing attention to the joint IAU–Magna Charta Observatory guidelines for developing an institutional Code of Ethics, which emphasise the need to "encourage social responsibility at the institutional and individual level, including the responsibility for promoting equity in access and success in higher education; sustainable development; human rights and democratic citizenship, among others": www.iau-aiu.net/sites/all/files/Ethics_Guidelines_Final_0.pdf (accessed on 25 July 2012).

and students in the aftermath of the 2010 presidential election in Belarus – as well as the role higher education has played in developing Norwegian democracy. As the country's only university for well over a century, the University of Oslo became a nation builder. Aasland emphasises that higher education can contribute to democracy today in many ways, for instance by promoting academic freedom, by developing knowledge, by encouraging staff and students to participate in public debates, by involving them in decision-making and by making sure that structural reforms are carried out with a view to the purposes higher education is intended to fulfil.

Ole Petter Ottersen, Rector of the University of Oslo, compares the development of his institution with the development of Norwegian society to demonstrate the link between higher education and democracy. It is not a coincidence that the university is three years older than the country's constitution. However, even well-established democracies need to be maintained and developed, and higher education has a vital role to play in avoiding "democratic decline".

Ira Harkavy contrasts the widespread desire to live in a democracy with the very real challenges democracy faces today in his home country, the United States, but also in other parts of the world; those challenges include poverty and its effects, rising inequality and declining civic participation. He underlines the fact that education and society are intertwined and summarises the relationship by saying "no effective democratic schooling system, no democratic society". Harkavy reminds us that – as the first President of the University of Chicago, William Rainey Harper said – education is the basis of all democratic progress. Today, we need to continue to see our education system as a coherent whole, from pre-primary schools to research universities, and that system must see the development and practice of democracy, for the good of our societies and not only of our economies, as its main mission.

Sjur Bergan takes as his starting point the public reaction to the killings in Oslo and at Utøya on 22 July 2011, when a nearly unanimous society met the attack against democracy with a call for more democracy. While several factors may help explain the reaction – including the fact that the terrorism was home-grown – the emphasis on democratic culture and values in Norway's education system is certainly an important part of the explanation. Urban riots and the financial crisis provide other examples of how important a culture of democracy is and how democracy cannot function if the approach to it is institutional only and does not include the development of values and attitudes of responsibility and respect. These examples all show that, though democratic institutions are essential, they are not sufficient to build sustainable democracies. Democracy needs an institutional frame but it will not function unless it also becomes a state of mind – and education is essential to achieving this. As the author says: "education should help us find a way but it should also help us find a why."

The second part of the book presents a series of chapters written from the perspective of policy makers at higher education institutions, representative organisations of institutions and students, as well as a former Deputy Minister for Higher Education.

Eduardo Padrón, president of the largest higher education institution in the United States as well as, at the time Chapter 8 was written, Chair of the Board of Directors of the American Council on Education, underlines the key role of learning in revitalising our democracies. Too often, we view education as a commodity and one whose price places it well out of reach for many. However, education is more of a birthright than a commodity. Taking issue with Plato, Dr Padrón suggests we need a "society of philosopher kings". Community colleges, often described as "open door colleges", play a key role in making higher education accessible to many who would otherwise never have the opportunity. Higher education must prepare students to live in and help shape not only the world of today but also that of tomorrow.

Srbijanka Turajlić – Deputy Minister of Higher Education in the first democratic government in Serbia after the fall of the Milošević regime, and president of the Alternative Academic Education Network before that – draws on the Serbian experience to illustrate the democratic mission of higher education. As the world is changing, so must democracy. Change and adaptation are also a vital part of the discussion of whether democracy can be exported – or imported. Many of the NGOs organised under the Milošević regime suffered from a lack of experience and took advice and assistance from bodies and organisations outside the country. When the regime fell, government responsibility in many cases fell to people from the NGO sector, who often found the challenge difficult and the learning curve a steep one. The author uses her own experience of reforming higher education in a new democracy to outline lessons learned and discusses their relevance for others.

Bert Vandenkendelaere was Chair of the European Students' Union at the time of writing. He contrasts the feeling of pessimism and even fear among today's students with the relative optimism of their predecessors in the 1990s. A future in which improved travel and the prospect of a European Higher Education Area held promise has been overshadowed by one that seems dominated by rating agencies and the threat of unemployment. An even greater challenge is the tendency for people to be passive and not engaged in the public space. In institutional terms, universities and other higher education institutions must engage in public debate and seek to influence our future. At what the author calls "micro-level", higher education must prepare its students for active citizenship not only by what it teaches but also by how it teaches.

Inga Bostad and Lars Løvlie take a philosophical approach in their chapter on "Deliberative democracy and moral disturbance". Against the background of the events of 22 July 2011, they stress that political awareness and education often begin with a personal experience. For an earlier generation, the assassination of President John F. Kennedy was such an experience. Upbringing, which is to a large extent informal education, and formal education both play an important role in deciding whether a person, in awakening politically, will go towards an extremist ideology or become committed to deliberative democracy, for which the authors sketch the philosophical background. The role of education is not only to set requirements in terms of knowledge and skills but also to provide context and discourse. An understanding of philosophy is therefore an essential part of education. In higher education, the goal must be to build a university that is responsible to society – locally, nationally and globally.

This second section closes with two related chapters based on the experience of two major US higher education organisations, the Association of American Colleges and Universities (AAC&U) and the American Association of State Colleges and Universities (AASCU). Caryn McTighe Musil draws on the AAC&U's recent report *A Crucible Moment*, which she wrote; Muriel Howard and Jennifer Domagal-Goldman describe and analyse AASCU's ongoing American Democracy Project. Both chapters outline what Dr Musil calls "higher education's twin obligations" – thinking about democracy and doing democracy. As in other parts of the world, in the United States higher education is under pressure and a narrow economic mission is strongly emphasised. Nevertheless, the civic role of higher education is also firmly recognised. Against a background of what the authors call "civic malaise", both organisations have carried on extensive work to develop civic-minded institutions and strengthen the contribution of higher education to developing and maintaining a democratic culture.

The third section of the book is devoted to a series of case studies. They span from Poland to the Pacific shore of the United States and from Norway to Australia. They represent classic universities as well as more specialised institutions. Together, the case studies illustrate many of the points made in the more conceptual contributions in this book. The cases have been selected because they are both unique and representative, and in each case the authors were asked to identify elements that could be of particular relevance to higher education policy makers and practitioners from other institutions and other countries.

Sev Ozdowski describes the University of Western Sydney's efforts to serve the highly diverse 2 million population of Greater Western Sydney with the aim of being "a vibrant and inclusive intellectual community and being connected locally and internationally", one characterised by equity of access, inclusiveness, collegiality and participatory decision-making.

Vidar Haanes and Helene Lund present a study of MF Norwegian School of Theology, which, as its name suggests, is an institution specialising in theology and religious studies. It educates the vast majority of pastors in the Norwegian Lutheran Church as well as a high proportion of the country's graduates in religious studies. It has developed a more ecumenical profile and the case study focuses on a project on Intercultural Methods of Community Development carried out with Catholic, Protestant and Orthodox partners from five European countries.

Henry L. Taylor describes the University at Buffalo, a large public research university in a major industrial city that has been hard hit by economic recession and more generally by extensive changes in the structure of the US economy. Buffalo has lost a large part of its traditional industry and with it more than half its population over two generations. The University at Buffalo, in particular through its Center for Urban Studies (CENTER), is playing a key role in solving the problem of neighbourhood distress and emphasises a participatory democracy model.

Paul Pribbenow's case study focuses on Augsburg College, a liberal arts institution in Minneapolis, associated with the Evangelical Lutheran Church in America. Located in a diverse neighbourhood, it engages with groups that are very different from the constituency for which it was established in 1869. Pribbenow describes the institution's reaction to the murder of one of its students, of Somali immigrant origin, in 2008 and how it succeeded in strengthening community relations in a crisis situation.

Giedrius Viliūnas describes the democratic mission of higher education from a quite different angle. Mykolas Romeris University was originally established as an institution to train police officers. After Lithuania became an independent, democratic country, it was faced with revising its laws and training new police officers, but also with changing the attitudes of those who had been trained in the Soviet period. At the same time, the university developed from a higher professional training institution into a fully fledged university.

Under the heading "act as though you live in a free society", Sondra Myers takes Adam Michnik's motto from the Solidarity (*Solidarność*) period in the 1980s, which resonated well beyond the borders of Poland, as her starting point for a personal reflection on the role of education in developing society. Her article also draws on her experience at the University of Scranton, a Jesuit institution in Pennsylvania. She emphasises the need for an interdisciplinary approach and puts forward a number of topics that could inspire student learning.

Gilbert Rochon and Thierno Thiam describe an institution with iconic status in the United States: Tuskegee University. Established through the efforts of Booker T. Washington, born a slave shortly before the Civil War, Tuskegee was a part of the second group of land-grant universities with a specific mission to provide higher education to the Black population in the still-segregated South. Rochon and Thiam describe how this mission has been carried out over the institution's history, as well as some of the controversies that have arisen.

Piotr Wilczek focuses on a European liberal arts experience – the *Collegium Artes Liberales* – an institution within a large, traditional institution: the University of Warsaw. On the basis of his experience in this institution and a series of initiatives in Poland over the past 20 years, the author describes how higher education can support democratic citizenship and democratic society by engaging local and regional communities in promoting democratic commitments and cultures.

Brian Murphy describes a Silicon Valley institution, but not one that fits the image most people have of Silicon Valley. De Anza College is a community college with some 24 000 students from across the region, many of whom are of immigrant background. The college plays an important role in widening access to higher education by providing opportunities to many who would otherwise not go to college – 80 per cent work full-time while studying, 65 per cent use another language in addition to English – laying the basis for a high proportion of De Anza graduates to go on to four-year colleges or university. De Anza also emphasises democratic participation on campus and includes democratic skills in its Institutional Core Competencies. It was one of the initial organisers and signatories of *The Democracy Commitment*, the document in which a coalition of US community colleges publicly declare that the development of democratic capacity among their students is one of their main goals.

Edward Ray describes the structural and content reorientation of Oregon State University in the face of severe fiscal constraint and cuts in public funding. A thoroughly revised strategic plan firmly states the goal that OSU should become one of the top ten land-grant universities in the United States; it also re-emphasises the commitment that comes with land-grant status to serve the educational and economic development needs of the state and the country. In taking steps to increase fundraising and restructure the institution, its leadership insists on a transparent and inclusive process to develop a statement of vision, values and principles.

David Maurrasse describes the Anchor Institutions Task Force (AITF), an association of individuals pushing ahead with co-operation among institutions, and between institutions and their communities, one that transcends the border between secondary and higher education. Anchor institutions are thus called because they are unlikely to move away even if their local communities are troubled: they are tied to their location and cannot easily be outsourced or relocated. Therefore they have the potential to become cornerstones in their local and regional communities. This potential can be realised through their commitment to collaboration and partnership; equity and social justice; democracy and democratic practice; and place and community. Maurrasse describes the development of the AITF and some of the challenges it faces as well as the potential relevance of this experience for other parts of the world.

Tony Gallagher describes the civic and social engagement of Queen's University Belfast. In a divided community and throughout the period commonly referred to as "the troubles", Queen's upheld a commitment to inclusiveness and to catering to both major components of the society of Northern Ireland, from which the university draws the vast majority of its students. Its importance can also be seen in the fact that many of the most prominent members of Northern Irish society, whether in politics, culture, business or other walks of life, are Queen's graduates. Gallagher describes how the university seeks to stimulate the civic engagement of students and also outlines some of the main challenges ahead.

The final section, labelled "Ways forward", analyses and builds on the discussions at the conference. In a commentary on the group discussion (and some informal discussion) during the conference, Gwen Dungy explores the answers the discussion gave to three fundamental questions: "What is democracy?", "What is the role of higher education in democratic societies?" and "What is the purpose of higher education and how will students and educators collaborate for student-centred learning in order to realise the aspiration of democracy?" Participants emphasised that, while democratic institutions are important, participation is the essence of democracy and universities should be role models in this sense. The question about the purpose of higher education brought forth a variety of responses, but they all tended to stress the democratic mission of higher education. The discussion led the author to put forward, as her conclusion, three issues that higher education leaders should address in order to help promote a culture of democracy.

Martina Vukasović provides much more than a conference report: she uses the conference to reflect on democracy and the contribution of higher education to furthering it. She discusses the basic characteristics of democracy on the basis of presentations made at the conference and on a critical reading of the Economist Democracy Index. Vukasović then discusses whether the university itself is democratic and points to the difficulty of providing measurable criteria to answer this question. Nevertheless, if higher education is to play an important role in furthering democracy, institutions must reassess the ways in which they function. The focus of university education must also be re-examined – or perhaps reimagined – so that it aims to educate the whole citizen. Not least, as she ends by stating: "conferences or publications on the university and its role in democratisation should not be used as an alibi for lack of continuous effort and pressure on ourselves and other colleagues, staff and students alike to further democratic principles, the rule of law and respect for human rights".

In a final, brief essay we, as editors, bring together some of the diverse ideas and examples provided in the book in order to identify what these highly varied contributions have in common and take a final look at how higher education might engage in a "democratic reimagination". Since there is not a single way forward but several roads that may be travelled, we have called this essay "thoughts for the road".

As always, the views expressed in the essays are those of the authors and commit neither the editors nor their organisations. That is, however, the essence of democracy: a commitment to public debate and to working in the public space for the greater common good, whatever our perception of that common good may be. As editors, we would like to thank all the authors, both those who wrote on the basis of their contribution to the conference and those who wrote specifically for this book. We would also like to thank the participants in the conference, most of whom engaged very actively in the debate and in this way also provided inspiration for the contributions to the book. A particular thank you goes to Sophie Ashmore of the Council of Europe's Education Department, who has kept track of us, different versions of the drafts and the very considerable correspondence between editors and authors, and has kept a keen eye on details we would have overlooked.

In our turn, we hope that this book will be read not only as a description of a state of affairs or even as a collection of interesting but separate essays. We hope it will provide inspiration for higher education policy makers and practitioners to continue to develop and improve the contribution of higher education to building the kind of societies in which we would like to live – and to tear down the resilient but unjustified myth of the ivory tower. The diversity of views, background and experiences reflected in the book will, we hope, in the true sense of the term stimulate readers to reflect and then act. Higher education should provide knowledge and understanding but also the ability and the will to act – to engage in public space, to act ethically and to consider the long-term as well as short-term implications of our actions and our priorities, and their impact on our local societies as well as globally. Only if higher education – institutionally as well as through individuals with a higher education background – engages in working for the common good will we be able to build the kind of societies in which we would like our children and grandchildren to live. This will require determination and imagination – as well as a solid dose of reimagination.

References

Bergan S. (2005), "Higher education as a 'public good and a public responsibility': what does it mean?" in L. Weber and S. Bergan (eds), *The public responsibility for higher education and research*, Higher education series No. 2, Strasbourg: Council of Europe Publishing.

Bologna Process (2009), "The Bologna Process 2020 – the European Higher Education Area in the new decade", Communiqué of the Conference of European Ministers Responsible for Higher Education, Leuven and Louvain-la-Neuve, 28-29 April 2009. Available at www.ond.vlaanderen.be/hogeronderwijs/bologna/conference/ (accessed on 23 August 2012).

—   (2012), "Making the most of our potential: consolidating the European Higher Education Area", Bucharest Communiqué.

Council of Europe (2007), Recommendation Rec(2007)6 of the Committee of Ministers to member states on the public responsibility for higher education and research.

Plantan F. (2004), "The university as a site of citizenship" in S. Bergan (ed.), *The university as* res publica, Higher education series No. 1, Strasbourg: Council of Europe Publishing, pp. 83-128.

University of Pennsylvania (2010), *University of Pennsylvania Financial Report, 2008-2009*, Philadelphia: University of Pennsylvania.

Overview and context

4. Reimagining democratic society: a political view

Tora Aasland

I am heartened that so many prominent higher education leaders and practitioners gathered at my old university for its 200th anniversary to discuss a topic very close to my heart.

Freedom of thought and freedom of expression are fundamental principles in any democracy. And nowhere in a well-functioning democratic society are these principles more apparent, obvious and also vitally important than at higher education institutions.

Freedom to pursue a line of research into any subject area and any topic regardless of whether the government thinks it suitable; the exchange of ideas and thoughts; the clash of different opinions between students and academic staff in lively and sometimes heated debates: these are what characterise higher education institutions in most countries and these traits should be the hallmarks of all higher education everywhere.

Unfortunately, as we know, there are regimes in the world where these principles are neither valued nor followed. To totalitarian and authoritarian regimes, academic freedom is usually seen as a severe threat to the chances of upholding the regime; and higher education institutions are considered as nesting places for independent and critical thinking, elements which are dangerous to such regimes. Under regimes like these, academics and students are in an exposed position, precisely because they represent critical and independent thinking. Higher education institutions become important arenas for forces wishing to challenge the present rulers, so academic freedom is restricted to try to prevent development and to prevent critical voices from reaching the surface.

In January 2011, I took the initiative to ask my fellow ministers for higher education in Denmark, Sweden, Finland, Estonia, Latvia and the Netherlands, as well as the Scottish minister,[6] to join me in approaching the Minister of Education in Belarus regarding the situation of academic freedom in Belarus. Following the unrest in the wake of the Belarus presidential elections in December 2010, we had been informed that a number of students and academics had been harassed, detained and prevented from continuing their work and studies. In our letters, we therefore emphasised that an independent Belarusian academic voice is of great value – above all to Belarus itself, but also as part of the European academic

---

6. Scotland, while a part of the United Kingdom, has a distinct education system for which the Scottish Government is the competent public authority.

community at large. We urged the minister responsible for higher education to help ensure that students and academics in Belarus are given the security and recognition they are entitled to, so that they can pursue their academic careers regardless of their political views. On behalf of our own academic institutions, we also offered partnership in expanding contacts and collaboration with the worldwide academic community.

I am pleased to note that various forums of the Council of Europe made formal statements on the situation following the presidential election in Belarus on 19 December 2010, and that these included the Steering Committee on Higher Education and Research.[7] The latter stressed the fact that: "A commitment to academic freedom, institutional autonomy and student participation is key among the fundamental values of the European Higher Education Area."

Depriving academic staff or students of the opportunity to pursue their quest for knowledge because they have expressed their political views is deeply unjustified. Moreover, it undermines the intellectual reservoirs that promote social and economic development in the country. Any regime taking action restricting freedom of thought and expression reduces the vitality of the academic community and seriously undermines the participation of the country in shaping the future of knowledge.

It must be a goal for all of us that participation in the global community of scholars is borderless. European borders are gradually losing their significance and the European Higher Education Area is now a reality. The Bologna Process, which includes most European countries, is an important expression of the aspirations for a borderless academic community.

We have seen from history, over and over again, that higher education institutions can become important arenas for reform movements and even resistance during wars. Conference participants all heard Rector Ole Petter Ottersen tell the story of how the University of Oslo came to be. In our own country, the students at the University of Oslo experienced retaliation from the Norwegian Nazi Government during the Second World War and, as a result, 650 students were tragically deported to concentration camps in Nazi Germany in 1943. This illustrates clearly the force of academic freedom and the fear it creates in a totalitarian regime.

There are also other reasons why the University of Oslo was a suitable venue for a conference focusing on the role higher education can play in reimagining democratic societies, in the year in which it celebrated its 200th anniversary. It was founded in 1811 as the Universitas Regia Fredericiana, the "Royal Frederik University", named after the Danish king who then ruled both Denmark and Norway. The university became a highly important factor in developments towards an independent Norwegian nation state and in the redevelopment of the Norwegian national identity. I use the term "redevelopment" because, prior to being ruled by Denmark

---

7.   Adopted by the CDESR at its meeting on 4-5 April 2011.

for about four centuries, Norway was an independent nation. Having our own university meant that Norwegian students no longer had to go to Denmark in order to study. The possibility to educate Norwegians for the civil service, as well as other vital professions for a nation state, ourselves, in our own country, were among the reasons for establishing the university, alongside Norwegian patriotism and an increased demand for knowledge. Nicolai Wergeland[8] even won a prize in 1810 in a competition to describe a new university in Oslo.

The University of Oslo started out with four faculties, seven professors and 18 students – quite a contrast to today's situation with some 27 000 students. It became a vitally important element in building the Norwegian nation in the 19th and early 20th centuries. It supplied the civil service with people educated in Norway, and research was carried out in subject areas like history, literature and languages, focusing on Norwegian contributions and elements. Over time, a lot of factors paved the way for Norwegian independence in 1905, but having civil servants educated in Norway was crucial for the success of independence, a well-functioning democracy and our first university, and later other higher education institutions.

In this connection, I should mention that our other host, the European Wergeland Centre, is named after the poet Henrik Wergeland, who was vital in making the anniversary of the 1814 signature of our democratic constitution into our national holiday. He wrote several speeches, poems and songs in connection with Norwegian Constitution Day, including the first national anthem for children. I would like to add that our constitution is very much inspired by the constitutions of the United States and France – both countries represented at the conference. Henrik Wergeland worked for the independence of all nations, not only his own. Likewise, he was an advocate for democracy and an eager defender of freedom of faith and expression.

As the background for this chapter was a Council of Europe conference entitled Reimagining Democratic Societies, it is fitting to recall that in 2005, in Warsaw, the Heads of State and Government of the Council of Europe underlined the importance of the values of democracy, human rights and the rule of law:

> We call on Europeans everywhere to share the values which lie at the heart of the Council of Europe's mission – human rights, democracy and the rule of law – and to join us in turning Europe into a creative community, open to knowledge and to diverse cultures, a civic and cohesive community. (Council of Europe 2005: final paragraph)

Higher education can contribute to these aims in a number of ways – through the promotion of academic freedom, through the development of new knowledge through research, through encouraging staff and students to participate in public debates, through the involvement of staff and students in decision-making processes that concern them and through strong legal rights for students.

---

8. Member of the Constitutional Assembly at Eidsvoll in 1814 and father of the poet Henrik Wergeland, mentioned later in this chapter.

This concern is for instance reflected in the Norwegian qualifications framework for higher education, which is inspired by the Dublin descriptors that were developed in the framework of the Bologna Process. Some of the learning outcomes are designed to make sure that all graduates can participate in academic, professional and public debates within their fields.

Another approach to the promotion of democracy through higher education concerns the duty of national authorities to ensure equity in access, participation and completion. This can be done in a number of ways, for instance by special measures for students from underprivileged groups. In Norway, concerns about equity underlie our policies on free provision of tuition on student welfare and on the grants and loans systems in the State Educational Loan Fund.

In the Bologna Process, the responsible ministers have voiced the importance of the social dimension of higher education, in the London (2007) and Leuven/ Louvain-la-Neuve (2009) communiqués. In the latter, their aspiration – our aspiration, as I was among them – was that:

> the student body entering, participating in and completing higher education at all levels should reflect the diversity of the populations .... This involves improving the learning environment, removing all barriers to study, and creating the appropriate economic conditions for students to be able to benefit from the study opportunities at all levels. (Bologna Process 2009)

The Council of Europe recommendation on the public responsibility for higher education and research (Council of Europe 2007) defines four objectives as equally important:

- preparation for sustainable employment;
- preparation for life as active citizens in democratic societies;
- personal development;
- the development and maintenance, through teaching, learning and research, of a broad, advanced knowledge base.

In addition, public authorities should ensure appropriate conditions for higher education and research institutions to fulfil their function as a service to society.

For the purposes of this publication, the objectives of preparation for life as active citizens in democratic societies and personal development are of particular importance. Higher education institutions indeed have an important role to play in promoting democratic values in society. In the Norwegian Act on Higher Education (2005: section 1-3), it is expressly laid down that all higher education institutions should facilitate the participation of their staff and students in the public debate.

Student participation is encouraged because experience has taught us that good student representatives actually contribute to better decision-making. An important way of assuring the participation of students in public debate is to give them the possibility to organise at national, institutional and local levels. In Norway, this is done through legislation and through the financing of student organisations.

Internationally, many forces have driven modernisation in higher education in recent years, among them new technologies, globalisation (which reduces the significance of national boundaries), the demand for equal educational opportunities for everyone and the fact that many more are enrolled in higher education than ever before.

These are forces that influence higher education and to which the higher education sector in all countries needs to respond. However, these are also forces that the global higher education community in turn can influence, precisely by recreating democratic societies and providing the graduates and qualifications needed for these societies.

I would like to take the opportunity to underline the importance of the contributions of the Council of Europe to European higher education and beyond. These are manifold:

- There is the important field of recognition of international higher education qualifications in co-operation with UNESCO, based on the Lisbon Recognition Convention and its supplementary texts and followed up through the ENIC network.
- There is the fundamental support of the Council of Europe for the Bologna Process and today's European Higher Education Area. This is given through:
  - special support for countries that joined the process late, particularly in South East Europe;
  - the special mandate from the ministers of the Bologna Process regarding implementation of the qualifications framework for higher education;
  - numerous high-quality contributions enriching conferences and seminars; and
  - special studies, like those on governance in higher education and on the public responsibility for higher education and research, which underpin the process by providing reflection and thereby help it to move forward.
- The Council of Europe is also important as a centre of reflection to help us see where we are going and particularly as the voice of conscience in higher education policy development, constantly reminding us of what really matters, namely intercultural dialogue, democracy, human rights and the rule of law.

I would like to return to the poet Henrik Wergeland, who has lent his name to the European Wergeland Centre. His masterpiece is a 720-page poem entitled "Creation, humanity and the Messiah" (Wergeland 1830), dedicated to the advocates of truth, freedom and love. It shows his belief in humanity's ability to improve and in the improvement of the human heart through Christianity and through freedom. On his deathbed he rewrote it as "Humanity", which ends by describing the coming ten centuries. In his vision, social need, religious strife, the power of priests, colonialism, slavery, war and borders are all abolished and replaced by gender equity, freedom of religion, freedom of the press, literacy, sustainable cultivation, creation of hospitals, disarmament, democracy and national independence. There are enough visions of global changes there to keep us going for the remaining 834 years of Wergeland's time frame.

Speaking of Wergeland's own practical contributions to improving the world, he is maybe best known for his fight to repeal a provision in the original Norwegian Constitution banning access to the country for Jews. In gratitude, the Jewish Society in Norway has had a statue of him set up at his grave. Wergeland fought this battle through articles and essays but perhaps most importantly through a poem and a short story that have brought tears to the eyes of generations of Norwegian schoolchildren.

As the conference was held in one of the buildings that Henrik Wergeland frequented as a student (he qualified as a pastor of the Norwegian [Lutheran] State Church at the age of 21 and also studied medicine for a couple of years), it is only proper to remind ourselves that it was as a member of the student association of the University of Oslo that Wergeland fought one of his initial battles for the right to celebrate our Constitution Day on 17 May.[9]

Despite writing a piece entitled "Why does humanity move forward so slowly?" (Wergeland 1831), he always retained his belief in the improvement of humanity – and so should we. I hope we can all find some inspiration from Henrik Wergeland, because we all want the higher education sector and new generations of students and graduates to promote academic freedom and democracy and be able to reimagine and shape our democratic societies.

We have important work to do.

References

Bologna Process (2009), "The Bologna Process 2020 – the European Higher Education Area in the new decade", Communiqué of the Conference of European Ministers Responsible for Higher Education, Leuven and Louvain-la-Neuve, 28-29 April 2009. Available at www.ond.vlaanderen.be/hogeronderwijs/bologna/conference/ (accessed on 23 August 2012).

Council of Europe (2005), Warsaw Declaration by the 3rd Summit of Heads of State and Government of the Council of Europe, Warsaw, 16-17 May 2005.

—   (2007), Recommendation Rec(2007)6 of the Committee of Ministers to member states on the public responsibility for higher education and research.

---

9.   Known as *Torvslaget* – the "Market Battle" – on 17 May 1829.

Norwegian Act on Higher Education (2005), Lov av 1. April 2005 nr 15 om universiteter og høgskoler [Act of 1 April 2005 No. 15 relating to universities and university colleges].

Wergeland H. (1830), *Skabelsen, Mennesket og Messias* [Creation, humanity and the Messiah].

—   (1831), "Hvi skrider Menneskeheden saa langsomt frem?" [Why does humanity move forward so slowly?].

5. The role of universities in reimagining democratic societies

Ole Petter Ottersen

In June 2011, I had the privilege of welcoming prominent university leaders from all over the world to a conference in Oslo on the topic of Reimagining Democratic Societies: A New Era of Personal and Social Responsibility?

Indeed, universities have played and are still playing vital roles in developing and upholding democratic principles worldwide. The relatively peaceful revolution that we have witnessed in Egypt started in Cairo University. Liu Xiabo, who received the Nobel Peace Prize in 2010 and is an activist calling for political reforms and the end of one-party rule in the People's Republic of China, is a university professor and was here in Oslo as a guest researcher in 1988. Students were also important in the civil rights movement in the United States in the 1960s. In Malawi, students who protested in support of academic freedom were tear-gassed by armed anti-riot police – and the University of Malawi was closed in April 2011. There are endless examples of how universities have inspired movements for freedom and democracy all over the world but there are also numerous examples of such movements being suppressed.

The University of Oslo

The University of Oslo often proclaims its important place in the birth of our Norwegian democratic system. The university celebrated its 200th anniversary in 2011 and is itself a result of a democratic process that began under an authoritarian regime. Its history is as follows.

If we go 200 years back in time, Norway was still in what we call a "union" with Denmark – that is, it was a part of Denmark but with some specific governance structures. The Danish-Norwegian king rejected the idea of a university in Norway, possibly for fear of Norwegian separation. It may be worth noting that in 1757 an institution called the *Bergakademiet* – literally "the Mountain Academy" but a more appropriate translation would be "the Mining Academy" – was established in Kongsberg, which was then the mining centre of the kingdom. In other words, a university was considered too dangerous an institution, but an academy of higher learning with a limited, professional orientation was considered safe. Danish rejection of the idea of a Norwegian university made higher education an important symbol in the struggle for Norwegian autonomy in the union with Denmark. Thus the decision to create a university in Norway was an important step in the struggle for independence. Establishing it became both the means and an aim of Norwegian autonomy. Three years after the university was founded, our country adopted its constitution. Our university is older than our nation, and this is no coincidence.

In fact, the University of Oslo came about in a rather peculiar fashion. All citizens were asked to contribute financially towards the establishment of a Norwegian university – literally out of their own pockets. This fundraising was immensely successful – perhaps the most successful ever in this country, in terms of participation and the total sum of money raised. The fundraising event served two purposes: it secured the financial basis for the university and also served as a referendum. The Norwegian voice was loud and clear – so much so that the King of Denmark had no choice but to give up his resistance.

When the university was founded 200 years ago, many of our professors were also politicians who played active roles in developing the young nation as a democracy. Indeed, the Economist Intelligence Unit's Democracy Index for 2010[10] stated that we Norwegians enjoy the most democratic political system on this planet! According to the 2011 issue of the index,[11] Norway scored a total of 9.80 on a scale from zero to ten, keeping its position from 2010, when it replaced Sweden as the highest ranked country in the index. However, we should beware of complacency, which is certainly the first step towards democratic decline. The very title of the Economist's 2010 Index is *Democracy in Retreat*.

It is really worrying that the report shows us that democracy is in decline – a decline that started in 2008. The report states that "The dominant pattern in all regions over the past two years has been backsliding on previously attained progress in democratisation". And the global financial crisis is given part of the blame. If this trend is real it means that in the years to come, more people than today will be faced with authoritarian regimes and violations of their human rights.

When I was preparing my opening speech for the conference, I was sincerely thinking that we – as university leaders – hold a special responsibility. There is absolutely no room for complacency and indifference. As part of a global university community, we have a responsibility to uphold democratic values, ideals and practices – and we shall continually support our colleagues from universities in non-democratic states.

The events of 22 July 2011

Only a few weeks after our conference in June, on Friday 22 July 2011, Norway experienced the worst attacks since the Second World War. The government

---

10. See www.eiu.com/public/topical_report.aspx?campaignid=demo2010 (accessed on 6 July 2012).
11. See www.eiu.com/public/topical_report.aspx?campaignid=DemocracyIndex2011 (accessed on 6 July 2012).

headquarters in Oslo were severely damaged by a massive bomb and eight people were killed. The terrorist continued to Utøya, where he killed 69 young people and wounded many more. He attacked the annual summer camp of the young Social Democrats. The attacks appear to have been fuelled by hatred of a multicultural society – a society where different religions, cultures and people can live together in security, confident that their individual rights are respected – and 22 July was an attack on our values of equality and non-discrimination, as well as other fundamental human rights and freedoms. I am proud to say, however, that the response of the Norwegian people to the terrorist attacks was a strong call for more democracy, more openness and more inclusiveness. Norway stands united in its determination to uphold the values of democracy, openness, trust and participation, regardless of background or belief.

Thomas Hylland Eriksen, professor of social anthropology at the University of Oslo, said about the legal procedure in the trial of Anders Behring Breivik, the perpetrator of the 22 July massacre, that this was a case study of democratic values. Furthermore, Hylland Eriksen stated that democracy is not a "what" but a "how". [12]

Democracy does not recommend a particular political position. It is about form rather than content, even if some kinds of content – notably hate speech – stretch the limits of democracy. It presupposes mutual recognition and the acceptance of divergences of opinion, of the right to be heard, of the obligation to listen to others and of respect for common norms of decency. The calm and reasoned way in which the Norwegian judiciary, the audience in the courtroom and indeed the population at large dealt with Breivik, allowing him to be heard and asking him to listen, should be viewed in this light. It does not imply that Norwegians lack passion or that anger and vengefulness were absent during the trial. What it says is that our values are fundamentally different from his.

After the terrorist attack we had to try to comprehend the incomprehensible. This is the university's task and responsibility. An important defence that can be raised in an open and successful democracy is a good education system that communicates the values on which our society is founded. These values must be internalised through active involvement in debates and the exchange of views.

Views must be brought to the surface, confronted with objections, and tempered with historical and cultural knowledge and understanding. Only then can we prevent views from becoming extremist and fostering hate and violence. Last autumn the University of Oslo therefore presented a lecture series called "After 22 July". Many of our leading professors in fields like psychology, law, political science and sociology gave open lectures in the university's Old Festival Hall. This is the very

---

12. See www.opendemocracy.net/thomas-hylland-eriksen/norways-trial-and-democratic-lesson (accessed on 6 July 2012).

same hall where the democratically elected representatives of the Norwegian population met in the years before the *Stortingsbygningen* – the Norwegian Parliament building – was completed in 1866. In a hall thus symbolising the Norwegian democracy, the university offered research-based knowledge at a time when many felt the need for reflection and deeper understanding.

On behalf of the University of Oslo I would like to thank the Council of Europe; the US Steering Committee of the International Consortium for Higher Education, Civic Responsibility and Democracy; the European Wergeland Centre, the International Association of Universities and the Norwegian Ministry of Education and Research for making the conference on Reimagining Democratic Societies possible.

Let me conclude with the words of *The Economist*: "Even in long-established [democracies], if not nurtured and protected, democracy can corrode." The understanding and appreciation of democracy must be continually renewed, for each generation and for each new class of students. Democracy requires constant vigilance. It is against this background that the responsibility of the universities must be defined: they have played and must continue to play a vital role in educating democratic citizens and upholding democracy.

6. Reimagining schools, universities and democracies

Ira Harkavy

Although more individuals live and desire to live in democratic societies than ever before, we write at a time of deep concern about realising a genuinely democratic future for all citizens. The problems of American democracy, for example, are quite familiar to my US colleagues:

- increasing poverty and its concomitants: ill health, unemployment, poor schooling;
- increasing economic, political, social and educational inequalities;
- increasing racism and xenophobia;
- declining trust in nearly all major societal institutions, including higher education;
- declining civic participation and engagement.

Given these and other problems, reimagining democratic societies is surely crucial. But reimagining is merely the first step in a two-step process. The second, more difficult step is to specify what should be done to help reinvigorate democratic societies in and for the 21st century. This book's focus on education, schooling and higher education is precisely, in my judgment, the right place to begin the process of reimagining, reinvigorating – indeed, of recreating.

Education and society

I strongly agree with the Chilean sociologist Eugenio Tironi that the answer to the question "What kind of education do we need?" is to be found in the answer to the question "What kind of society do we want?" (Tironi 2005). Education and society are dynamically interactive and interdependent. If human beings hope to maintain and develop a particular type of society, they must develop and maintain the particular type of education system conducive to it. To cut to the chase: no effective democratic schooling system, no democratic society.

Perhaps John Dewey's greatest contribution was his farsighted observation that, during the 20th century, the schooling system would function as the strategic subsystem of the increasingly complex industrial and post-industrial societies produced by the post-1800 economic and communication revolutions. To use the term now in vogue, Dewey predicted that the school-based operations of "civil society" would become more important than the traditional functions performed by the state in solving "the difficult problems of life". Just as Dewey saw citizenship expanding to take on functions that were beyond the capacity of the state in an advanced capitalist society, he saw an expanded role for the school in preparing citizens to assume those functions.

Extending Dewey's observations, particularly in the 21st century, it is not the judicial, legislative and administrative state, but rather the complex schooling system of American society – from early childhood centres to elite research universities – that 1. must function as the strategic subsystem of the society; 2. has performed that function poorly – in the past and present – at all levels; 3. must radically improve its performance, at all levels, if we hope to solve the problems of American life in the 21st century; and 4. can only be radically reformed if questions about its performance – in the past, present and likely future – are given the highest priority by action-oriented researchers and administrators dedicated to advancing learning and knowledge for "the relief of man's estate" – which Francis Bacon long ago specified as the goal of science (Benson, Harkavy and Puckett 2007).

Higher education has the potential to powerfully contribute to the democratic transformation of schools, communities and societies. Higher education institutions possess significant human (and other) resources, play a leading role in developing and transmitting new discoveries and educating leaders, and play a pre-eminent role in shaping the schooling system, notably through the education of teachers. The American higher education system, in my judgment, does not sufficiently contribute to the development of democratic schools and communities. American research universities, for example, significantly contribute to an elitist, hierarchical schooling system. Moreover, as the International Consortium's Democracy Project has shown, American higher education has largely failed to effectively educate its students for democratic citizenship (Dubin 2007). [13] But the times and American higher education have fortunately been changing. Campus Compact, a national coalition of community college, college and university presidents dedicated to civic engagement, has grown from three institutional members in 1985 to over 1 100 in 2009, about a quarter of all higher educational institutions in the United States. The vast majority of Campus Compact members are engaged in partnerships with schools in their local communities (Harkavy and Hartley 2010).

Participatory democratic schooling is mandatory for a participatory democratic society. Simply put, unless the schooling system at all levels from pre-kindergarten through to research universities is transformed into a participatory democratic schooling system, America will continue to fall far short of functioning as a decent,

---

13. Max Dubin was an undergraduate honours student of Henry Teune, Professor of Political Science at the University of Pennsylvania. Professor Teune, who died in April 2011, made indispensable contributions to the development of the International Consortium for Higher Education, Civic Responsibility and Democracy (IC) and the partnership between the Council of Europe and the IC, serving as a principal investigator of the Universities as Sites of Citizenship research project and the Democracy Project. Henry Teune was my teacher (since my freshman year in college in 1966), colleague and friend. This essay is dedicated to his memory.

just, participatory democracy. The transformation of higher education – the most influential, strategic, powerful component of the schooling system – is crucial to the transformation of the entire schooling system and the education of democratic, creative, caring, contributing democratic citizens. Simply put, the path to effective democratic schooling and large-scale, significant, societal systemic change must run through American higher education, particularly the American research university.

I think it axiomatic that the schooling system functions as the core subsystem – the strategic subsystem – of modern information societies. More than any other subsystem, it influences the functioning of the societal system as a whole; it is the subsystem that, on balance, has the greatest "multiplier" effects, direct and indirect, short- and long-term. I think it equally axiomatic that universities function as the primary shapers of the overall American schooling system. The major role of research universities stems not only from their enormous prestige and power – they serve, in effect, as the reference group that defines and shapes the entire schooling system – but also from their role in educating teachers. In short, what research universities do and how they do it, what they teach and how they teach, have enormously complex and far-reaching impacts on the entire schooling system and on society in general.

The idea that universities played the central role in shaping the schooling system, and therefore American democracy, inspired William Rainey Harper when he served as the first president of the University of Chicago (1892-1906). For Harper, the university was the "prophet" and "the Messiah of the democracy" (Harper 1905). To realise in practice the promise of American democracy, Harper worked tirelessly to develop pedagogy as a university discipline of distinction and to make teaching at all levels a profession "equal to any other". In 1896, the year Dewey began the Laboratory School at Chicago, Harper proclaimed his "desire to do for the Department of Pedagogy what has not been undertaken in any other institution". Even more telling, when criticised by a university trustee for sponsoring a journal focused on pedagogy in precollegiate schools, Harper emphatically asserted, "As a university we are interested above all else in pedagogy" (McCaul 1959, in White 1977: 15). His devotion to pedagogy derived logically from two propositions central to his vision for the University of Chicago in particular and for American universities in general:

1. Education is the basis of all democratic progress. The problems of education are, therefore, the problems of democracy (Harper 1905: 32).

2. More than any other institution, the university determines the character of the overall schooling system: "Through the school system, the character of which, in spite of itself, the university determines and in a larger measure controls ... every family in this entire broad land of ours is brought into touch with the university; for from it proceeds the teachers or the teachers' teachers (Harper 1905: 25).

The societal, indeed global, reach of universities also makes them particularly important partners in school-system and community-wide reform. In this era of global information and communication, local school systems are powerfully affected by the larger national and global schooling systems. Local changes cannot be sustained if they remain only local and unconnected to broader national and global developments. Significant systemic change not only must be locally rooted and generated, it must also be part of a national/global movement for change. For that to occur, an agent is needed that can simultaneously function on local, national and global levels. Universities are simultaneously the pre-eminent local institutions (embedded in their communities) and national/global institutions (they operate with an increasingly interactive worldwide network).

The research university, in my judgment, must constitute the primary component of a highly integrated schooling system [14] that could function as the primary agent of democracy in the world and in the United States in particular. All American colleges and universities should explicitly give a very high institutional priority to solving the problem of the American schooling system; their contributions to its solution should count heavily both in assessing their institutional performance and in responding to their requests for renewed or increased resources and financial support. Actively helping to develop an effective, integrated, genuinely democratic schooling system, pre-K through to higher education, should, I contend, become a collaborative primary mission of American universities and colleges.

The advancement of learning

When we view this book, *Reimagining democratic societies*, in historical perspective, its potential significance is better appreciated. Viewed in historical perspective, I believe, the book could constitute an important development in the progress of the Scientific Revolution that Francis Bacon worked to promote in the early 17th century.

Heated controversy continues to exist about Bacon's contributions to modern science and modern philosophy of science. Almost everyone agrees, however, that his eloquent, passionate prophecy of the great good that would result from development of a highly collaborative, genuinely experimental science of inquiry powerfully contributed to the Scientific Revolution and the idea of progress it helped inspire and spread. To John Dewey, Bacon ranked as one of the great figures in world intellectual history.

In his major book calling for *Reconstruction in Philosophy*, Dewey hailed Bacon as "the great forerunner of the spirit of modern man", a "prophet of new tendencies" and the "real founder of modern thought". Bacon's devastating criticisms of the "great body of learning" and aristocratic idealist theories and methodology handed down from antiquity, as well as his devastating criticisms

---

14. The schooling system as defined here covers what North Americans call "pre-K through 20" – every stage from pre-kindergarten through to doctoral studies.

of the quarrelsome, parochial, tradition-bound universities that transmitted and perpetuated antiquated learning and methodology, Dewey observed, powerfully helped revolutionise scientific inquiry and effectively began modern thought (Dewey 1920: 28-32). Among the major "defects" Bacon attributed to universities, their internal divisions – and the failure of "all the different universities of Europe" to collaborate closely – ranked high. I quote the most relevant passage from Bacon's critique of universities in his great 1605 work on *The Advancement of Learning*:

> as the progress of learning consists not a little in the wise ordering and institutions of each university, so it would be yet much more advanced if there were a closer connection and relationship between all the different universities of Europe than now there is. For we see there are many orders and societies which, though they be divided under distant sovereignties and territories, yet enter into and maintain among themselves a kind of contract and fraternity, in so much that they have governors (both provincial and general) whom they all obey. And surely as nature creates brotherhood in families, and arts mechanical contract brotherhood in societies, and the anointment of God superinduces a brotherhood in kings and bishops, and vows and regulations make a brotherhood in religious orders; so in like manner there cannot but be a noble and generous brotherhood contracted among men by learning and illumination, seeing that God himself is called "the Father of Lights". (Sargent 1999: 53-4)

This present book, in my judgment, can be characterised as a positive response to Bacon's proposal that higher educational institutions collaborate across cultures and national boundaries to advance learning and human welfare. I believe that the authors have done a most impressive job reimagining democratic societies and developing new ideas – ideas that, when put into practice, could contribute to creating and sustaining genuinely democratic universities, schools and societies for all.

References

Benson L., Harkavy I. and Puckett J. (2007), *Dewey's dream: universities and democracies in an age of education reform*, Philadelphia: Temple University Press.

Dewey J. (1920), *Reconstruction in Philosophy*, Boston MA: Henry Holt & Co.

Dubin M. (2007), "Educating undergraduates for democracy and efficacy and the 2006 Penn Democracy Project", *CUREJ: College Undergraduate Research Electronic Journal*, University of Pennsylvania, http://repository. upenn.edu/curej/48 (accessed on 29 June 2012).

Harkavy I. and Hartley M. (2010), "Pursuing Franklin's dream: philosophical and historical roots of service-learning", *American Journal of Community Psychology*, Vol. 46, Nos. 3-4: 418-27.

Harper W. R. (1905), *The Trend in Higher Education*, Chicago: University of Chicago Press.

McCaul R. L. (1959), "Dewey's Chicago", *School Review* 69, quoted in W. T. White (1977), "The study of education at University of Chicago", unpublished PhD dissertation, University of Chicago.

Sargent R.-M. (ed.) (1999), *Francis Bacon: selected philosophical works*, Indianapolis/Cambridge MA: Hackett.

Tironi E. (2005), *El Sueño Chileno: communidad, familia y nación en el bicentenario* [The Chilean dream: community, family and nation at the bicentenary], Santiago de Chile: Taurus.

7. Reimagining democratic societies: what does education have to do with it?

Sjur Bergan

The topic of this book, and of the conference that gave rise to it, is the role of higher education in reimagining democratic societies. Why would we need to re-imagine democratic societies? Do we not have democracies that are already up and running and that need little, if any, repair? As they say: "if it is not broken, do not fix it."[15] Are our democracies really broken?

These are appropriate questions to contemplate at the 200th anniversary of a university, as we did at the conference co-organised by the Council of Europe, the International Consortium for Higher Education, Civic Responsibility and Democracy, the European Wergeland Centre, the International Association of Universities and the University of Oslo as part of the latter's bicentenary celebrations. Perhaps 200 years is not old when compared to some universities, but the University of Oslo, like many universities across the world, played an important role in imagining and developing the society of which it is a part. It is no coincidence that the University of Oslo is just three years older than the Norwegian Constitution.

Violent reminders

The pertinence of those questions was brought home to conference participants, and to people all over the world, less than a month after the conference, when on 22 July 2011 people in downtown Oslo and soon afterwards on the small island of Utøya became victims of terrorist attacks. The bombings in Oslo were directed at today's democratic government, as the car bomb destroyed the buildings that house government offices, while the shooting spree at Utøya, where Labour Party Youth held its annual summer camp, aimed to cut off recruitment to tomorrow's democratic government. Many of those killed were politically active students engaged in the public arena to try to develop our future society in accordance with their ideals.

I use the word "our" not only because I am a Norwegian citizen, but because I am a citizen of Europe and of the world. Whatever nationality we are and whatever passport we carry, what the terrorist tried to extinguish is ours – not only Norway's, but Europe's and the world's. This horrific incident was not about a specific party, a specific government or a specific country, even if the physical effects were felt

---

15. In the original vernacular: "If it ain't broke, don't fix it".

in Oslo and Utøya. It was an attack on the fundamental values and ideals on which our societies have been built and on which they must continue to develop.

Herein lies a gleam of hope in the middle of the horror. The reactions of both the political leadership – across party lines – and of the public at large were amazing and heartwarming. Even before it became clear that the terrorism was home-grown rather than imported, that Norway was faced with the equivalent of Oklahoma City, Columbine and Winnenden all in one – rather than with 9/11, *el once de marzo* (11 March) or 7 July – the reaction was that we cannot and must not let violence set the agenda of Norwegian society. The immediate reaction could easily have been a demand for stricter security measures and closed borders; instead it was an affirmation that we need open, democratic societies and that we will not be driven by fear into a different system. The reaction was a reaffirmation of a commitment to democracy. We received a second reminder about two weeks later, when urban riots erupted in London and then spread to other cities in the United Kingdom. Again, even if the urban riots were limited to one country, they were of concern to the whole continent and beyond. Whatever gave rise to the riots, the use of blind violence cannot be justified and must be firmly condemned. Violence is incompatible with solving even the most severe problems in a democratic society. At the same time, police force alone – however much it might be needed as a first reaction to stop the violence – cannot address the underlying reasons for it. Trying to understand the reasons for violence is not incompatible with condemning it firmly, as shown when President Lyndon B. Johnson appointed the Kerner Commission to draw lessons from the riots in major US cities during the summers of 1965-67.

A third reminder came at about the same time as the urban riots, when the world seemed to balance on the brink of another financial crisis. Policies and practices in both Europe and the United States contributed to it, and the problems were partly political. In the United States, the two major parties failed to come together to face an impending crisis, whereas in Europe national leaders failed to find a common solution within the zone sharing a common currency, at least one that was credible in the eyes of the market. Yet at the same time, the market failed to behave in ways that were credible in the eyes of the broader public, in other words to the larger society. Most members of society agree that a well-functioning market is a key element of democracy, but most members of society also agree that a well-functioning market need not be one without oversight and restraint, in which speculation is rife and consideration of how economic activity will influence the longer-term development of our societies seems absent.

Understanding how democracy works and what is needed for it to work better is, of course, a fundamental task for higher education. It includes understanding why democracy can seem on the verge of breaking down, as well as understanding the sometimes amazing forces that give it life. It includes understanding why democracy can seem unattractive, as well as understanding what is needed to ensure it remains attractive. That may at times be done by depicting the alternatives, all of which are considerably less attractive. But a lasting commitment to democracy cannot be founded solely on the conviction that democracy is the least bad alternative. A lasting commitment to democracy must be founded on the conviction that individuals committed to the public good can and should make a difference. It has to be founded on the conviction that politics is important and that civil society is vital to the success of our societies. We need the knowledge economy but we also need the wisdom society. [16]

Democracy: attraction and challenges

If we go back only 20 – not 200 – years to 1990, Europe showed very clearly that democracy has great attraction. Europe was in the middle of a democratic transformation, symbolised by the fall of the Berlin Wall but perhaps even more importantly by the fall of many political, legal and mental barriers. Civil society came alive in countries where it had previously had no place other than as window-dressing serving the purposes of undemocratic regimes. Civil society demanded democracy, and civil society cannot live without democracy.

Now, some 20 years later, Europe has made great strides. Developments that seemed utopian a generation ago are commonplace today, including the fact that the organisation this author represents is no longer the Council of half of Europe but the Council of all of Europe, with the sad exception of Belarus. Even in Belarus, however, democracy is a model and an ideal, kept alive by higher education staff and students as well as by other members of civil society.

In reimagining democracy, we should not forget that democracy is under threat. In May 2011, the Council of Europe published the report of the Group of Eminent Persons chaired by former foreign minister Joschka Fischer, called *Living Together: combining diversity and freedom in 21st-century Europe* (Council of Europe 2011). This report spelt out eight main risks:

- rising intolerance;
- rising support for xenophobic and populist parties;
- discrimination;
- the presence of a population virtually without rights;
- parallel societies;
- Islamic extremism;
- loss of democratic freedoms; and
- a possible clash between religious freedom and freedom of expression.

These eight elements form a set of risks that we need to take very seriously if Europe is still to be a continent of vibrant democracies a generation or two from now.

---

16. A term for which I am indebted to Professor Paolo Blasi, former Rector of the University of Florence as well as a former member of the Board of the International Association of Universities.

Imagining and reimagining democracy

We have also advanced in our thinking about democracy. Traditionally, democracy was thought of as institutions and procedures, as parliaments and elections. These are of course crucial and we cannot have democracy without them. However, even if institutions and fair procedures are essential, they are not sufficient. Democracy is about more than voting every three or four years. Democracy is about participating in the lives of our societies every week of the year and every day of the week. [17] Civil society is more than a reserve of voters that can be called forth when needed. Civil society is the very life and blood of democracy. Apathy and lack of interest are as strong threats to democracy as active opposition to it. I would personally add apathy to the eight risks identified by the Group of Eminent Persons because if all people of good will wait for others to do good deeds, nothing will happen.

Therefore we also speak of "reimagining" for, 20 years after the fall of the Wall, there is – we must admit – disillusion and fatigue. There is little taste in Europe for trying a system other than democracy, but there is also insufficient taste for putting in any personal effort to make democracy work. Too many of us focus almost exclusively on our own little private spheres, too few engage in the public sphere – in how to improve our societies – and too many think that social responsibility and politics are for others to take care of, reserving to ourselves only the right to complain. Not least, too many of us take national borders to set the limits of our own responsibility to others or to indicate the borders beyond which there is little to learn.

At the same time, the idea of democracy knows no borders. If we needed a reminder of that, we got it through what has come to be known as the "Arab Spring". True, the situation is not uniform throughout the Arab world, just as it is not uniform throughout Europe. Egypt and Tunisia have already lived through relatively peaceful regime change, whereas in Libya change was bloody and in Syria attempts at change meet with bloody resistance and, at the time of writing, are still unsuccessful. In other countries, the jury is either still out or has not yet convened. Democratic institutions are not easy to set up, but developing the democratic culture needed to make them work is immeasurably more difficult.

Nevertheless, what strikes us about the Arab Spring is not the difficulty of the exercise but the power of the ideal. Many Europeans believed the seeds of democracy would not grow in Arab soil. Luckily, they were proved wrong. We who are policy makers and practitioners in higher education will play an important role in deciding how Europe and North America can best help in bringing the Arab Spring to fruition. This will not be by trying to impose policies, but by sharing our ideas and analytical skills, by being open and honest about what has worked in different contexts and what has not. The Arab world will need to decide for itself what

---

17. I am indebted to Ira Harkavy for pointing out that this point was central to John Dewey's work and at the heart of his debate with Walter Lipman.

solutions will best further democracy in their countries, but we can help by sharing what has worked to advance democracy in ours.

Living together

In the 19th century, Norway sent a larger share of its people abroad, as emigrants, than any other European country except Ireland. Emigrants, however, become immigrants when they reach their destination. In the case of those who emigrated from Norway, the destination was most often the United States: the plains of the Midwest and the shores of the Pacific northwest. In the case of other European countries, the destination was often the United States but they also went to Latin America, Australia and other parts of the world, sometimes at the expense of those who lived there already. Today, we are proud of the European heritage of the Americas or Australia. We look with pride on the Irish heritage of Boston and the Italian contribution to Buenos Aires. Why, then, are we so sceptic of the Indian community of Cork or the Vietnamese community of Catania? Can we seriously believe that only European migrants contribute positively to their adopted communities?

Enabling us to live together is one of the Council of Europe's top priorities. In 2008, we published the White Paper on Intercultural Dialogue, called *Living Together as Equals in Dignity* (Council of Europe 2008). As just mentioned, in May 2011, the Council of Europe published the report of the Group of Eminent Persons, also on the theme of living together. With the International Association of Universities, the Council of Europe has explored the contribution of higher education to intercultural dialogue (Bergan and van't Land 2010).

These are important contributions to what this book aims to do, namely reimagine democratic societies. Can we imagine them as societies looking inward, closing themselves off from the broader world? Can we imagine such societies believing that they have little to learn from those whose backgrounds and experiences are so different from our own and foregoing the pleasure of intellectual and cultural discovery and interaction?

If we answer "no" to this question – which I admit is intended as rhetorical, but which would certainly not be seen as such by all – we also begin to make the link between democracy and education. Why should higher education reimagine democratic societies?

If we accept that, however important democratic institutions are, they will not bring democracy unless they are underpinned by democratic culture, we are talking about the importance of education. If we say that democracy requires its citizens not only to vote but also to engage actively in the public domain, we are talking about the importance of education. If we say that democracy is about the will and the ability to live peacefully with those whose backgrounds and opinions are different from our own and being enriched by the experience, we are talking about the importance of education.

Democracy as a state of the mind

It has been said that democracy cannot be built on empty stomachs; but nor can democracy be built on empty minds. Education is about conveying knowledge, understanding and the ability to act – the classic definition of learning outcomes. But education is also about developing attitudes. I may be able to do things that I should not do, and because I realise that these actions may be unethical or otherwise indefensible, I refrain from them. I may find it difficult to do things that I know I should do, but because I am convinced it would be right to do those things, I persevere and try to find a way to do them.

Education should help us find a way, but it should also help us find a why.

In Europe, the education debate focuses strongly on the role of education in furthering economic development. This is an important debate, but it is not the only debate we should have on education. There is no contradiction between developing competences and developing values. Rather they go together, as emphasised in the concept of "converging competences", which was at the heart of the previous conference the Council of Europe organised in co-operation with our friends in the International Consortium (Bergan and Damian 2010). Education must, as the Council of Europe says in its recommendation on the public responsibility for higher education and research, do four things, all at the same time (Bergan 2005, Council of Europe 2007):

- prepare for sustainable employment;
- prepare for life as active citizens in democratic societies;
- provide for personal development; and
- provide our societies with a broad and advanced knowledge base.

These are not contradictory purposes, but complementary – to say that preparing for democracy is important is not to say that preparing for work is not – but, in European public debate, we too often hear about one purpose alone: economic development. Higher education must contribute to developing our economy, but even more, it must help develop our societies.

Reimagining democratic societies

The question, then, is not whether higher education should contribute to the development of democratic societies, but how. This is a practical question as well as a philosophical one. Reimagining society is something our forebears did on several occasions. Today it is our turn to imagine how we, as members of the higher education community as well as being members of broader society, can imagine a better society for tomorrow. It is also our turn to imagine what we must do today to give our children the kind of society in which we would like them to live tomorrow. I hope this will be a society in which they can move even more freely than we can today, in which the value of an idea will be judged on where it will lead our society rather than on from what part of our society it comes. I hope it will be a society in which the barriers will fall that still keep some citizens of Europe as well as of other parts of the world within the borders of their home countries either because their own governments are afraid to let them leave or because other governments are afraid to let them come. Above all, I hope it will be a society in which the barriers of the mind will fall – the barriers that make us afraid to think that we can learn from others very different from ourselves, creating informal barriers even when the formal borders are made easy to pass. Who can imagine such a society if not those in higher education? Who can make such a society a reality if not those in higher education?

In Norway, the poet and singer Alf Prøysen wrote one of his most famous songs about the promise of being given a new day tomorrow – *du skal få en dag i mårå* – with clean sheets of paper and a new set of colour pencils. No matter how often you fail, there is an opportunity waiting when you wake up to a new day. Those same clean sheets of paper and those same new pencils are being offered to us as members of the higher education community, but they come with a responsibility. They come with a responsibility to look back, not to reminisce about how things were better in the old days, but to be conscious of how we sometimes failed in our old ways. They come with a responsibility to look forward, to imagine the future in ways that are ambitious but realistic, in which fundamental values count for more than value added and in which the success of the future builds on the achievements of the past, as well as on a vision of the future.

Those who established the University of Oslo 200 years ago could not imagine a new society without a university. Today the university – as an institution and as a community of scholars and students – must play a crucial role in designing the kind of society we want, one based on true values, relying on the involvement of its citizens and able to maintain dialogue with all parts of the world.

In many cultures it is a sign of wisdom to think first and act later. We are called upon to imagine today, but then we also have to act upon our imagination – not just tomorrow but all the days that will follow tomorrow.

References

Bergan S. (2005), "Higher education as a 'public good and a public responsibility': what does it mean?" in L. Weber and S. Bergan (eds), *The public responsibility for higher education and research*, Higher education series No. 2, Strasbourg: Council of Europe Publishing.

Bergan S. and Damian R. (eds) (2010), *Higher education for modern societies: competences and values*, Higher education series No. 15, Strasbourg: Council of Europe Publishing.

Bergan S. and van't Land H. (2010), *Speaking across borders: the role of higher education in furthering intercultural dialogue*, Higher education series No. 16, Strasbourg: Council of Europe Publishing.

Council of Europe (2007), Recommendation Rec(2007)6 of the Committee of Ministers to member states on the public responsibility for higher education and research.

—   (2008), *Living together as equals in dignity*, White Paper on Intercultural Dialogue, Strasbourg: Council of Europe.

—   (2011), *Living together: combining diversity and freedom in 21st-century Europe*, Report of the Group of Eminent Persons, Strasbourg: Council of Europe.

Higher education perspectives

8. Reimagining democratic societies: a new era of personal and social responsibility

Eduardo J. Padrón

Democratic societies harbour a dicey tendency towards complacency. We assume our traditions will endure but in fact the importance of crafting and sustaining democratic societies remains the most fundamental of challenges for democratic societies. The challenge is heightened by our living in a time with little precedent in its great potential or its great uncertainty. Our human ingenuity has given rise to a new dimension of global communication, one that is reshaping the world of knowledge and learning. And, in the very same moment, our human foibles are on display, along with our ignorance. Our differences and our diversity, the very raw material of democracy, prove too often divisive; our sense of common purpose often seems frail enough to collapse completely.

But the great potential of this new era is strikingly apparent, particularly in our academic institutions. At this critical time in history, education – translated into authentic learning that nourishes mind and spirit – offers a crucial saving grace for this high-octane era. More to the point, those who embody that quality of learning offer the energy to revitalise our democratic roots. Study after study has confirmed that higher education, clearly the prime variable in advancing economic standing, is also the principal factor in civic participation and community-building (Verba et al. 1995; National Center for Public Policy 2003). Having said that, however, I fear it will take more than casting a ballot to re-energise our democratic traditions.

In this, the age of information, it is safe to assume that the ancient Greek philosophers are attracting smaller crowds in our classrooms than they did previously. But it was Greek society that gave us some of the earliest attempts at citizen democracy, and it can serve us well to reflect not only on their success but also consider their criticism.

Plato took issue with Greek democracy. He doubted the body politic's grasp of – or interest in – the details of economics, military strategy or domestic policy. He felt the citizens of his time were also vulnerable to the cunning and nebulous talk of politicians, whose commitment to the common good Plato seriously doubted. His remedy was the philosopher kings, gifted individuals who would rule with both wisdom and practical intelligence. Though his utopian ideal never came to pass, he has left us with much to think about today.

First and foremost, we should elevate our view of education. Too often, it is a commodity, and one that is priced well beyond the reach of many in societies around the world. As the Harvard political philosopher Michael Sandel suggests, the marketplace is not meant to answer every question, yet market values too often are overriding civic practices (Sandel 2012: 5-6). The opportunity to learn, right through to completing college, is more birthright than commodity. No more fundamental instinct exists within a human being than to learn. We are thinking and feeling beings who make decisions drawn from values and understanding. Democracy is at its best when these traits are nurtured and at its worst when they are neglected.

Our challenge then, in a manner of speaking, is to prove Plato wrong. We need to cultivate an entire society of philosopher kings, not merely a privileged class. And we need to court a much broader swath of the community and ensure that they take up the challenge of being citizens of a new order. Far beyond mere entry into a world of learning, our students need to emerge from our institutions with an unparalleled combination of understanding and competence. When we speak of democracy, too often we are holding a conversation about systems and constructs of governance. But it is a house of cards if the residents of this democratic household lack the enrichment to be genuine participants. Society cannot guarantee prosperity, but it is required to provide opportunity. Providing an avenue to learn for each member of society is, perhaps, the civil rights challenge of our time.

American higher education includes institutions referred to as "open door colleges". This is a literal descriptor, because they offer the opportunity of a college education to any student who has completed high school. It is an inclusive approach to higher education, not a selective one. Our motto reflects an abiding belief that "opportunity changes everything".

The institution where I reside offers a telling case study. Miami Dade College (MDC) was born at the intersection of two historic moments, the desegregation of American society and the Cuban revolution. The first began the painstaking work of altering the very nature of American democracy and the second remade, in no time, the demographic of Miami and south Florida. Miami Dade College became the doorway of opportunity for many low-income, minority and immigrant residents who had never dreamed that a college education was possible. To this day, more than half of MDC's students are the first in their families to attend college, and those original students have long been the established leadership in every facet of community life.

MDC is today the largest institution of higher education in the United States. It is also, unquestionably, the central point of educational opportunity and workforce development in south Florida. For many in the community, it is the only option if they wish to pursue a college education because of the affordability of MDC's programmes. In a community of 2.5 million residents, the college has welcomed nearly 2 million students in its 50-year history. In a very real sense, it belongs to the south Florida community. In that same sense, it is the most democratic of institutions.

American community colleges have focused historically on offering two-year degree courses and specialised short-term training to meet workforce demand. Two-year associate degrees prepare students to transfer to four-year institutions to complete their baccalaureate degrees or to directly enter the workforce on graduation. In recent years, these colleges have added their own four-year degrees, but in each case those degrees have been responsive to the labour needs of their geographical regions. The mission of the American community college remains clear: to provide excellence in higher education to the full range of residents in its surrounding community and to work closely with industry and professional partners to ensure a ready workforce.

Based on the educational ambassadors we have hosted from countries around the world for many years, this is a model of education very much in demand globally as well. MDC has established partnerships in China, Saudi Arabia, India and countries throughout Latin America. It is a model that has proved essential in stimulating developing economies and identifying educational priorities. When you consider that the combined population of India and China is 2.5 billion – and that more than half are under 25 years of age – the doorway to college will need to open wide if those nations are to prosper.

Our mission statement reads "changing lives through the opportunity of education" (Miami Dade College 2012). Changing lives – is this not the fundamental promise of democracy? In posing this question, I am taken back to an exceptional essay by the American philosopher Jacob Needleman. He called it *Two Dreams of America*, and in it he suggested that the purpose of this grand American experiment in democracy was to provide a sheltering environment, as he put it, "to seek the conditions and the companions necessary for the inner search" (Needleman 2003: 3). The American Dream has since been too often defined by material prosperity, but the original purpose of American democracy was to be an incubator of understanding. That applies not only for the purpose of governing but also to address the intrinsic needs of the people within that society.

Our democracies are far from perfect today. But no matter their condition, there remains an undercurrent of possibility and the hope for a better life. Higher education and the ideals of democracy are allies in this aspiration. Opening the door to higher education for a much broader expanse of the population is an essential step in enriching the democratic conversation.

But beyond the challenge of access, the critical responsibility of the education community today is to ask questions of value: To what ends shall we employ our new technology? What does it mean to be a citizen of this new world? What is required to reinvent our civil discourse? Not least, how are we to see beyond the lethal divisions that lay waste to so much human possibility?

Plato insisted that the general public was ill-prepared and easily misled. What are we, then, to make of the challenges our students face today? In this new order they are assaulted by an unrelenting volume of information and opinions. They are growing up in a global network that has no precedent in our lives. They are, as Massachusetts Institute of Technology professor Sherry Turkle recently wrote in the *New York Times*, enamoured of the multiple and constant connections afforded by today's social media, but too often at the expense of real conversation. As she said, "Many sips do not add up to a gulp" (Turkle 2012). But when they enter higher education they begin to engage in a different quality of interaction. They become accountable for their thoughts, their feelings and their actions, the depth and implications of which are often lost in the abbreviated world of social media. Hence, their engagement and thoughtfulness is equally important to the content of their particular field of study.

It follows that our responsibility is to ensure that they are challenged and prepared for a volatile workforce environment. But that is not enough. College learning should be transformative. Students should leave our institutions having contended with a diversity of viewpoints and having honed their capacity to shape their own point of view. Learning relies on the dynamic of conversation that is often missing amid the acceleration of daily life. And that dialogue, with a range of ideas and people, is an evolutionary dynamic. Conversations unfold. They take time and they encourage the skills of listening, patience and persistence.

These qualities are the everyday casualties of a combustible and partisan world. It is this brand of partisanship that has capitalised on the 24/7 multimedia onslaught. This is the back-and-forth soundbite war that has lost touch with the north star of every democracy, the common good. Our students must understand what many in the halls of democratic institutions have forgotten – that there is a tariff to pay for your ideological zeal and that tariff is the commitment to listen, to be open to the views of others.

On a worldwide scale, the lethal results of these passionate movements are all too evident. Blind partisanship is a half-step from intolerance, and that amounts to denying the richness and nuance of each individual, of each new possibility, of each new idea. It is a form of ignorance that contents itself with labels and their convenient stock of meanings.

Few of us are naïve; the problems we face today are complex and confounding. Those who navigate the political rapids, lives in the balance, have responsibilities that differ from most of us – but, as educators, our work has never been quite so crucial. We are compelled to understand the turmoil in human terms. Human beings – not systems of governance or belief – embody the ignorance – and the wisdom – that mark history's movement. To forget this fundamental fact is to forfeit any chance of resolution.

The simple rebuttal to this madness of mind is learning – deep, authentic learning that requires each student to question assumptions and discover their own self, and not merely their own intellectual prowess. Most importantly, this quality of learning offers the chance to discover a fundamental commonality, even in the midst of great diversity. If we can encourage this quality of dialogue among our students, then they will depart our institutions with a far more meaningful certification than any degree can confer.

Having said that, there is obvious importance to the range of programmes our institutions offer. The Industrial Age has long since given way to the Age of Information and that has produced something we call the "knowledge economy". To be sure, this is a moving target and keeping pace is a formidable challenge for everyone in higher education. And this critical intersection between business and higher education – the one that produces meaningful work – is a central tenet of a flourishing democratic society.

Times of economic decline take a serious toll on the spirit of a democratic society. The lack of meaningful work affects people exactly as the words imply, in the area of meaning and enthusiasm. Our institutions are the key component in preparing a pool of talent to match the economy that has shifted before our eyes. A report titled *Across the Great Divide* (Bridgeland et al. 2011) estimates that nearly 70 per cent of new jobs in the USA will require college-level learning and the USA will need to produce 3 million additional college graduates by 2020. A second report, by the McKinsey Global Institute projects (McKinsey Global 2011), predicts that the USA could face a shortfall of 2 million technical and analytical workers and several hundred thousand nurses and doctors. The list of STEM – science, technology, engineering and mathematics – realms that are forecast to have labour shortages is truly alarming.

Two points should be made in response to these very real challenges: First, preparing students to be successful in this emerging work environment will require flexibility and agility from our institutions. From our adherence to credit–hour units and semesters to our insistence on baccalaureate degrees, we may very well be limiting our contributions to the economy. If we are to maximise the synergy of higher education and the business sector, one size will not fit all. Our academic traditions will, indeed, survive, as they must, but our liberal arts and sciences backbone can and should bend to meet the demands of a new global work environment. And our partnerships with business and industry should be very real, enabling us to craft learning pathways that lead to jobs and growth in the new economy. The work of reimagining our democracies is complex, especially when it comes to connecting with the energy of economic forces.

Every available study suggests that our recent graduates will change jobs or even careers more than 10 times in their working lives. They are entering an economic setting in which entire industries and career paths can appear and disappear seemingly overnight. In a very real and practical way, we are preparing them in the early years of college for jobs that do not yet exist.

Our students, then, will need a toolkit of navigation skills. MDC's faculty have crafted a set of 10 learning outcomes [18] – among them, competences that still owe much to the traditions of liberal learning, particularly in vital areas of communication and mathematics. But they also ask students to expand their awareness on the issues that are quickly defining the new century. Clarity on the interplay of cultures, environmental sustainability, the need for civic engagement and mastery of technology are just a few of these formal learning outcomes.

While our students intuitively understand the changes unfolding, what they really want, beyond the tools to change jobs, is the chance to change the world. While we are busy criticising the superficiality of social media, young people have slipped through the looking glass. Facebook is a community of nearly one billion people. [19]

---

18. See www.mdc.edu/learningoutcomes/ (Miami Dade College 2012).
19. See http://connect.icrossing.co.uk/facebook-hit-billion-users-summer_7709 (posted 11 January 2012).

If it was a country, it would be the third largest in the world. The number of text mes-sages sent – each day – is greater than the population of the entire planet. Diminishing the staggering implications of these new avenues of commerce is foolish.

A 140-character Twitter post has obvious limits but the connectivity, mobility and speed of the entire IT complex is freakish. Our students have the unprecedented po-tential to alter the conversation – political, economic, social – you name it. They have created a social network that defies all manner of borders and classifications; they are defining themselves differently from the traditional descriptors of occupation, country and ethnicity. Their reach is second nature by now, and they have proved they can bring the titans of the established order to their knees with a single keystroke. Clearly, they are not ready to settle for the choreographed politics of recent years.

Of course, the possibility exists that they will be swallowed up. The same network of connection also serves to increase the velocity, the irreverent momentum of our times. And this is where the wisdom of age and time and patience has a historic role to play, for it is never enough to be adept. It does not matter if you talk into a tin can or a satellite telephone; it is the conversation that must change. Yes, our students can leap across the universe in a digital moment but it may be the smaller, more private moments that determine their course and the future of our democratic institutions. We can craft our learning institutions to ensure that these conversa-tions occur on a regular basis.

Young people are at a moment in their lives where the boundaries are fewer and the possibility of recognising the value of commonality and shared interest is ripe. That commonality occurs in classrooms with the most diverse groups of students, and they are fascinated and excited by their collaboration. They are not nearly as mesmerised by the demarcations and divisions of their elders. They are less in-clined to adopt ideologies; they would rather see things as they are.

You and I can attest that they may not always feel this way. They can fall prey to a range of necessities, not the least of which is poverty and joblessness, a grow-ing threat in so many countries. Their freewheeling belief in the impossible is a vulnerable asset. And so it is that we, as their teachers and mentors, have a limited time to be of help to them, to support their impossible dreams. Our students reas-sure us that we do not need to reimagine our democratic institutions. They embody all that is needed, and our institutions can be the vehicles to reinforce their best instincts. Indeed, they are our best hope.

References

Bridgeland J., Milano J. and Rosenblum E. (2011), *Across the great divide: per-spectives of CEOs and college presidents on America's higher education and skills gap*, Civic Enterprises/Corporate Voices for Working Families.

McKinsey Global Institute (2011), *An economy that works: job creation and America's future*.

Miami Dade College, Department of Institutional Research (2012), www.mdc. edu/main/about/mission_vision.aspx.

National Center for Public Policy and Higher Education (2003), *Measuring Up 2002*, San Jose CA: NCPPHE.

Needleman, J. (2003), *Two dreams of America: essays on deepening the American dream*, Kalamazoo MI: Fetzer Institute.

Sandel M. (2012), *What money can't buy: the moral limits of markets*, New York: Farrar, Straus & Giroux.

Turkle S. (2012), "The flight from conversation", *New York Times*, 21 April 2012.

Verba S., Lehman Scholozman K. and Brady H. E. (1995), *Voice and equality: civic voluntarism in American politics*, Cambridge MA: Harvard University Press.

9. Reimagining democratic societies in challenging circumstances: the role of higher education

Srbijanka Turajlić

> "Will freedom be able to sing as beautifully as the oppressed sang about it?" [20]

Is democracy a good that can be exported?

The world we live in is a world of change, driven by the unprecedented development of technology, which is shaking up completely a number of paradigms. Thus we are forced to rethink and reimagine almost all the concepts in which our societies are rooted. In our efforts to define this new world, which is changing shape so rapidly, some major areas of discussion are globalisation and its influence on the world economy, the knowledge-based society – in which knowledge and innovations are perceived as the raw materials that shape a country's economy – and the information technologies that have penetrated not only our professional lives but our private lives as well.

Of the various changes that can be identified in almost every human activity, probably the most significant relates to our understanding of time and space. A century ago we were led to accept that time and space are relative. We were told that we need not dwell particularly on it, since this concerns only extremely high speeds outside the scope of everyday life. However, all of a sudden we seem to be achieving those speeds. Information technology (IT) has reduced the whole world to one point, the time span to one tick. Indeed with conference calls and similar IT tools, we seem to be everywhere on this planet. We share business ideas, friendships, concerns, even small talk all around the globe. It might be said that we, for the first time in human history, have started to consider this entire planet as our home. Yet this home does not look familiar. It is strangely divided into small parts where people speak different languages, believe in different gods, have different traditions, consider themselves to be members of different nations, and have different economic means and different aspirations. Despite such fragmentation, if this is indeed our home, then we do have our share of responsibility for its well-being. Hence, we have to find out how one should live and behave in a home that is so unlike the home we are used to.

Faced with the challenges posed by so many differences, it seems natural to look for a common denominator. After the collapse of the USSR, with its so-called socialist

---

20. Branko Miljković (1934-1961), Serbian poet.

regime, it seems that, at least for the western hemisphere, democracy remains this common denominator that can connect us all. Formally, we all live, or aspire to live, in a democratic society. This may be defined as meaning that we have a form of government in which the supreme power is vested in the people and exercised directly by them or by their elected agents under a free electoral system. This implies that once you manage to organise free elections your society is transformed into a democratic one, which may be understood as one characterised by formal equality of rights and privileges. More formalised definitions of these terms – as for instance stated in various dictionaries and other reference documents – do not concern themselves with the problem of converting this "formal equality" into a "real equality".

Regardless of the ambiguity of formal definitions, we now start from the assumption that only a democratic society can be considered a decent one; as a result, we are witnessing all around us the process of exporting and/or imposing democracy. Sometimes it is delivered through different types of co-operation, sometimes by force, but always with the true conviction that in the long run it will bring a decent life and prosperity to citizens.

To this end there seem to be two points that call for further clarification. The first one concerns the concept of democracy as it has been in existence in a number of Western societies for over a century. Is it possible that it remains basically unchanged in a time when everything else is rapidly changing? I believe not. I am convinced that it requires serious revisiting in the light of the new circumstances which guide our world. However, having no direct experience of living in such societies I can rely only on my perceptions as an outsider, based on my experience of Serbia and former Yugoslavia.

The second point is related to the export or introduction of democracy in countries that have no democratic tradition. Since I happened to be not only at the receiving end, but an active participant in this process, I believe my experience can throw some light on this endeavour. As a person responsible for reforming the higher education system in Serbia at the outset of the transition period, I was in a position to witness in practice what went wrong and why.

Living in the state-provided cradle

Serbia's transition started at a point when those who had an active memory of living in a democratic society were aged over 80; for the remaining population this was just an abstract notion. In spite of the fact that we were living in a one-party society, the majority was quite content with it. This was mainly due to the ever-improving standard of living, increased personal freedom and extensive social care enjoyed by the entire population.

The one-party system imposed after the Second World War, and the socialist revolution that came with it, was characterised by stable institutions, clear rules and a strong sense of where it was headed. The state took care of basic needs like employment, housing and health care. Personal freedom, in terms of travel and cultural activities, was also visibly improving. Over time professional skills started to matter more than party membership in all professions except those in the domains of humanities and social sciences. Hence there was a large area of activity around which one could organise one's professional activities without any reference to the actual regime.

The majority of those who had opted for careers in the humanities and social sciences succumbed to the given rules. As a consequence, those who were willing to oppose the regime and engage in dissident activities were not only in the minority, but often did not get any support or even understanding from others.

To sum up, we were a society in which people were never forced to take responsibility for any substantial personal or social decision, or indeed were aware that they would be better off if they did not try. In addition, those who were not party members had no experience in running the government or any other public institution.

In the context of a society organised in such a way, education was orientated towards developing academic and professional skills. This meant that our youngsters were taught, but not educated. Again, social sciences and the humanities suffered more, not only because education is their primary role but also because strong party control did not leave much room in their curricula for modern policies.

Having all this in mind, it came as no surprise when in December 1990, in the first free elections for over 40 years, the ruling Socialist Party headed by Slobodan Milošević took an overwhelming victory. Though this may be partly attributed to rising nationalism throughout the region, it is also evidence that people were reluctant to change and opted to remain in a state-provided cradle. We were living in a country where democracy was not a major issue.

Fighting for, learning about and dreaming of democracy

During the 1990s, wars and atrocities throughout the region, instigated and perpetrated by our government, followed by increasing corruption and economic decline, brought together groups of people who were ready to fight against it. Naturally the regime became more oppressive and totalitarian. Elections were largely rigged, so the question of what could be changed – and how – arose.

The regime had outwardly started to destroy one public institution after another. Draconian laws regulating the media, the judicial system and education were introduced. Out of sheer despair, people started to organise into groups around similar professional interests (including human rights, legal issues and education). Forced to function outside (and often parallel to) official institutions, gradually these groups registered as NGOs, though the majority had never heard this term before. They only knew that they had to do something to overthrow the regime and at the same time preserve some core values in society.

In spite of all the energy and the willingness to bring change, those NGOs lacked basic knowledge and experience of such activities. Help came from funds and institutions outside the country. The nascent NGOs – from those offering alternative education to those supplying legal services to disenfranchised sectors of society, and others acting as independent think-tanks formulating policy proposals – were recognised as groups who might bring change and deserved to get help in this endeavour. Through various seminars and projects we learned how to organise and got the means to do it. In addition, we got the opportunity to learn what changes were taking place in the outside world. Consequently we were eager and ready to initiate serious reforms and take our part in the transition.

On 5 October 2000 the regime was finally overthrown by a huge mass movement. Most people expected that, through a change of regime, they would also see a change towards a more decent society. Somehow all of us, including those who were taking over, believed that it could be done overnight. Going to sleep in a deeply destroyed society we expected to wake up in a rich, safe and sound environment with well-being, "liberty and justice for all". The overwhelming assumption was that it would suffice to elect a new government, which would take care of everything, much as before, so that the majority of the population could go back to doing their jobs and not being concerned with anything else. It seemed that the majority longed to be able to, once again, enjoy pleasant irresponsibility.

Going down the bumpy road of transition

The first transitional government was very eager to initiate major reforms and got strong support for that, within the country and from the world beyond. There was no lack of major reform policies because the NGOs that were formed in the 1990s joined forces with the government. However, the major drawbacks were lack of experience in governance, unskilled administration, corrupt institutions such as the police and the justice system, and empty state coffers.

Just when it seemed that the first government was ready to start delivering, the prime minister, Zoran Djindjić, was assassinated. The reform process was ended before it had even started. Taking into account that over half its term of office had already passed and that the first government introducing major reforms is inevitably doomed to lose the next election, there is still a question: would things have evolved differently had the prime minister survived?

The subsequent government was more right-wing and remained on the same course only in its declarations. In practice it took power but was unable or unwilling to start developing institutions, stop corruption and improve the standard of living.

The major problem seems to have lain in the fact that their concept of "being in power" was a carbon copy of the only government – the socialist one – they had ever seen. They considered it their right to place "loyal" party members in all vital and even ordinary positions. Public company CEOs, governing boards and similar posts were openly divided up while concluding the coalition agreement. Other public positions, such as those of judges or police management, were divided up surreptitiously.

With full awareness that the public expected some reforms, they engaged in perfunctory changes. New laws were constantly introduced under the pretence that they were adjusted to EU norms. However, there was no willingness to put them into operation and definitely no idea that they should apply to all citizens. As a consequence, all institutions were weakened and their authority devalued.

To sum up, the ten years of transition have not led us where we expected to be. At the moment we are witnessing liberal capitalism in a pauperised society. The ever-decreasing social benefits – such as deteriorating health care and no state-provided housing, accompanied by huge unemployment – can hardly be welcomed as a democratic achievement. In addition, privatisation, combined with increasing corruption, has created a large divide between the majority of the population, which has no decent living conditions, and a few tycoons who, together with party officials, are becoming increasingly rich.

Yet we have regular, free elections every fourth year. The overwhelming impression is that, in spite of the fact that people can choose, the problem lies in a poor offer. Regardless of the agreed definitions of terms, practice has shown that free elections do not suffice to establish a democratic society. A closer look at one particular reform process that did not succeed may indicate what might suffice, or at least might bring some improvement.

What went wrong, and why?

Efforts to reform the higher education system, which I was appointed to lead, can serve as an example of what went wrong and why. Those of us working with an educational NGO, [21] which I had the honour to lead, thought that after a few years we were ready to start the reform process. In our mission statement, we declared that we wanted to establish a modern higher education system in accordance with the Bologna Process. When applying to join the Bologna Process, we stated that "the academic community strongly endorses the notion of a European Higher Education Area and unanimously is voicing support to join it".

The starting premise was that it would suffice to draft a new modern higher education law so as to create the framework that defined the final goal and to help in its

---

21. The Alternative Academic Education Network (AAEN).

implementation. We believed that, given the freedom, academics would grab the opportunity to perpetuate reform almost on their own. Consequently, while drafting the law we launched a number of seminars and conferences to introduce the new concepts and explain what should be done and why.

Along the way we understood that we were wrong. To begin with, we overestimated the academic community, whose members were definitely not ready to understand their responsibilities and take on their new roles. Their attitude to the process was one of ambiguity between the feeling that something had to be changed and the fear of a possible loss of established status, which was disguised behind a stated need to preserve tradition. Hence the gap was widening between the declarative stance about reforms and their implementation.

The second drawback lay in the wrongly defined role of the NGOs. Instead of being at the forefront of the reform process on the academic side, they acted in the name of the first government as if incorporated within it. The underlying rationale was that the government had no internal strength to carry out reforms. This was further underlined by the fact that all support from outside turned to the government, signalling to the NGOs that the "new society" did not need them any more.

While it is hard to dispute the given rationale, the net result was that the NGO position within the academic community weakened. As a consequence, when the first government was replaced by a more conservative one, the new government did not meet any opposition when introducing an article in the new Law explicitly forbidding higher education NGO members to take part in any higher education governance or managerial bodies.

Since the new government did not seriously intend to continue with the reform process, it completely renounced its natural role in shaping higher education and left the academic community to draft the first "Bologna" Higher Education Law. In the absence of any pressure, the academic community drafted the Act to provide ample space for different interpretations. In a way it may be said that it reverted to the two-part maxim learned in the socialist past: "No higher education strategy (or Law), even the worst one, can force the academic community to ruin its higher education system" – this is damage minimisation – "and no higher education strategy (or Law), even the best one, can force the academic community to improve its higher education system" – which is effort minimisation.

This example clearly shows that, in addition to free elections, freedom and opportunity also do not suffice. Changes, no matter how declaratively supported, are rarely done willingly; there has to be somebody to promote them. It also asks the question as to whether it is possible to reform any subsystem as if it were an oasis within society, or does each subsystem have to reflect the whole picture?

Lessons learned

At the beginning, when we were instigating higher education reforms, we made the following SWOT analysis.

Our strengths were:

– the formal decision of the country to join the European Higher Education Area (EHEA) and European Research Area (ERA), and awareness – at least, an abstract awareness – of the benefits this might offer;

– our human resources in terms of professional capacity, experience in working on joint research projects and experience of co-operation with industry.

Our weaknesses were:

– human resources in terms of mindset, a wait-and-see mentality, reluctance to change;

– no experience in decision-making and taking personal responsibility;

– no government pressure to reform.

The opportunities were:

– the EU motivating us to conform to the accepted role and shape of the higher education system, as well as a possible source of major support in reform;

– the possibility of taking part in a number of projects and activities within the EU.

The threats were:

– an inherited ability to make perfunctory changes and then present them as serious ones;

– a public misconception of the notion of autonomy – missing the link with accountability and responsibility.

Ten years later this analysis is still valid. Even more so, it is valid in a broader sense, which means that the notions of EHEA and ERA can easily be switched with EU or democratic society, and the notion of "autonomy" with "democracy".

Why strengths and opportunities were not enough

There seems to be no doubt that up to now the weaknesses and threats have prevailed. There are several reasons why we were not able to profit from the strengths and opportunities.

First, governments tend to opt for short-term strategies that can be realised within the time span between elections. They are not willing to undertake major reforms that will antagonise certain influential groups. Instead, they prefer to use the media to promote and approve their activities. In addition, it is a sad truth that governments will always find support within the intellectually corrupted elite. Democracy is sidetracked. The best way to beat this can be citizens saying no to such changes, gathering in groups or NGOs to fight the injustice and the abuse of their right to democracy.

Unless they are unbearably oppressed, citizens tend to try to organise their life within the boundaries given. If possible, they will use the existing system to their benefit or try to go around it when necessary. Moreover, the lower the standard of living, the greater the focus on themselves. They somehow lose the perspective that their conditions might improve if they managed to force the government to introduce some changes.

A strong civil society seems to be the only one that can provide a consistent and continuing effort to introduce new policies and reshape society. Unfortunately, during the transition period our civil society has been almost completely marginalised with the assistance of those who had initially helped to build it.

During these ten years we have learned that democracy does not possess a magic wand to change reality into paradise. It requires responsible citizens ready to make decisions and take their own future in their hands. It also calls for well-organised, firmly structured, transparent institutions. It cannot be established overnight; it is a long process that requires a collective effort to reshape society.

There are things that can be done immediately. Relief in food, medicine and money can be delivered by any means, even from the sky. However, building democracy is not on that list. The "democratic dawn" cannot come from the sky. Though it can help in ousting a dictator, it is more accurate to view it as the last chapter of an oppressive regime. To mistakenly view it as the first chapter of a democracy brings, in the long term, only destruction, death, wounds, frustration, mistrust, hatred … and chaos.

The right to freely elect the government does not by itself constitute a democratic society. A trip to the voting booth every four years only presents an opportunity and an obligation for citizens to monitor governmental actions, to react promptly, to promote values and reinforce public opinion. But this cannot be achieved without a developed, firmly rooted civil society that constantly provides vision and motivation.

10. Europe's democracy under threat: how education can save our societies

Bert Vandenkendelaere

Scarred by the impact of the governance of our societies by their parents' generation, students of today are in doubt about the level of welfare they will be able to enjoy and the shape of the democracy in which they can participate in the future. Europe is suffering from a growing indifference among its young and a passivity threatening our societal development and democratic system. In this chapter I wish to give voice to the concerns of more than 11 million students represented by the European Students' Union (ESU) and to demonstrate how higher education can serve to overcome the increasing passivity in our young communities.

The irresponsible decisions and excesses of the governing baby-boomer generation have let their countries slip into a modern-age depression and one could expect revolutionary and angry reactions from the people who will have to suffer from their legacy. Younger people, however, in general remain passive in the face of this situation. I see the cause of this attitude in a fatigue resulting from governance failure, a defective positioning of the university in society and an indifference fed by the current teaching methods in higher education.

After I have clarified the context and the causes of this indifference, I want to explain how the university at the macro-level needs to play an important role as a watchdog and an institution of independent wisdom. I will also address how university teaching is crucial in creating and shaping the attitudes of society. The university can be both a reflection of the democratic organisation of our society and a training institution for its citizens. The introduction and development of student-centred learning can once again spark active citizenship in students and create the statesmen and -women who will be needed in the near future to lead our societies towards more tolerance and high-quality, democratic governance.

Swirling through the current problems in Europe and their effects on higher education and its students, I include a warning about some tendencies that are visible and I offer an alternative solution through socially responsible, engaged and student-centred higher education.

A time of concern

Another brick has been added to the wall of fear built up in the past decade. Whereas the 1990s knew prosperity, and students were happy to witness the world opening up to them, the first decade of the new millennium was one of paradoxes, of fear, of concern.

This chapter is based on a presentation at the conference Reimagining Democratic Societies: a New Era of Personal and Social Responsibility? – organised in Oslo by the Council of Europe, the US Steering Committee of the International Consortium for Higher Education, Civic Responsibility and Democracy, the International Association of Universities, the University of Oslo and the European Wergeland Centre. Less than a month later, in the same city and at a summer youth camp on Utøya, Anders Behring Breivik proudly took responsibility for killing 77 people, most of them students, in a "master plan" to warn the world about what he claimed to be the demographic and other warfare by Islam in Norwegian society. It is sadly yet another example of the developments discussed a month earlier in that city, in that conference. It unfortunately gives students yet another reason to worry about our future.

Ten years ago one would probably have been much more optimistic about the then-prosperous European society. At the time the mere idea of studying in an internationalised classroom and living abroad was not obvious. Low-cost airlines knew the same boom as European higher education: travelling became easy and cross-cultural exchange very welcome. Students were discovering the benefits of academic mobility, eager to open up our systems for neighbouring students, eager to live in a connected academic society. Those students saw the birth of the Bologna Process, a promise to establish a European Higher Education Area in which we could travel, study and work freely in a stronger Europe, in welfare and harmony.

Today, however, European students are worried: worried about their future, concerned about their society and upset about what previous generations have done to it. We have to face a future where prosperity is distributed by rating agencies (Tett 2010), where our travel will be restricted by new border controls (Pascouau 2011) and where education becomes a mere trade-off between the need to have a degree on the job market and the ever-increasing cost of it. We unfortunately have to face a future in which multiculturalism has been declared a failure (BBC 2011, Siebold 2010) and in which a tolerant citizen becomes a rare phenomenon.

This future needs to change. We, European students, are not content to live in a society where we are starting to be afraid of every news cycle, of every next day, where we are scared of our neighbours, for attacking us, for pulling our economy down or merely for stealing our chance of education. We are not content to go down in history as the first generation of modern Europeans that can expect to "benefit" from fewer opportunities than the previous one – whether it be from a significant age gap in wages, high risks of dropping out, post-graduation unemployment or limited support in starting a new home and a new family. We are also not content to be passive in the face of this new and sad reality.

A peak of passivity

We live in a society where being passive is becoming a habit. The baby-boomers have grown up and 1968 is far behind us. Europe is suffering from growing indifference, with citizens tired of reforms and the economic setbacks that we have inherited from an irresponsible baby-boomer generation. Just as the genocide in Rwanda in 1994 was for many "just another African mess", we have likewise become indifferent to suicide attacks and death tolls, but also to the economic downfall of our neighbours. Every crisis in one European country or another makes us more indifferent to the next one.

This indifference or no-questions-asked attitude is in my view a breeding ground for populism and for the shift to the intolerant right we are currently experiencing. Whereas ten years ago the European Students' Union would have had no problems in demanding an open and accessible Europe, it now has little hope that Europe will become more tolerant in the next few years, let alone that European integration will continue. The political balance of Europe is heavily tilting towards extremes, and in many countries elections are won on the basis of nationalist arguments, euro-scepticism and protectionism.

We are indeed living through what Bruno Kaufmann calls an "ethno-nationalistic backlash" in many countries: from Finland to Bulgaria, from Austria to Denmark, right-wing nationalist populism is gaining ground at the cost of tolerance, and very often at the cost of the social dimension in our societies (Kaufmann 2011). Why are citizens more open to right-wing propaganda than they were before? Did tolerance and solidarity and cross-cultural interest – or better, curiosity – just disappear?

The fact that a society can be played upon by populist politicians is to me a clear consequence of the indifference that means people no longer care for the poorer, for the attacked, for the sick, for the refugees – for their fellow citizens. What I want to outline in this chapter is how we as students, in co-operation with the academic leaders of today, would like to change this tendency, the likely future, and most importantly how higher education is the key to any of these changes. Although my opening paragraphs might have sounded rather pessimistic, I, together with the European students that ESU represents, still foster hope and intend to show what members of society – through higher education – need to do to change this situation for the better, how we can help our democracies to take intercultural understanding and active citizenship to the next level.

I want to discuss the role of higher education in the "reimagination of our democracies" on two levels: a macro- and a micro-level. The macro-level is named thus because it describes macro-politics, the public debate on the great questions and discussions in our democracies. Macro-level questions are political and societal questions connected to society as a whole. The micro-level concerns the individual and changes within the individual. The micro-level here is disconnected from larger group behaviour or other influences and is purely meant to discuss the position and role of an individual in the society.

In what follows I aim to show how education can serve as both lighthouse and watchdog at the macro-level, when – with no intention to make it sound elitist

– the educated citizens in our society are guiding others in wisdom. But I would mainly like to demonstrate that, even though I am part of a university that actively contributes to the dialogues of society as an institution, I believe the real change will have to come from a changed approach towards the individual. The individual student has to learn active citizenship from the start of his or her academic enrolment. To bring new democracies into practice, universities can indeed contribute by speaking out on certain topics as an institution, but they should first and foremost contribute by educating the critical voices of society. For this the teaching and learning practice in many higher education institutions has to change, and this chapter tries to argue that much larger things than simply the quality of teaching will be affected by this new teaching practice.

Democracy, although it actually originates from very common values and a feeling of governance that is justified through history, is something that is in my view now rather taught than found/rediscovered as the ideal form of governing and cohabiting. When we see the way Europe is voting, and how the level of democracy is declining in many countries, we have to look at what is being taught and, as I aim to show, at how things are being taught, to reimagine our democracies and to make people "find" democracy again as a natural, justified way of governing.

The macro-level: the university in our society

As a first step I want to discuss the university at the macro-level, as a player in our society taking part in debates about democracy and other topics, as a force that can steer or at least be heard and hopefully influence the public debate.

Higher education is crucial in maintaining our conscience of a collective history and in transferring that conscience between generations. It helps us learn from mistakes in the past, it teaches us about the birth of human rights, it makes us understand the acts, values and world views of different cultures and it should help us to live together in peace. Higher education should henceforth be accessible for all in accordance with their abilities and aspirations, without any discrimination, so learners from all levels of our society have access to this history, to knowledge, and can be shaped as active citizens.

Higher education should furthermore serve as the guardian of our democracy and the values that once made Europe such a peaceful and pleasant place in which to live and study. We as students truly believe higher education should be at the centre of our communities, because it creates educated citizens that serve as a reference in our societies, the people that other citizens depend on and trust for the creation and guidance of our societies in a democratic way.

One can somehow compare the role of higher education in society with the role of the Council of Europe. The latter focuses on human rights, democracy and the rule of law and serves as a promoter, through various reflective publications and initiatives, and as a protector, through the judgments of the European Court of Human Rights and the political action of the Secretary General. In the same way as the Council of Europe tries to promote the values it is built upon and serves as a centre of reflection on those values, higher education should try to promote the outcomes of its research, the values built by wisdom. Should it not promote, it should at least serve as a centre of reflection and propagation of the wisdom it has gathered. Or, as the Norwegian Minister of Higher Education and Research, Tora Aasland, puts it, universities are "nesting places for independent and critical thinking" (Chapter 4, above).

The university can and should play a significant role in public debates. Admittedly, the time when the university was regarded as the most important opinion-maker or the main source of wisdom is over. Rightly so, because the emancipated input from the business world, civil society organisations, trade unions, non-governmental organisations and the like, has its place next to the opinion of academia. The time when lawmakers or business leaders, let alone the great public, listened and often blindly agreed to what the "educated elite" thought about an event is long-gone history. But this does not mean that a university, its leadership and community can no longer play a large role in the public debate. They remain as centres of knowledge and, if they were to emerge from the restrictions put upon them by their current structures and financing, they could bring a significant added value as steady and independent reference points for "the educated answer" in public debates. Higher education should remind us citizens of what is important, away from markets, away from politics – especially as our societies become more complex: culturally diverse, economically interlinked and vulnerable. I do not want to pretend that logical reasoning, market interests and political views do not have a place any more in the governance of our society, but it becomes increasingly important to have subject-specific knowledge as well as transversal competences when taking part in these public debates of our complex societies.

It is therefore sad to see that in many places rectors or vice-chancellors are giving away their power to the presidents of boards of trustees, to regional economic leaders, to more managerially profiled leaders, who are often more short-sighted and focused on short-term needs of the labour market than are rectors with their academic and cultural baggage. It is not the only sign of a slowly decreasing independence of academic institutions, but the decision-making structures and financing models of higher education are changing in many countries. I want to consider this symptom of the decreasing independence of institutions and their lower profile in the societal debate. It is unfortunately logical, though: when the priorities of higher education institutions become those of basic economic survival, or even those of profit, and when the leadership has private interests to defend, the consequence is that the leadership and hence the university as a whole has little interest in mingling in the public debate. It does this less and less, all over Europe, and if the dual role of the university as watchdog and lighthouse is still existent, it is under threat.

Essentially, if our academic governance gets dominated by short-term economic needs dictated by the market, who will ensure the independence of the academics working there, and who will ensure the university's independence in thinking as an institution and as a lighthouse for the society around it?

Moreover, not only for the sake of quality education but particularly also for the sake of our democracies, higher education should maintain its independence from any short-sighted market powers. Many European governments are now examining how to withdraw from public financing for higher education or are already reducing the involvement of the state budget in financing higher education. By treating education as a commodity and by looking to students or business to finance the whole cost of education, they are undermining the entire idea of the university as a nesting place for independent thinking. They make it more difficult for academia to choose wisdom and research as its main priorities when forming an opinion in the public debate. Putting this enormous financial pressure on universities makes their leadership more and more powerless to independently participate in those debates and serve as a reference in the democracy, even if that leadership has not already been replaced by a "neutral" management structure, not personally committed to the university's values and not especially interested in where society – the democracy and society in which the institution nests – is going.

It is thus critical that some European governments take a step back from where they are going now, and invest in academic freedom, in the financial and scientific independence of their institutions. Besides, they are pushing their students away from their societies and taking away the last fresh blood they had for their future democracies.

Fee exodus

Because of the steep rise in tuition fees, ESU's members in the United Kingdom are vigorously seeking other European destinations where education is available at a cheaper rate, and there is no guarantee that they will return to work and contribute to British society. The tuition fees in many British universities rose from £3 000 to about £9 000 per year, following a decision by the Conservative–Liberal Democrat coalition. This leaves the graduate who then studies for a master's degree with a typical cost of £45 000 in tuition alone, which is not sufficiently backed up – and this is even more true in the United States – by grants and other scholarship systems. The change will force students to take study loans or reconsider going on to higher education at all. Already, part of UK society is undoubtedly pulling out of higher education, and the youngest are giving up on their dream of going to university because they will never be able to afford it or earn the investment back.

As discussed above, our democracies are increasingly complex and hence their governance relies on educated citizens. Structural innovation can only come from strong higher education and from progress in the development of our best-educated citizens. But the harsh increase in tuition fees that was implemented in the United

Kingdom has the consequence that young people are fleeing (and rightly so) to havens of cheaper education. Unless the decision is reconsidered or a suitable social support package is provided to remedy the enormous flaws in the current financing system, other young citizens will not flee but simply give up the idea of tertiary education. Instead of paying large amounts for formal education, they will turn to informal or non-formal education and learning by practice. Notwithstanding the advantages and qualities of informal and non-formal education, this will reduce the number of students receiving the important collective history and (generalising) the highest quality of education to which they have the right.

The British turn-around is unfortunately serving as a model for other European governments and, as fast as ethno-nationalism is conquering European parliamentary assemblies, the idea of privatised higher education and student contributions is being put into practice. The introduction of high tuition fees – or raising them if they are already present – in other western European countries will create many more streams of "free-movers" that will lead to an education deficit in the countries they leave. Among the likely tangible problems that come to my mind are reduced brain-circulation, restricted student mobility, protective education entrance exams or requirements, infringements on the free movement of persons (and the Devil's advocate would mention free trade too) and the reaction of the taxpayers who pay for all the free-movers coming to their country if more and more European education systems focus on tuition fees, apart from the huge drought in intellect in the democracy, leaving society more open to populism and intolerance. The argument would not be the same if all systems became fee-dominated, though that would mean these free-movers seeking access to higher education according to their financial capacity would no longer find that access and would be prevented from entering higher education. Both options lead to an education deficit.

If these governments do not urgently start treating education again as a public good and a public responsibility, we as students fear a diminution of intellectual advancement and, in the long run, of innovation, prosperity and democracy.

The micro-level: the society in our university

We already face a reduction in democracy. In 2010, the Economist Democracy Index went down in 91 out of 167 countries listed, in comparison to its 2008 edition (Economist 2010). What could come as a surprise to some is that these countries were not necessarily "just another African mess", but central European powers such as Italy and France.[22]

---

22. By again referring to "just another African mess" I have no intention at all to denigrate African countries or their citizens, but rather refer to the prejudices many Europeans hold and the indifference that exists to persistent problems in African countries. It rather brings hope and beats prejudices to see Mali and Ghana, for example, climbing in the Democracy Index from hybrid system to flawed democracy – the same level as France and Italy.

According to this index, Norway is now the most democratic country in the world, but many European countries have become flawed democracies, subject to market influence and to corruption. It is – for me, and I assume for most young citizens – appalling to see that the European Union allows the level of democracy to decline, and is – more realistically speaking – powerless against the larger market powers. The richer leaders in its "union" are ironically the ones reducing the level of democracy. To quote Srbijanka Turajlić, former Deputy Minister for Higher Education of Serbia and former Chair of the Alternative Academic Education Network: "the best way to beat this can be citizens saying no to such changes, gathering in groups or NGOs to fight the injustice and the abuse of their right to democracy" (Turajlić, Chapter 9 above).

Unfortunately, though I very much wish it was otherwise, the burning desire for change that once made Serbia become a flawed democracy (Economist 2010) instead of a country ruled by an authoritarian regime, is lacking today all over Europe – even in Serbia.

I come from a country where, due to negotiations between political parties and cultural communities, we had no government for 541 days. You would imagine protests, riots, a furious civil society reclaiming their votes, demanding a solution. But no, in Belgium – which, ironically enough, is symptomatic of a much larger part of Europe – the citizens do not necessarily care. Over more than a year (and actually the situation had been very difficult for over three years) there has been one protest and a few "funny" actions to raise attention, but all these actions remained rather unpopular. Few care, and certainly not enough people think they should think about it! If they cared even a bit, and learnt to actively pursue their societal welfare, things would not look the same.

That is why the European Students' Union believes that, alongside the macro-level, with the higher education institutions as guides for our democratic development, a lot can be done on the micro-level, within the institutions and focusing on the individual. Activating the individual is to activate the basis of our democracies.

Active citizenship arising from student-centred learning

In a simplistic approach, obviously, higher education can be of great importance in steering democracy: "learning" pluralism, transmitting the right set of values to the leaders of tomorrow. Whether the values and tools learnt in higher education are used for the right purpose also depends, I admit, on the personal interest of the leader in question, but nobody will question the benefits of a broad education resulting in a pluralistic attitude. It proves how important it is that the right values are chosen for transmission in higher education and that independence and academic freedom are maintained by a market-independent leadership.

But, more important than its leaders, higher education should provide the basic knowledge and understanding with which all citizens can question their leaders and make democracy function as a peaceful dialogue between leaders and active citizens, who are fully involved in their society and concerned with the way that society is developing. Aristotle defines citizenship in many ways. One definition of a citizen in his *Politics* goes as follows: "A citizen pure and simple is defined by nothing else so much as by the right to participate in judicial functions and in office" (Aristotle 1999 web edition). Building on this and mainly alluding to it – as the entire context of this passage from *Politics* and the ancient Greek *polis* is different from what concerns us here – I would postulate that a citizen pure and simple is defined by nothing else so much as by the possibility and willingness to participate in public life, the larger political life of the *polis*, the big questions of our democracies. A democratic society is nothing unless its citizens can be actively involved. But even more, and Aristotle would be deeply worried to see this in our modern societies, a democracy cannot live without the empathy, the interest of its citizens in the welfare of society as a whole, in the positive development of their democracy. This is what is genuinely lacking in many European countries.

It is easy to find a source of this new behaviour and this indifference to the way we are organising higher education and hence skilling young citizens for an active life in society. If you are only taught to listen to what the teacher has to say and copy that for your examination, it is only normal that the citizens this education brings forward are not as critical as they could be and are rather passive towards all societal development. The way most higher education is being delivered to students is *ex cathedra*, a one-way street dominated by the teacher, with little room for debate or questions. This is already improving in western and north-western Europe, but unfortunately as with many changes in higher education we must note that southern and eastern Europe are lagging far behind in activity-based learning and other forms of student-centred learning (European Students' Union 2010a: 105). With the experience of members of the European Students' Union in mind, it is appropriate to emphasise that, though the situation is slightly improving, in most European countries this passive form of teaching is still the rule, with sometimes dramatic forms of bureaucracy, classroom hierarchy and formality in (southern and) eastern Europe.

As Sjur Bergan, Head of the Education Department of the Council of Europe, says (Chapter 7, above):

> Democracy is about more than voting every three or four years. Democracy is about participating in the lives of our societies every week of the year and every day of the week. ... Apathy and lack of interest are as strong threats to democracy as active opposition to it.

Or, as a student on the discussion panel at the Oslo conference put it (Chapter 26, below):

> Democracy is not only about having institutions in place and having fair procedures and elections, but it's about the daily participation of citizens in a society, and apathy, lack of interest is the biggest threat to our democratic development.

The education that Europe knows in many places today fosters this apathy for the majority of the students. Apart from the deeply engaged student who actively seeks more knowledge than is provided in the classroom, European universities have become battery cages in which students are fed information with little opportunity for interaction and independent thinking. When thinking about the primary reasons for this phenomenon it seems difficult to ignore the reality that a lot of it is caused by austerity measures adopted because of the financial crisis and even more so by the "massification" of higher education, which has turned a privilege for the elite into a programme for many, but all too often without the appropriate budget alteration. Nonetheless, even given austerity and massification combined, a lot of it is caused by the reluctance of teachers and university leaders to try something new. Teachers blame it on a lack of support measures for them to start working on better forms of learning; as I shall clarify below, I agree with this argument. It is, however, not the only reason and a real paradigm shift is needed, despite austerity measures or the lack of a supportive environment. If Europe maintains these passive forms of learning, fostering apathy among students, this will severely affect the well-being of our society.

To be precise, the product of this kind of education is, with notable exceptions admittedly, citizens open to populist propaganda, without questions asked, and indifferent to what is done to the democratic society they live in. Once again coming back to eastern Europe, there is a looming danger that societies there, already troubled by the fact that many of the most brilliant brains are leaving their country for a higher-quality education or employment elsewhere, will be filled with passive citizens, obedient to hierarchy and easily convinced by the arguments of populist politics.

Whereas people who do not live in a democracy know what they are fighting for, European citizens today are not sufficiently aware of what they can lose again if they do not fight for their democracy or at least stand up for it. And our higher education can change this. Our higher education can once again create a generation of involved citizens, by getting them involved from the start in the classroom. By introducing student-centred learning, higher education institutions could stimulate students to become active citizens again, ask questions, seek improvement and become active contributors to the welfare of their societies.

This also came forward as an ambition of the European ministers of higher education in the 2009 Leuven/Louvain-La-Neuve Ministerial Communiqué of the Bologna Process, now renamed the European Higher Education Area, which stated (Bologna Process 2009):

> Student-centred learning and mobility will help students develop the competences they need in a changing labour market and will empower them to become active and responsible citizens. ... The aim is to ensure that higher education institutions have the necessary resources to continue to fulfil their full range of purposes, such as preparing students for life as active citizens in a democratic society; preparing students for their future careers and enabling their personal development; creating and maintaining a broad, advanced knowledge base and stimulating research and innovation.

The extract shows that the demand for student-centred learning is very legitimate and that the connection with active and responsible citizenship is also made by the higher education ministers of the European Higher Education Area. For a while it remained a question, though, what exactly was meant by "student-centred learning" and how we can implement it, in large groups, despite austerity measures being put in place. Even in times of mass higher education, the European Students' Union believes student-centred learning is paramount for students to fully develop their potential, for universities to skill the future workforce and to create the best leaders for tomorrow. It hence also created, in co-operation with the global teaching staff union, Education International, a Toolkit for Student-Centred Learning, in which the idea was defined and translated into practical proposals and tools (European Students' Union 2010b). According to this, student-centred learning can be defined as follows:

> Student-Centred Learning represents both a mindset and a culture within a given higher education institution and is a learning approach which is broadly related to, and supported by, constructivist theories of learning. It is characterised by innovative methods of teaching which aim to promote learning in communication with teachers and other learners and which take students seriously as active participants in their own learning, fostering transferable skills such as problem-solving, critical thinking and reflective thinking.

It takes students out of their ordinary situation of listening and reproducing what they have heard, and transforms them into actors in their own education, guided to excel beyond their own expectations but allowed to do that on their own in co-operation with their colleagues. Certainly after receiving a broad introduction they define and decide how and what they want to learn. The teacher then knows the expectations of the students, and the students are more autonomous in creating their own curriculum and progress. They will feel more committed, more involved, and have ownership over their curriculum. They will question the established knowledge and find their own truth. It is often used as a platitude, but it is a fact that students should answer the questions themselves. They do not need someone to preach a truth; they need guidance on what tools to use and how to use them in search of the answers to their questions.

Academic governance usually sweeps the idea off the table because it would be too expensive to hire enough staff for a decent interaction with the students. However, even with a very bad student/staff ratio it is possible to organise it. I also raised this at the 2010 OECD Institutional Management in Higher Education conference, Doing More with Less, though actually the exercise aimed to produce a more efficient work environment with less time spent in lectures, fewer examinations and more self- and peer-assessment. [23]

---

23. See www.oecd.org/dataoecd/22/54/45950511.pdf (accessed on 27 May 2012); the speech was not published.

The conventional methods of teaching have failed and one should rethink the role of a teacher entirely. After all, I doubt that teachers have ever enjoyed long, repetitive readings of their material without interaction. I doubt if it was the most efficient way of teaching, and surely it is not the most qualitative one. The new way of learning should be independent and problem-based. It should send the students out in the field to collect data, teach them and help them to digest this and transform it into academic knowledge.

Khan Academy

There are more and more online modules of university courses, but why not more in a form like the one promoted by the Khan Academy? This spontaneously-begun Internet platform contains already more than 2 400 freely accessible teaching videos from Extraneous Solutions to Radical Equations and The French Revolution to Economics of a Cupcake Factory. [24]

Students start at basic levels and can advance to more difficult video classes when they are ready. In the Khan Academy system, evaluation results give an overview of where each student is in the classroom for that subject. The stronger students can advance; the weaker students need some repetition or help from stronger students, who hence become teachers for less strong students; their peer work, with thorough mentoring, can become as valuable as a classic academic course. The Khan Academy takes place entirely online, so students from Brazil who are good at mathematics can help students from Azerbaijan to get the picture. This is not the place to go into further detail but, fully in the spirit of the Khan Academy, there is a video that can far better explain the system and benefits invented and shared by Salman Khan. [25] It is worth watching and then asking if this system could not easily be implemented in higher education, where students already should be more apt to learn independently and teach colleagues in need.

To give students the construction authority over their curriculum and the freedom to learn how they want it through projects with peers is a risk. The student-centred model thus does not exclude the teacher from education. Clearly a lot of support is still needed at the entry level, but there are examples of universities that have even abolished examinations and leave the students themselves to work on projects and assess each other's performance in later years.

All this is mentored by a teacher, but the student learns to be independent and entrepreneurial. The student also learns how to debate with colleagues and how to develop ideas, gaining those valuable transferable skills that are needed to function in any labour market and society. It makes us, as students, think outside the box and perform

---

24. See www.khanacademy.org (accessed on 27 May 2012).
25. S. Khan, "Let's use video to reinvent education", www.ted.com/talks/salman_khan_let_s_use_ video_to_reinvent_education.html (accessed on 23 August 2011).

in the interdisciplinary environment around us. And more importantly, it makes us question the information that is given to us, and we become people who go out into society ready to change what is going wrong and protect the values we adhere to. It activates the student, and it teaches the citizen inside the student how to be active.

This may of course sound like a very idealistic idea that institutions and governments will not be able to afford and teachers will never accept. This is absolutely not the case.

Firstly, we are talking about a paradigm shift, a total change of mentality, a shift in education and curriculum design by which both the teacher and the student have to arrive in the classroom with a different attitude. The teacher has to want to know what students expect and what their background is when they start. The student needs to be willing to pursue knowledge and actively engage in his or her educational career. It might provoke some reluctance from all parties when they first get to know the concept of student-centred learning, but that reluctance is mainly based on the fact that we are still stuck in a different paradigm, fearing the unknown. All it takes is the ambition to jump to higher-quality higher education, an ambition which has to be shared by the governance, the staff and the students.

Secondly, this change will never happen at one fell swoop and it will not be brought about through articles and essays. It needs to be hands-on. Rectors and academic directors can start tomorrow, by taking the checklist from our toolkit to see how their institutions rate on the scale of student-centred learning. Measures are proposed to improve that rating, and to create a student-centred learning environment even in the largest classrooms or for the poorest institutions.

More is needed of course, in particular to build a supportive environment in which to create student-centred learning. I still hold that league tables and university rankings are a malicious and simplistic way of measuring quality, but it would already be a slight improvement if they would also value the teaching mission, teaching innovation and student satisfaction in the institution, rather than being mainly based on research output. As Phillip Altbach says: "the problem is that these criteria still do not actually measure teaching and not even come close to assessing the quality of impact" (Altbach 2011). It is sad but true that institutions everywhere (but, from my experience, especially in eastern Europe) focus on league tables to determine their strategy and budget allocation in the hope of becoming "the world's best university". Hence – and again, this is regrettable – if rankings took into account teaching quality and teaching innovation, the institutional governance bodies could have an eye – and a budget – for it. Research is what brings universities to the top of the rankings in most cases today. The natural consequence is that teachers have to perform in those fields that affect the league table standing and have little time or stimulus to do well in the fields not relevant to that. I hence reiterate that rankings are no tool to assess or inform students about the quality of education. They furthermore form an obstacle to the implementation of student-centred learning, an ambition laid down in the larger framework of the European Higher Education Area.

Rankings are, however, not the only reason why teachers are not able to work on student-centred ways of teaching. It is also a matter of internal institutional governance, and the European Students' Union is seeking revision of the evaluation methods for career progress.

Judging the quality of academic staff by assessing research output and capacity is still a widespread way of deciding which staff members should be promoted. Apart from the entire administrative burden that is already being put on teachers – especially in the Bologna reforms period – they are forced to produce research output in order to climb the ladder. It might be derived from the ambition of being a world-class university, it might be part of the mission of the university to perform in research or it might simply be an unquestioned habit. In any case, the habit can be changed and even a world-class, research-orientated university cannot produce new generations of excellent researchers without high-quality teaching.

But why would a teacher these days invest time in teaching innovation, in getting extra training for their teaching mission, and in the teaching mission itself, when his or her academic progress is in most cases dependent on research performance and output?

Only by evaluating fulfilment of the teaching mission and allowing time for teaching innovation will teachers be able to devote themselves more to this than to their research careers. Only by valuing the teaching mission more than we do today, will we be able to balance the activities of the teacher and create time to foster the first sparks of active citizenship in the classroom.

Tolerance through student and staff mobility

We have already touched upon the macro-level, with the role of the university in society, and the need on the micro-level to implement student-centred learning for active citizenship beyond the study years. While activity and project-based learning should already enhance the tolerance and understanding of the individual, one should still seize every opportunity to promote the benefits of student and staff mobility, because there is nothing so effective in enhancing tolerance and understanding.

Educated citizens are in general more tolerant citizens. They will, again in general, be less easily influenced by right-wing extremist propaganda. Making students work together with colleagues during their study time will, especially in internationalised universities, add further to their level of tolerance. But nothing compares to what students and staff experience when going abroad for a relevant academic exchange or study period.

First of all, there should be more support for academic staff to be mobile. This is still a painful point in the European Higher Education Area that needs proper attention. The change of attitude that staff can bring into the classroom and day-to-day contact with students is enormous. It is important to note that only about 5 per cent of students are currently mobile.[26] While the Bologna target is to raise that number to 20 per cent by 2020 (Bologna Process 2009), even in the best-case scenario that would still keep 80 per cent of the students in their country for the entire duration of their studies. It is also financially impossible, and even not wished by some students, to aim at 100 per cent mobility among students, but the mere impression that can be made by having international members of staff or "internationalised" teachers from the home institution and country is a standard every institution should be working towards. It is consequently paramount to send teachers abroad and for authorities and academic leadership to allocate resources to this.

Many works have already been written about the benefits of student mobility for the personal development of students and for the opportunities of those students on the labour market. In the light of this chapter, and the problems of right-wing populism and extremism raised previously, it is fitting to restate how far more individual students will automatically become more tolerant from going abroad than could be achieved by simply having a mobile teacher. Thus, if staff mobility is and will remain of great importance for the ones staying at home, and for the quality of education for all, the ambition should indeed be to send at least 20 per cent of students abroad by 2020. The main obstacle to achieving the benchmark is unfortunately the financial capacity of students to go abroad for a period of their studies (Vossensteyn et al. 2010: 4). To fulfil these promises a lot of investment will have to follow because, with the current state of mobility support and plans to make students pay for it, the level of mobility among students is more likely to stagnate or even decline in the coming years. Reinvented democratic societies need these active and tolerant citizens and hence need students to travel and study abroad as much as possible to form their personality. The cross-cultural exchange that takes place in a mobility period and the increased tolerance it brings cannot be taught in any other form of education.

The university as a reflection of our democracies

Finally, apart from the tolerance created through student mobility, the active citizenship created through student-centred learning and the societal welfare created through an active university in the public debate, the university can also be a model of democratic governance. The European Students' Union sees it as an absolute right of students to have a say in the development and evaluation of their academic curriculum. For many students it is their first

---

26. Bernd Wächter at the ACA Seminar, Mobility under a Magnifying Glass, 3 December 2010, Brussels, and based on ACA, CampusFrance, DAAD, Hochschul-Informations-Systems GmbH (HIS), U. Teichler, U. Lanzendorf and S. Bürger, *Mapping Mobility in Higher Education* (formerly known as *EURODATA II*).

chance to take part as an "active student" in their academic society and get to know forms of democracy in practice. It is also obvious that the only way in which we will keep our higher education institutions sensitive to these societal frustrations and the only way we can find acceptance for the much-needed university reforms is by listening to and working with students in the governance of our universities.

Giving student representatives access to the highest levels of decision-making in the university is a must and is, in the context of this chapter, a vital factor to set the right tone in the perception of democratic governance and active citizenship in students' development. The recent trend of withdrawing public funding for higher education adds to the idea of students being marginalised as users of higher education, rather than treated as equal partners. Creating a system in which students follow the laws of pure consumerism is fatal for our societal development. If this happened (as Lord Browne of Madingley and his commission foresaw in their report *Securing a Sustainable Future for Higher Education*), there would be many questions to ask about the quality of our higher education (Browne 2010). Apart from that, consumerism in higher education can in my view also affect the way citizens look at societal governance. Consumerism is easy in politics: party-shopping and populism go hand in hand, but they are a threat to the quality, the welfare and the sustainability of our democracies.

The university should thus play a role as a model for our societies, teaching how to interact with governance and how to change what is not going well, through joint decision-making. This will skill the students to become involved and significant citizens themselves, rather than easily influenced consumers of a flawed democracy.

Conclusion

Education on the macro-level can be the lighthouse for what goes right and wrong in our societies and for what history has taught us. Education on the micro-level can bring forward active citizens who question the way in which society is being run and have the courage to do it better themselves. With these two roles of education fulfilled, our democracy should know more actively involved students. If those students have experienced how other societies shape their community life, those actively involved citizens will also be more tolerant and open towards other cultures in society. They will be able to listen to and work respectfully with others, even when they are from different backgrounds or of different opinions. Apart from the importance of primary and secondary education, which lay the foundation of our core values, our way of living in society can be shaped by experience of democracy in higher education: with students and staff in equal partnership with the governance of the institution and the authorities the right "model" for societal debate and true democracy is set. Students will respond to the opportunity of joint decision-making and will not turn as easily to consumerism and populism in their political life as a citizen.

The ESU believes the Council of Europe can be crucial in promoting this in its member states and should be the first organisation to protect and support both the macro- and micro-level tasks of higher education. We will not experience true democracy, we will not be able to enjoy our human rights and the rule of law, if it is not injected into and safeguarded by our higher education systems, which have been the origin of democracy and will be the saviour of it.

Ira Harkavy, Chair of the US Steering Committee of the International, Consortium for Higher Education, Civic Responsibility and Democracy, cuts to the chase: "no effective democratic schooling system, no democratic society" (Chapter 6, above). I would even go one step further by saying: no active and mobile students, no active and tolerant citizens.

References

Altbach, P. (2011), "Rankings season is here", *International Higher Education*, 62 (2011): 2-5.

Aristotle (1999 web edn), *Politics*, III, 1275a, 20, www.perseus.tufts.edu/hopper/text?doc=Perseus%3Atext%3A1999.01.0058%3Abook%3D3%3Asection%3D1275a (accessed on 23 August 2011).

BBC (2011), "State multiculturalism has failed, says Cameron", BBC News (5 February), www.bbc.co.uk/news/uk-politics-12371994 (accessed on 23 August 2011).

Bergan, S. (2012), "Reimagining democratic societies: what does education have to do with it?", Chapter 7 in the present volume.

Bologna Process (2009), "The Bologna Process 2020 – the European Higher Education Area in the new decade", Communiqué of the Conference of European Ministers Responsible for Higher Education, Leuven and Louvain-la-Neuve, 28-29 April 2009. Available at www.ond.vlaanderen.be/hogeronderwijs/bologna/conference/ (accessed on 23 August 2012).

Browne of Madingley, Lord (2010), *The Browne Review* (12 October 2010), http://webarchive.nationalarchives.gov.uk/+/hereview.independent.gov.uk/hereview/report/ (accessed on 23 August 2011).

Economist (2010), *Economist Intelligence Unit's Democracy Index 2010*, http://graphics.eiu.com/PDF/Democracy_Index_2010_web.pdf (accessed on 23 August 2011).

European Students' Union (2010a), *Bologna at the Finish Line, 2010*, Berlin: Laserline.

—   (2010b), *Student-Centred Learning – toolkit for students, staff and higher education institutions*, Berlin: Laserline.

Harkavy I. (2012), "Reimagining schools, universities and democracies", Chapter 6 in the present volume.

Kaufmann B. (2011), "Beyond the 'European dream" (27 June), http://euobserver. com/7/32552, 2011 (accessed on 23 August 2011).

Pascouau Y. (2011), "Internal border controls in the Schengen area: much ado about nothing?" (28 June), www.epc.eu/documents/uploads/pub_1309_ internal_border_controls_in_the_schengen_area_-_much_ado_about_ nothing.pdf (accessed on 23 August 2011).

Siebold S. (2010), "Merkel says German multiculturalism has failed" (16 October), www.reuters.com/article/2010/10/16/us-germany-merkel-immigration- idUSTRE69F1K320101016 (accessed on 23 August 2011).

Tett G. (2010), "Rating agencies in a bind as pressure mounts", *Financial Times* (16 December), http://www.ft.com/intl/cms/s/0/f420a838-092e-11e0- ada6-00144feabdc0.html#axzz2ACNgmmnz (accessed on 23 August 2011).

Turajlić S. (2012), "Reimagining democratic societies in challenging circumstances: the role of higher education", Chapter 9 in the present volume.

Vossensteyn H. et al. (2010), "Improving the participation in the Erasmus Study Programme" Brussels: European Parliament, www.europarl. europa.eu/meetdocs/2009_2014/documents/cult/dv/esstudyerasmus/ esstudyerasmusen.pdf (accessed on 23 August 2011).

11. Deliberative democracy and moral disturbance

Inga Bostad and Lars Løvlie

The background: 22 July 2011

A vivid and healthy democracy is not only built upon education; it must be aware of the difference between an educated person and someone with insight, capable of using knowledge to create a better world. A better world means a world with equality, dignity and freedom, as well as a place for critical reflection where political, religious and moral discussions are encouraged. We have seen through history too many examples of educated citizens who have misused their knowledge, acted against democracy and in the extreme ended up as perpetrators, oppressors and terrorists; they show us that education in itself is not a guarantee against violence, humiliation and abuse.

In the summer of 2011, shortly after the conference on democracy at the University of Oslo, a terrible and horrific event took place. Altogether 77 people, at the government headquarters in Oslo and on the island of Utøya, some 40 kilometers away, where engaged youth were participating in a political camp for social democracy, were brutally killed by a terrorist – the vast majority of them at Utøya. The nation went into collective shock but, instead of meeting the events with fear and demands for revenge, more police and armed security, it seemed as if the people of Norway gathered around democratic values such as more openness and more solidarity. And shortly after the killings, the streets of Oslo were covered by roses, in front of the Lutheran cathedral, Parliament, the government buildings, City Hall and the Royal Palace.

But then the reflection started. How may our society be inclusive and at the same time defend its own values? How can we express even more clearly respect for human integrity and our inherent value as humans? How can our society make room for unpopular and extreme opinions, while being sensitive to the fear of terror? And not least: how do we combine fruitful and sound nationalism with global solidarity? To answer these questions we need to take better account of the aggressive and radical Internet discussions on immigration, national identity, violence and culture. We need to confront the uncomfortable ideas that exist in our society and in this confrontation refine our views on tolerance and intolerance.

The events in Oslo and on Utøya in the summer of 2011 add an important dimension to the need for reimagining a democratic society. The terrorist's own ideology showed distaste for weakness and a romanticising of violence, combined with a desire to be a uniformed hero. This terrorist was also a product of our society and his ideas have their roots in the middle of our ordinary lives. How do we confront ideologies of this type, how do we build up resistance to such inhumane actions and how do we create a public culture of debate and action that appeals to a diverse and modern society?

Education is a part of the answer, but we cannot "teach away" the terrorists. In this chapter we argue for an education that seeks to foster critical, reflective, moral individuals, people who are first and foremost morally capable of creating moral disturbance when confronted with the current global dilemmas, or with the classic questions in science and society, and who have internalised the academic virtues of being analytical, critical and ethical – arguing with precision, care and sufficient knowledge. Such dramatic experiences as those of summer 2011 in Oslo and Utøya may open two windows to give academic society a clearer view: one window is a liberal education, backed by the historical and multidisciplinary knowledge that universities nurture, that we need if we are to cope with any unknown event in the future; the other window is an awareness of what is lacking in today's democracy. The core task of an open society is to develop and develop, again and again, for every new generation, a public dialogue – a dialogue broad enough to face uncomfortable dilemmas.

Reimagining democratic societies: deliberative democracy

Political education often begins with personal experiences of infringement, injustice or lack of respect for oneself and others, being drawn into political movements and organisations, or with dramatic political events. It may also come down to the more commonplace influence of a good friend, an inspirational teacher or an absorbing book. In any case, it seems to begin *in medias res* – in the middle of things, by time and by place: the assassination of President John F. Kennedy in Dallas in 1963, the attack on the World Trade Center in 2001 and now in Oslo and on Utøya on 22 July 2011. A person does not become politically-minded out of the blue but through their upbringing, which makes us part of a society of political institutions. Even when we are children, the past is engraved in our minds in the form of attitudes, customs and concepts. But it is the incident that ignites our perception of history, making a difference and thereby becoming significant. Utøya was one of these instances.

We will let the incident of 22 July lead us into the subject: education in a democracy. The bombing of the government block and the massacre on Utøya increased the significance of what is known as deliberative democracy, based on the concept of a political debate in which everyone, in principle, has a right to their opinion, and in which people follow common rules of objectivity. In terms of methodology, the deliberative is based on a dogma of objectivity, while it is clear that a political education is more than a mere skill and an instrument. It is the everyday world that makes the dogma of objectivity and political debate possible, and it is tradition that provides cultural resources. If we are to talk of democracy in the Western sense, then we require concepts and values such as freedom of expression, solidarity and tolerance.

Moreover, we relate to such values in a rhetorical field in which irony, paradox and deconstruction all form part of political education. But let us begin at the heart of the reality of 22 July. The attacks were carried out by a 32-year-old ethnic Norwegian, born and brought up in Oslo, who to everyone's astonishment was operating alone. We cannot begin to explain Anders Behring Breivik's actions. He made the impossible possible, but we cannot prepare for the impossible. We can improve the upbringing provided by schools, but we cannot "teach away" the terrorists. If psychological diagnoses result in the increasing isolation and stricter treatment of potential offenders, if measures to guard against the impossible move us further towards a surveillance society, if the news media fuel people's fear and loathing, and if the reaction of schools is to indoctrinate, then we are moving towards the very totalitarian society that Breivik wanted. Breivik is a neo-fascist ideologue, urging us to fight against what he perceives as a back-door Islamification of Europe. His ideology is based on the premise that a Muslim invasion is supported by the governing political elite and the public media, and that the political youth organisations of Norway are continuing this tradition.

On the day he carried out the attacks, Breivik published a 1500-page political manifesto, cut and pasted from various sources and supplemented by his own comments. In this context three features of Breivik's position are worth mentioning, features that lead to the question of how we envisage education in a deliberative democracy. The first feature is ideology and it is tied up with viewpoints that are as common on populist immigrant-sceptic Internet fora as on Europe's extreme right wing. Those who envisage what they call Eurabia do not necessarily lack political knowledge. The flaw in their argument lies in the facts, in a logic that concludes with the absurd, in a judgment that is warped. The second feature is immunisation, which is on an emotional level and can act as a motivator for extreme actions. This is about the "big conspiracy", the alleged Muslim plot to take over political power in the West, an intrigue in which the Western elite is a willing participant.

What are the typical features of this kind of conspiracy theory? Naturally, it is immune to criticism. Counter-arguments against the theory are by definition part of the big conspiracy. They only reinforce the belief that the other party is embracing the whole pack of lies. This paranoia and lack of trust preclude any actual objective discussion. The third feature is self-imposed isolation and denial of reality: withdrawal from interaction with family, schoolmates, friends and colleagues. This creates a social and mental void that limits any recognition of others and means that family and authorities can have only limited influence. What insights do we gain from this? Firstly, that knowledge is not enough. It must be disciplined by a communicative, discursive rationality and controlled by reasonable procedures. Secondly, that faith-based immunisation prohibits the discursive public that Kant in his day envisaged, where people have the courage to express themselves based on personal autonomy and a healthy examination of reality. Thirdly, that self-imposed isolation leads to real isolation and lack of judgment; for judgment is another word for social common sense, and we develop this by interacting with other people. These conclusions can be summarised in the concept of a deliberative or discursive democracy.

Some history

The word "to deliberate" roughly means to evaluate, discuss and reflect, but has no immediate function in everyday language. The word "discursive" can be substituted for the word "deliberative" and we may differentiate between three different types of discussion. The first type is when we verify statements of fact, to find out whether they are true or false; the second type is when we make normative statements, such as right or wrong; the third is about values, in other words the issues and qualities with which people identify, that they esteem and want to preserve. Empirical and normative statements in speech, writing or images are in principle free, public and available to all. Verification is a form of criticism that does not reject other people's statements, but examines them in a public debate that must adhere closely to facts.

The same premise applies to the question of how we should act towards other people in a multicultural society that is based on the principle of complying with what is right and what is fair. However, discussions of values cannot be approached in the same way as letting the cows out in spring, as if points of view can be allowed to roam in different directions until they run out of energy, or where people can choose to live by certain criteria, for example by what is fair play at work, good music in a concert or suitable content for the school curriculum. A complete concept of democratic education must therefore be extremely extensive. The debate can then range from the formal research seminar to newspaper articles against discrimination and even to the question of what is a nation. It can take place in all its variations within a common horizon, using everyday language as a medium. There is nothing to prevent the classic trio of that which is true, right and noble from forming the basis of political education.

Historically, deliberation or discourse goes back to the European Enlightenment and can be found in Immanuel Kant's concept of "publicity", in Edmund Burke's idea of parliament as a "deliberative assembly" and later in John Stuart Mill's proposal for "rule through discussion" (Elster 1999: 1ff). Discussion in our sense includes the constitutional state and civilian society, and ranges from Stortinget (the Norwegian Parliament) to voluntary organisations such as Save the Children. We can differentiate between three different practices in our democracy: representative, participatory and discursive practices – or, if you prefer, choice, negotiation and debate. We achieve the first on Election Day, the second in salary negotiations and the third by justifying moral and political statements. John Dewey's republican ideas, in books such as *The Public and Its Problems* from 1927, of the state as a "political public" created by "common activities" and "articulated" by selected representatives (Dewey 1927: 67), covers these areas. His proposal of education based on general logic as a means of solving problems, a "logic of inquiry", has similarities to Jürgen Habermas' idea of justifying a linguistic philosophical profile by the use of arguments. On a more general note, the Second World War led to a general requirement for Scandinavian education to offer a more political upbringing and knowledge, to such an extent that it is possible for us to talk, with Adorno, about education before and after Auschwitz (Adorno 1971).

Discourse and education

Education is not achieved solely by setting requirements for knowledge and skills. Having a reading list and ensuring that skills are learnt are both of course essential, but introducing a regulation for education in the form of the European qualification framework – a key element of the Bologna Process – creates a quasi-legal governmental regime with formal obligations and sanctions. The framework itself is not open to debate. The problem may be illustrated by the most recent upper-secondary school curriculum in Norway. While it was being developed in 2005 and 2006, several drafts of the Norwegian plan were published on the Internet. One of them proposed that the issue of the canon, which is the basis for the prescribed reading list, should be included in the curriculum, thereby making it an issue not only of contents but also of scope. The proposal was removed in the next draft and the curriculum thereby lost its self-critical function, which is to address any differences or rough edges in its own concept and system.

We do not know why the proposal vanished but we have two hypotheses. The first is the view that this "metalogue", to use Gregory Bateson's term (Bateson 1972), could create conflict for the teacher or be too difficult for the students. The second is that, as long as the students are acquiring knowledge and skills, the teachers are doing their job. Schools should prepare students to criticise, but do not need to criticise themselves. Both are problematic. Traditionalists view education as an initiation into the ways of the bourgeois middle classes – a way of getting the barbarians inside the walls of civilisation, as the British educationist R. S. Peters once put it (Peters 1972: 107). But children are not primitive beings living in the wilderness; they do not live as barbarians before they can talk or heathens before they are christened, but from birth – and even before – they are actually living among us adults inside the four walls of our houses. Over a period of time, education is there to cultivate attitudes and mentalities that promote independence and criticism. It imparts political insights that make students aware of simple and more subtle power mechanisms in society and thereby help to increase their political and moral understanding and judgment.

The line between initiation and social criticism is not easy to define. The American philosopher Richard Rorty tries to solve the conflict in one fell swoop, and he does this by locating the conflict in various educational phases. In his article "Education as socialization and as individualization", originally published in 1989, he suggested that up to the age of 18 or 19, education for most people should be about socialisation, about instilling traditional values: "getting the student to take over the moral and political common sense of the society as it is" (Rorty 1999: 116).

After students have left school and gone on to college and university, it is time for their "rebellion" against indoctrination and for them to realise themselves as individuals. This view seems to hit two stumbling blocks, one psychological and one logical. Firstly, young people are capable of social criticism based on their own experiences and on what they learn at home, at school and from their friends. Since socialisation goes hand in hand with individualisation, the solution of postponing children's criticism does not seem to be a particularly good idea. Furthermore, children have more inquiring minds than adults. Let us move on to the stumbling block of logic. It seems no less impossible to believe that the transition from indoctrination to criticism comes as a surprise on one's 18th birthday than it is to believe that knowledge is transformed into action as if by magic. Students are developing their critical repertoire at the same time as they are learning facts, acquiring good habits and using the ability to evaluate what is part of a critical debate.

These observations require us – parents, teachers and citizens – to take responsibility for an early, multidimensional schooling in critical thinking. This schooling takes place in the form of indirect encounters with democratic ideals, by demanding respect for children's boundaries and encouraging them to speak rather than strike, to accept rather than bully, and to include rather than isolate. Criticism feeds on diluted authority, for example allowing teachers the freedom to design their own methods and curricula; this would free teachers and pupils from rules and regulations that create lifeless routines and absolve the parties of everyday responsibility for themselves and each other. Moreover, when students are valued using double descriptions: as self-centred yet social, reckless yet cautious, or unreliable yet responsible, teachers may find that it is a hard balancing act to choose between demonstrating a point of view and leaving it open, or between standing by their authority or accepting their fallibility. Responsibility for one's own opinions, the *Mündigkeit* ("authority" but also "coming of age") mentioned by Kant, cannot be put on hold; it should be cultivated over time through usage and experiences shared by teachers and pupils. This is an educational view and the basis for a broad discussion of a discursive democracy as an educational project.

The need for rationality

It is no new discovery that democracy is a vulnerable institution, nor that, in the long run, objectivity is a good and preferable safeguard against fear, discrimination and hatred. Kant's Enlightenment Age contribution was his concept of what we could term a regime of rational discussion. Regimes like this set strict boundaries for a reasonable debate. One example is Arne Næss' principles for a fair debate in preliminary tests in philosophy, which later became the *Examen Philosophicum* (a one-semester introduction to philosophy and logic previously required of all university students in Norway). In his little book *En del elementære logiske emner* (1941), he defined the field of objectivity as avoiding irrelevance, ambiguity and irony. Now irony does not have to be subjective. It can be a particular way of relating to the world, as we find in Richard Rorty's irony, in which the ironist appreciates what is contingent or random in his own convictions and in which this doubt is tied up with the hope that it may be possible to reduce the cruelty of the world. Similarly, ambiguity does not mean several ways out of the fox's den, so to speak; it refers to the complexity of interpretation and rhetoric.

We have outlined a concept of objective discussion that ranges from the requirement for unambiguous, consistent thinking and its relatively strict rules on arguments, to discussion by topic, which has room for interpretation, irony and paradoxes. It is one thing to verify empirical statements, but another to justify normative selections and a third to interpret a text and lead value discussions. But then we are also talking about maintaining the scope of the practice that we know as education. In the introduction, we mentioned that knowledge is not enough, but that empathy (having a personal experience of something as unjust, unfair or against personal or collective values), political sense and the ability to tackle an objective discussion are also needed. When knowledge is on the table, it should be verified and justified in an argument involving two or more people in a conversation or discourse. In a dialogue there are always two or more participants who need to listen to each other, argue and justify the validity of their ideas and theories – and they need to engage in each other's positions. There is always a counter-argument, always another way of looking at things and always another human being with rights, convictions and dreams.

Educationists are prone to perceive language as a means of communication, something that we use to make ourselves understood and influence others. This is interrelated with the current focus on knowledge and skills, in which language skills – you must be able to read and write – become part of a person's competence, enabling them to succeed in a professional environment. Traditional rhetoric may support this view. Quintilian's *Institutio Oratoria* was used by the Roman upper classes as an educational methodology. In addition, languages exist in the plural, and having language skills could now mean mastering, for instance, Norwegian, English and French. But language also exists in the singular, language as a background and medium, the cement of society. According to what is known as the linguistic figure of speech, society is not based on man's awareness or on society's institutions, its basis is not Kant's "I think" or Hegel's concept of *Sittlichkeit* or ethical life; it is rather everyday language. Here we will identify and examine some linguistic uses of "reason", and attempt to reconstruct them. Your and my uses of reason pass from being pure thinking to becoming public and communicative, put on social display and realised in Richard Rorty's "conversation of mankind". We can make this conversation or dialogue more specific, using the grammar encountered by children in their first years at school. In the expression "I think ...", I use the first person to address another person from within an originally physical and musical relationship between child and carer, but now based on a generalised expectation that the other person will answer and thereby take responsibility for the social relationship.

The educationalist and linguist Wilhelm von Humboldt had faith in the individual and claimed that *Bildung* is a *Selbstbildung*, an education of the person or self. He assumed firstly that language is not simply a means to make oneself understood (*Verständigungsmittel*), but also an expression of an individual's "soul and perception of the world" or *Weltansicht* (Humboldt 1827: 135). He then stated that we as people develop in the living environment in which we participate, but that this participation has its motive in the fundamental social relationship between the "I" and the "you". We now see in this relationship "the deeper and nobler feelings, which in friendship and love and in every spiritual fellowship bind the two together in the deepest sincerity" (ibid: 140). Individual and society are not pitted against each other here; the differences between the two rest on a linguistic fellowship (a fellowship that may consist of words or body language). The purpose of upbringing is an independent self that cannot be considered to be isolated from mankind as such (ibid: 135). I and you are abbreviations of the self that is already interacting in a world that is maintained and conveyed by language. The grammatical conjugations of "I am", "you are", "it is" actually direct us towards the relationship between self-awareness, the other person and the rest of the world.

Reflective education

Reimagining democratic societies is about self-reflection and self-scrutiny. We have to look at our own history and our own institutions critically. What kinds of value are present in the universities' curricula, and how do we express the core values on the university campus and in seminars? How seriously do we debate with radical opponents? How open to all political and ideological views is the society of the university? And how do we as teachers act as role models when it comes to being inclusive and caring – while at the same time encouraging intellectual inquiry?

From one perspective education is formal: that is, it is something you have or do not have, in contrast to the process of understanding and reflecting on what you have read and heard and said, an understanding of knowledge on behalf of which you act. From another perspective education is static and has a given duration, though our use (and misuse) of this education is a never-ending process of making knowledge meaningful – a process of maturation that takes place in each individual (Bostad 2009 and 2010a).

With references to classical philosophy, not least through Plato's Academy, we see a notion of general education or *Bildung* emerging that is related to the concepts of virtue or capability: mastering life is a matter of refining one's personality or character (Bostad 2012).[27] In Plato's ideal school, general education does not occur through

---

27. Official Norwegian Report NOU 2007: 6, *Objectives for the Future. Objectives for Kindergartens and Education and Training. Report from the committee appointed by Royal Decree on 2 June 2006.*

passive acquisition of facts and skills, be it science, law or policy, but rather through a unique matter of self-knowledge. Even if the platonic ideal of education lifts the rational, free individual up as an ideal citizen, his or her concept of general education may be fruitful in our current context, in the sense that it is about being deeply convinced of a claim, a reason or an argument, as opposed to being persuaded. A person who is persuaded has accepted facts or skills without reflecting on them, perhaps repeated something more or less automatically, whereas a person who is deeply convinced understands why and has a considered, personal relationship to the knowledge they have acquired. In other words, the teacher convinces the student, not only by showing the student the pros and cons – the arguments behind the arguments as well as the counter-arguments – but also by being in the unknown, the open arena, with the students. This implies a fundamental shift in the way of looking at the relationship of teacher and student – it is not purely a "student-centred" way of learning, it is an "inquiry-centred" approach to academic knowledge where the common aim for both teacher and student is to succeed with a serious inquiry. The teacher and the students are in it together, trying to go deeper into an unsolved problem, analysing a concept together, looking at it from shifting perspectives. It is an essential democratic element in the dialogue that shifting perspectives are encouraged and lifted up as an ideal.

The philosophical dialogue may be structured in different ways, depending on the curriculum, age and cultural background of the students, but the common method follows a specific pattern intended to lead the parties in the dialogue to greater clarity and understanding of general issues related to human life, primarily by uncovering problems but also by searching for good, tenable arguments, viewpoints and perspectives. This inquiring method is open and invites a range of creative and impulsive hypotheses. Ideally, the structure of the dialogue has no room for ready-made solutions or predefined answers; ultimately it rests on the possibility that individuals can draw conclusions that may well be changed in the next round of discussion.

Presented to the Ministry of Education and Research on 8 June 2007. Chair: Inga Bostad. The mandate for the Bostad Committee in 2008 to formulate new objectives for kindergarten, primary and secondary schools was: What should the purpose of education be? What values should be upheld and promoted in modern schools, and what kind of views of learning, maturation and general education should teaching be based on? Are there any common values that the whole of society agrees on? It was a democratic process where representatives from different religious, political, ideological and social groups were present. The discussions in the committee showed there was little support for attempts to be value-neutral, which was regarded as synonymous with indifference. Cultural heritage had to be regarded as dynamic – that it shapes us and we shape it, and that the next generation's cultural heritage will consist of the things we have been involved in giving content to and conveying – elements we have picked out and valued. Lastly, cultural heritage is, if not cacophonic, then at the very least extremely polyphonic. The committee ended up formulating some core values that were to provide a direction for schools and express a common consensus, a process that also allowed the individual members of society to justify the values in their own way – on the basis of their own religion and beliefs. It was essential that schools should be based on respect for human dignity, intellectual freedom, charity, equality and solidarity, while at the same time the principles of religious freedom and non-discrimination were included. Religious and philosophical freedom is protected by several human rights conventions that also ensure the right to teaching and education without preaching and indoctrination.

In practice, this does not undermine the position of the privileged teacher and her authority. To lead this type of academic dialogue presupposes authority and knowledge of both the subject and the method of inquiry where the teacher/ conversation leader encourages new quests (Bostad 2006, Chapter 6), disturbing the students, asking provocative questions and making them think in new terms. But, in addition to the platonic ideal of a search for truth, a modern university needs to be continually aware of, and reflect upon, the environment that determines any learning situation: that the students are persons with a body, a gender, a personal history, a religion or a personal conviction, at a specific place and time.

In other words; the *praxis* of philosophical inquiry is a "happening", as Hannah Arendt puts it (Arendt 1958: 297), something unpredictable, uncontrolled and unexpected, which challenges every theory and method of pedagogy. To ask and make inquiries in a dialogue is to place the question itself out into the open, in contrast to repeating what is a common truth; to ask open questions makes the topic itself and its different possibilities "floating", as Gadamer puts it (Gadamer 2004: 348-9) and reveals the distinction between understanding and reflecting or thinking, which also implies the process or understanding that something will never be understood.

The tradition of "mindful" pedagogy, encouraging and accepting thoughts and emotions that are revealed in a learning situation (Hansen 2008), is to be distinguished from philosophical *praxis* of critical, creative or humorous inquiry into knowledge, wisdom, beauty and meaning. This *praxis* is not part of the tradition of mindful pedagogy concerned with care and upbringing, according to the Danish philosopher Finn Torbjørn Hansen – it is more rebellious and unpredictable. Even if Hansen's concept of "being in the open" is a fruitful perspective on the process of understanding and grasping knowledge as something different from thinking (which often implies being silent and in wonder), a framework of care and dignity is missing in his philosophy. Participating in an academic dialogue requires an environment of academic values, such as respect, equality, autonomy, sincerity and a sense of the unity in diversity. It is naïve to believe that education is free, that it sprouts and grows in every individual as long as we ensure that reflection is open and inquisitive (Bostad 2009). The social reproduction of education is one of the major challenges to education today, as Hilligje van't Land stated in her presentation at the Oslo conference. Another challenge is the power relations that exist in all forms of learning, which require an understanding of existence and use of the cultural capital in society for instrumental perspectives on learning pressure and learning outcomes.

The arguments

We now return to Næss' dogma of objectivity, since it centres on the formal requirements for conversation as a means of argument, and it is relevant to our discussion for three reasons. The first is that Breivik's manifesto has confirmed how fatal are the labyrinths in which some mavericks lose their way. The second is that discussions since 22 July have related to truth and justification. The third is that the incidents confirm the need for a political education to contain methods that objectively legitimise political statements and programmes.

Statements about Muslim terrorism are closely related to statements about the alleged back-door Islamification of Norway. The first kind of statement can be refuted relatively easily by referring to facts. But the second kind becomes part of a wider discussion, about a conflict of civilisations, about Muslims speaking with forked tongues, and therefore about conspiracy. This makes a difference. It is one thing to check facts against sources, but quite another to set values against culture. The latter requires broad interpretations and historic rationalisations.

The background culture, a mutual horizon of ideas, must be taken into consideration. It is not possible to exchange views about what is reasonable and fair without a mutual understanding of national and local traditions, including customs, rituals and interpretations that are not necessarily part of the discussion. This implicit lifeworld has already given us customs, metaphors and concepts that make individual interpretations possible. Shabana Rehman is a Norwegian writer of immigrant (Pakistani) origin. Her consistent critique of the oppression of women in the Norwegian-Pakistani community was based on the idea of the autonomy of the individual and the universal right to think out loud in public, on behalf of oneself and others – a living assertion of Kant's principle of thinking. These days, many people who are involved in the immigration debate expose a similar degree of oppression in Norwegian culture, for example of discrimination in the workplace. Since 22 July, deeply rooted prejudices have started to appear in the political arena, as ideologies and rhetorical manipulation – and people have become more aware of this. The extreme right-wing bloggers with their back-to-front perspective have more than reminded us that politics is language and that talking may lead to action. The rules of the argument stand out as a civilising factor in a multicultural society that depends on the agreement of the people – and if necessary, on their right to disagree.

What criteria are necessary for objectivity? Here are a few random examples: play fair, allow your view to be open to criticism, admit that your assertion has been repudiated before you put forward another one that backs up your main point ("I didn't really mean Europe, I meant global terrorism"), do not generalise one case to all ("Some immigrants are villains, therefore all immigration is bad for Norway") and take the consequences of losing the argument. But as von Humboldt implied, the linguistic figure of speech is to the detriment of Næss' doctrine of objectivity, at any rate as a pure method. A method is a tool that needs to be justified by something other than itself; it needs more than a decision from the education authorities and a proposal in the curriculum. The universal validity of politics is not good for local traditions based on the idea that personal autonomy easily goes hand in hand with community responsibility. In the objective discussion, in principle everyone can join in, even if in reality the discussion is limited by culture, gender, class, education and in some cases just bad luck. It is these limitations that make people write off argument as an attempt to cast people in the same mould, created by an elite and an expression of the West's intellectual lust for power. But then we have people like Shabana Rehman, who demands individual independence for all, and Abid Qayyum Raja, who managed to get hot-headed young people together into a political discussion at Oslo's House of Literature after demonstrations against the Israeli Embassy in 2009, thereby introducing them to discussion as an important part of democratic political practice.

We have suggested that political education must be based on knowledge and an objective treatment of the facts, based on rules that we may summarise in a dogma of objectivity. What is needed, then, is the knowledge and skills to enable us to lead a conversation according to mutually accepted rules; in other words a method or system to focus and guide us through the process of solving problems. Examples from political parties show that the requirement for objectivity is often weakly represented in election campaigns, for example, and that the issue of what is right and what is fair loses out to political expedience. In fairness, Norwegian politicians did unite during the autumn 2011 local elections and agree to be "nice", without in any way minimising the differences between the parties, perhaps an admission that democracy must be protected and that objectivity must come before expedience. Surprisingly enough then, it turns out that the events of 22 July have weighed in with more stringent demands on political rhetoric – we will see how long these last. But political education inside and outside the arena of party politics should be examined against a content that is detrimental to knowledge and skills. What we would call the pragmatic-linguistic figure of speech introduces something new here, namely an analysis of what we must expect when we enter into an objective discussion. This is about clarifying what is implicit in our speech acts, without falling back on subjective experiences and blind faith in our own opinions or in research institutions and communications experts, but relying on the bonds of everyday language.

Why examine these bonds, which are not the bonds of law or regulation? It is primarily to see how a practical fellowship, in this case a fellowship of language, can be described as education. Within certain boundaries, we can defy the law's rules and replace them with others, and that is what happens when people protest against laws that give to the rich and take away from the poor. We can also forget some skills and replace them with other, more adequate ones, and this has happened with the introduction of the computer. But the general contention now is that certain prerequisites need to be present if we are to be able to talk about a moral discussion at all. Without these prerequisites, we end in absurdity. To put it differently, some prerequisites can be regarded as norms that are constitutive or essential prerequisites of conversation between people. These can be identified using a philosophical reconstruction reminiscent of a psychoanalyst's work on memory, except that here it is the use of language in a social context that is being examined.

Identifying the obvious

Jürgen Habermas suggests this type of reconstruction of things that already have to be in motion when we are involved in a discussion of right and wrong. We must presume:

- that the other person's understanding of the words we are using is roughly the same, in other words that we share an interpretation horizon and an unambiguous vocabulary;
- that the other person is of sound mind, that is, that they are an independent or autonomous person, someone who can speak for themselves; and
- that they are truthful and not speaking against their better judgment.

Yet these norms are obviously idealisations, since we cannot assume that these prerequisites will actually have been met in every discussion. On the contrary, reconstructing them serves to identify – in the manner of Heidegger, as it were – the prerequisites for a serious political discussion. And it is here that we find the suggestion for a political education within the framework of our democracy: the fact that education not only implies norms but also explicitly relates to them, and still practises a form of self-criticism. In a way, this then confirms what we implied at the start: that a given culture has already formed its students and that eager educational agents can also say that they are making the understood understandable. Education is not just a content that we should acquire, a method we should use or a result that we should achieve, but a reflection of something that we already have to understand if we are to participate in an informed political life.

The Norwegian philosopher Gunnar Skirbekk has pointed out that we should reject the classic German *Bildung* idea of the perfection of man, and admit instead that we are under a certain obligation to realise discursive norms, in the certainty that we are fallible. Of personal autonomy, in the Kantian sense of thinking for oneself, he says that it is "a question of graduality, not of perfection" (Skirbekk 2009: 98). Participants in serious discussions must recognise their mutual fallibility and thereby accept "a gradual autonomy which needs improvement". The requirement of arguing without manipulating then goes together with the mutual need to reinforce personal autonomy. The idea of personal autonomy is constitutive in the sense that without it (the second of the prerequisites listed above) we may well have a conversation of one kind or another, but no discussion. Since the idea of autonomy prescribes a task that can never be completely achieved because of human fallibility, it can only be possible to live by an ideal that is by definition beyond the reach of man, and which must have a nature of expectation or hope – that is, a utopia.

Skirbekk introduces the thought of man's biophysical existence, with all its vulnerability and inadequacy (Skirbekk 2009: 169). He advocates a concept of personal autonomy not as fact and perfection, but as an ongoing draft or project that is controlled by thoughts of "more or less" and "little by little", and of the transition from something that is poor to something that is better. What is important for this educational project is the idea of improving people's independence by protecting them against personal infringements – he allows this thinking to fall under the banner of "meliorism". This is not about lofty ideals or strong formalisations, but about idealisations in a pragmatic and existential setting.

Rehman's requirement that we should be treated as independent, authoritative individuals and Raja's invitation to talk instead of climb the barricades both introduce implicit validity requirements and include everyone who allows themselves to be persuaded by those values that we hold in esteem in a democratic society. But the intention of achieving the political ideal and turning utopia into reality brings two potential evils into play. The lesser evil is paternalism or knowing it all, which allows figures of authority, such as politicians, bureaucrats, head teachers or teachers, to tell you what is best for you. The greater evil is achieving the perfect discursive democracy, since that ends in the same totalitarian state that Fascists dream of. To think in idealisations is to think counter-factually, yet that does not mean ignoring facts or putting reality on hold; it is rather about avoiding a concretism that ignores the place of idealisation in everyday life. Habermas puts it like this: "The point is that if we want to enter an argument, we have to take the argument's prerequisites as a *fact*, even if they have an ideal content that we can only get close to in reality" (Habermas 1993: 164). In other words, these premises exist as an "as if" in objective discussions and this hypothesis or expectation appears as a practical requirement.

There is an obvious example. The Norwegian Education Act's first paragraph, which describes the objectives of Norwegian schooling, contains strong ideals of intellectual freedom, equality and solidarity.[28] If we take these values at their word, and wish to achieve them in a specific set of quality-assured qualifications, we encounter a new paradox: the paragraph outlining the objectives cannot be turned into reality in the form of specific learning objectives unless it abolishes itself. The reason for this is that values are not the same thing as knowledge, skills or individual expertise, but idealisations woven into language and existence. This paradox is also the paradox of education. From 2013, the national qualifications framework will apply to all higher educational institutions. The idea of a common qualifications framework is try to standardise education so that it will be possible to compare achievements measured on an individual level with the results from other countries. But the better we are able to define education through learning outcomes and institutional rankings, the less we tend to be able to reflect on the type of institutional practice.

---

28. "Even if we see a modification of the egalitarianism of the Norwegian people in an ongoing research project at ESOP ..., University of Oslo, where groups of people from different places in the world were asked to share an amount of resources, and the conclusions were that the Norwegian group were not more egalitarian than for instance the African": speech by Kalle Moene, Forskningstorget [the Research Agora], September 2011, University of Oslo.

In a way, the argument is an invisible institution since it has no address, no offices and no budget. It contains a formalisation of everyday discussions and is a mode or practice that we can elect to use when political opinions, values and objectives come into conflict, requiring further justification. Discourse can generally apply to the boundaries of freedom of expression, the market or state intervention in the private sphere, but applies more specifically when university researchers protest that the results of their contract research are falsely presented or when teachers protest against the increasing amount of testing in schools.

Let us summarise some of the potential educational benefits of a deliberative practice. Students are trained to develop inquiring minds, to see statements as hypotheses that must be tested in discussion and to see the results of an argument as provisional and open to further discussion. To argue requires the skill of putting forward a problem, grasping significant aspects, bringing in different contexts, formulating a view, working towards potential agreement, respecting the rights of others to disagree and accepting the better argument, even if it means giving up a cherished conviction. Conflict is not necessarily an evil. At best, a discussion of the objectives and meaning of schooling will not only improve people's ability to justify their views, but can also create the trust that is engendered when people recognise each other as responsible citizens and honest debaters. These are some of the qualities that are included in what Habermas calls the democratic education of opinions and will. The argument has its limits, which we have touched on while discussing this subject. But it permits judgment, thinking for ourselves, and it disciplines thinking without making its results all-encompassing. Democracy is an unfinished project.

Democracy and access to knowledge

Democracy in the broad interpretation as participation and involvement on all levels, in all discussions, especially when it comes to minorities, disabled persons and so on, fits neatly into the Norwegian version of democracy. As in the other Nordic countries, our current economic and social model is based on democratic principles such as openness and transparency, equality, egalitarianism and extensive welfare benefits, and political organisation based on the right of participation. As Nina Witoszek says in her book *Norske Naturmytologier*, the special Scandinavian form of social democracy is a tradition based on values stemming from Christianity. It is a form of social democracy that has promoted egalitarian ideas and placed a focus on the weak and underprivileged, while at the same time promoting a pragmatic worldview. Today, we see a political tension in the national policies for education between the right-wing parties' effort to develop tools for the best students and the leftist parties holding on to the values of reducing social inequalities.

Social reproduction is an ongoing challenge in all education, seen primarily by focusing on the relationship between good grades and mastering of the curriculum on the one hand and privileged background on the other. This implies that children from less privileged backgrounds are not able to fully develop their potential. In other words: there is nothing wrong in following up the "best" pupils or the best students with high demands, as long as there are equal opportunities for all to get there. Education is regarded as the most effective institution to reduce social inequalities in society, but there is no clear and simple answer to the question of how to reimagine democratic societies. The formal conditions are free access to education for all, no or low school fees and a strategic policy of public education, but the political-philosophical goal is to develop attitudes and ways of thinking that promote independence and critical abilities.

Knowledge and education have been – and most certainly will be in future – closely connected to power and social inequalities. Throughout history, access to education has been reserved either for the elite, for men, or the privileged. Likewise today we see that the policies and ideology for education in a society are a mirror for the government and elected representatives in parliament.

A responsible university

A good university must acknowledge and take responsibility for its ability to influence both the development and the spread of knowledge globally. And the only way to succeed is to understand the potential of universities as a nexus for global solidarity. A university that is firmly rooted in academic freedom is an independent body able to criticise, propose radical ideas and challenge dominant paradigms. This is why political and social movements often start, or find a nurturing environment, at universities. Although it might seem so obvious that it does not need to be stated, a university is a place where ideas are exchanged across the sometimes rigid boundaries of academic disciplines. It is a place of synthesis and discovery, and a place that out of necessity encourages openness to free thinking – because, at any given time, a great discovery may be sitting right under our noses.

According to Geoffrey Boulton the challenge for universities now is to articulate clearly what they stand for, to speak the truth to the authorities and to be steadfast in upholding freedom and autonomy as crucial values safeguarding the future of society (Boulton 2009). But a responsible university is also a place where students are aware of their right to participate in every committee and where engagement is seen as an obligation to a common social goal.

To reimagine democratic society we must also search for the correspondence between freedom and education, or freedom in education. What parts of the learning methods and curriculum ought to be elective and decided by the school, the single teacher or the pupil – and how much should be compulsory and a part of a common culture and a historical-social canon? How should the rights of every child to be guided into their cultural heritage be balanced against the right and freedom of the parents to raise their children according to their own religion and faith?

And how should the protection of an individual's right to intellectual and spiritual freedom be balanced against the recognition that the values may be expressed and reasoned for differently in different religions and belief systems? The answers to these questions depend on the ability of schools and universities to stimulate and create autonomous individuals – who think independently, pose critical questions, make ethical choices and participate in social debates (Bostad 2010b).

As we have seen in the recent debate on general education in the United States, intellectuals like Anthony Kronman and Martha Nussbaum have argued for a new non-profit perspective on higher education, Kronman with an existentialistic approach and Nussbaum with a moral quest – both of them by appealing to humanistic values. Where Kronman sets out to meet the future of universities by giving the students an existentialist room of inquiry and wondering, Nussbaum argues for a new humanism where education is a moral tool not only for respecting diversity, but for improving our understanding of the current complexities in society. General education is needed for the ability to solve transdisciplinary problems in a just and informed way, according to Nussbaum. In Kronmans' view, it is a means for the personal transformation of being an individual and finding a way to master our own life (Kronman 2007; Nussbaum 2010).

The goal for higher education is not merely tolerance, but understanding. [29] To engage with the other person is crucial and this takes courage; to disagree with someone is often challenging, due to the framework or the settings. We must teach and encourage the student to be critical by seeking confrontations with people they disagree with – visiting other cultures and religions and trying out their way of looking at the world.

In 1972 the Norwegian social scientist Nils Christie wrote a book about Norwegian prison guards in concentration camps in northern Norway during the Second World War. This book has been ranked as one of the 25 most influential works in Norwegian social science ever. Christie shows the effect of seeing others as human beings – and more importantly why humans are capable of violence and torture. Prison guards who had even the minimum of personal contact with the prisoners did not participate in torture; reading letters the prisoners wrote, knowing they had a family back home, made the guards aware of the human nature and dignity of the prisoners and put restrictions on their primitive view of the prisoners as animals.

Christie provides important insights into what constitutes a society. And he asks: how do we create a society where everyone contributes and participates? Such knowledge of human behaviour is also important for scholars of democratisation, mainly because it looks at core values also central in human rights and the modern welfare state, such as the intimate relationship between a social right and a social duty. In her book *Not for Profit* Martha Nussbaum argues for a new humanism

---

29. Linda Alcoff in a lecture at the conferring of honorary doctorates by the University of Oslo, 30 August 2011.

where education is a moral tool for "the ability to think critically; the ability to transcend local loyalties and approach world problems as a 'citizen of the world'" (Nussbaum 2010: 7), and finally "the ability to imagine sympathetically the predicament of another person". In this way, higher education may contribute to and stimulate a modern democracy for our time – seek to be the room for inquiry that matures the students as well as society as a whole.

References

Adorno T. W. (1971), "Erziehung nach Auschwitz" [Education after Auschwitz] in T. W. Adorno, *Erziehung zur Mündigkeit. Vorträge und Gespräche mit Hellmut Becker 1959-1969* [Education for Coming of Age. Lectures and Conversations with Hellmut Becker 1959-1969], Frankfurt am Main: Suhrkamp.

Arendt H. (1958/2004), *Menneskets Vilkår* [originally published as *The Human Condition*, 1958], Oslo: Klim forlag.

Bateson G. (1972), *Steps to an ecology of mind*, New York: Chandler.

Bostad I. (2006), "Filosofi som metode" [Philosophy as a method] in I. Bostad and T. Pettersen (eds), *Dialog og Danning*, Oslo: Spartacus.

— (2008), "Synlige verdier og usynlig dobbeltmoral – hva skal være opplæringens formål for framtida" [Visible values and the invisibility of double standards – what should be the objectives for the future of education?] in Å. Røthing and O. Leirvik (eds), *Verdier* [Values] Oslo: Universitetsforlaget.

— (2009), "Dannelse med tellekanter" [*Bildung* with counting edges], *Samtiden* (February), Oslo: Aschehoug.

— (2010a), "Annerledeshet og frihet" [Difference and freedom] in J. Kristeva and E. Engebretsen (eds), *Annerledeshet – sårbarhetens språk og politikk* [Difference – the language and policy of vulnerability], Oslo: Gyldendal akademisk forlag.

— (2010b), "The university in contemporary society: what is the core of the university?" Lecture given at the Unica Student Conference, Rome 22-25 September 2010, published in the Proceedings from the conference by Università Sapienza, Roma Tre, Tor Vergata and Foro italico.

— (2012) "Existential education and the quest for a new humanism: How to create disturbances and deeper thinking in schools and universities?" Proceedings of the 2011 Comparative Education Society in Europe conference, Amsterdam: Sense for CESE.

Boulton G. (2009), "What are universities for?" Lecture EUA Prague 2009, *University World News*, 3 August 2010.

Christie N. (1972/2010), *Fangevoktere i Konsentrasjonsleire* [Prison guards in concentration camps; 1st edn 1972], Oslo: Pax forlag.

Dewey J. (1910/1997), *How we think* [1st edn 1910], New York: Dover Publications.

(1927), *The Public and Its Problems*, Chicago: Swallow Press.

Elster J. (ed.) (1999), *Deliberative democracy*, Cambridge: Cambridge University Press.

Gadamer H.-G. (2004), *Sandhet og Metode* [Truth and method; originally published as *Wahrheit und Metode*], Århus: Systime.

Habermas J. (1993), *Justification and Application: remarks on discourse ethics*, Cambridge MA: MIT Press.

Hansen F. T. (2008), *Å Stå i det Åpne: dannelse gennom filosofisk undren og nærvær* [Standing in the open: *Bildung* through philosophical enquiry and presence], Copenhagen: Hans Reitzel.

Humboldt W. von (1827/1963), *Über den Dualis* [On duality; 1st edn 1827], Werke, Band 3, Stuttgart: Cotta.

Kristeva J. and Engebretsen E. (eds) (2010), *Anderledeshet og Sårbarhetens Politikk* [Being different and the politics of vulnerability], Oslo: Gyldendal akademisk.

Kronman A. (2007), *Educations Ends: why our colleges and universities have given up the meaning of life*, New Haven CT: Yale University Press.

Næss A. (1941/1982), *En del Elementære Logiske Emner* [Some elementary logical topics; 1st edn 1941], Oslo: Universitetsforlaget.

Nussbaum M. (2010), *Not for Profit: why democracy needs the humanities*, Princeton NJ: Princeton University Press.

Peters R. S. (1972), "Education as initiation" in R. D. Archambault, *Philosophical Analysis and Education*, London: Routledge & Kegan Paul.

Plato (1989), *Gorgias*, Oslo: Samlaget.

Rorty R. (1999), *Philosophy and Social Hope*, London/New York: Penguin.

Skirbekk G. (2009), *Rasjonalitet og Modernitet: essays i filosofisk pragmatikk* [Rationality and modernity: essays in philosophical pragmatics], Oslo: Universitetsforlaget.

Witoszek N. (1998), *Norske Naturmytologier* [Norwegian nature mythologies], Oslo: Pax forlag.

12. Thinking about and doing democracy: higher education's twin obligations

Caryn McTighe Musil

Democracy needs to be born anew every generation, and education is the midwife.[30]

In most democracies, whether ancient or modern, there is a link with centres of knowledge and inquiry, which go hand in hand with the emergence of democratic societies. In the United States, for example, the establishment of the young republic only intensified the importance of having universities. Benjamin Franklin and Thomas Jefferson, two of the US founding fathers, launched universities as well – the University of Pennsylvania and the University of Virginia respectively. Each saw these institutions as essential resources for strengthening the fledgling democratic nation. The close connection between democracy and higher education is underscored by Norway's similar experience, the creation of the University of Oslo influencing the establishment of the Norwegian Constitution three years later. In one of the newest democracies, higher education again was seen as critical to nation building in South Africa's non-racial democracy.

But in the United States at least, the gravitational pull of other priorities for colleges and universities began to reduce education for democracy to a peripheral concern, more like an afterthought.

In the past half century, though, an ever-increasing civic reform movement serving democracy has slowly gained momentum in US colleges and universities as well as elsewhere in the world. In the USA, it was spurred first by the social justice movements in the 1960s and 1970s, which changed the profile of college students in terms of colour, class, sex and other categories. To a lesser extent the overall diversity profile of faculty, staff and administrative leaders changed as well. All of this contributed to the unprecedented democratisation of higher education in the United States by the end of the 20th century.

The civic reform movement in higher education was then carried forward by student activists eager to make the world a better place, especially through service to the community; through new academic disciplines like ethnic studies and women's studies; and through global studies that linked academic inquiry to justice-seeking political movements. Another significant wave of robust civic engagement has come from establishing partnerships with local and global communities as a new, vibrant academic arena where students can apply their knowledge to address pressing issues in collaboration with people and groups outside the academy.

---

30. John Dewey, "The need of an industrial education in an industrial democracy" (1916).

Most recently, prioritising education for civic learning and democratic engagement has been fuelled in the USA by growing evidence that American democracy is in the midst of a civic recession at least as dangerous as its economic one. For example, the United States ranked 139th in voter participation of 172 democratic countries in 2007 (McCormick Tribune 2007: 6-7), only 10 per cent of citizens contacted a public official in 2009-10 (US Census Bureau 2010) and only 24 per cent of graduating high school seniors scored at the proficient or advanced level in civics in 2010, which was fewer than in 2006 or in 1998 (NCES 2011). Data on college students show an equally bleak picture. Among 14 000 college seniors surveyed in 2006 and 2007, the average score on a civic literacy exam was just over 50 per cent (Intercollegiate Studies Institute 2007); just over one third of college faculty surveyed in 2007 strongly agreed that their campus actively promoted awareness of US or global social, political and economic issues (Dey et al. 2009) and only one third of college students surveyed in 2007 strongly agreed that while in college their civic awareness had expanded, their civic skills to change society had increased or their commitment to improve society had grown (ibid.).

This state of civic malaise caused the US Department of Education in 2010 to fund an initiative to examine the state of civic learning and democratic engagement in colleges and universities and set an agenda for advancing both. The Association of American Colleges and Universities (AAC&U), with its 1 250 colleges and universities across all sectors, in partnership with the Global Perspectives Institute (GPI), was awarded the competitive contract to lead the project Civic Learning and Democratic Engagement (CLDE).

Over the course of a year, we invited 150 civic practitioners, scholars, college and university presidents, civic organisations, disciplinary societies and other stakeholders to participate in a series of national roundtables to assess where progress had been achieved and could be accelerated. This chapter draws extensively on the findings from that year of investigation. The result of year-long research by the AAC&U and GPI, along with white papers, roundtables and public discussions, was the release of a national call to action entitled *A Crucible Moment: college learning and democracy's future*. I authored the volume on behalf of the CLDE National Task Force, and AAC&U published it for the collective and formally released it at the White House on 12 January 2012. *A Crucible Moment* is available in hard copy from AAC&U or can be downloaded at www.aacu.org/civic_learning/crucible/index.cfm.

As the Council of Europe's Sjur Bergan says, "The question, then, is not whether higher education should contribute to developing democratic societies, but how" (Chapter 7, above). *A Crucible Moment* makes a similar argument. Its national call to action offers a set of recommendations on how to make civic learning and democratic engagement an essential rather than optional outcome of all students' college education. This chapter will focus squarely on how colleges and universities in the United States are trying to do that. *A Crucible Moment* delineates the foundations that have been laid in higher education to cultivate civic learning and democratic engagement through the curriculum, scholarship and pedagogies, as well as in campus life and partnerships with local and global communities. But the report recognises that such opportunities are not available to most students. The challenge of the next decade is how to make such learning an expected and routine part of college learning, repeated in many forms in and out of class and across all disciplines over time.

Contemporary definitions of education for democracy

Before colleges and universities can decide how to educate for informed, responsible democratic citizenship, they need to agree in general about what they mean by civic learning and democratic engagement. The two phrases were deliberately chosen in *A Crucible Moment* to suggest that learning needed to be coupled with doing. Such a coupling defies many traditional practices in higher education. But it represents cumulative findings about how applying knowledge to complex, unscripted problems in real-world contexts accelerates and refines student learning. Learning is internalised not only by thinking about the complexities of democracy but also by practising democracy in its many different forms and forums.

Research for *A Crucible Moment* identified a growing consensus about the abstract and practical components of what educating for democratic citizenship requires in a century distinguished by diversity, globalisation and contention. While older definitions of civic learning are still embedded in the more comprehensive 21st-century definitions, those narrower goals are no longer sufficient. Higher education's challenge is to reorganise itself so it can provide the broader capabilities needed as well as the hands-on engagement that will further refine democratic learning.

As the chart below indicates, a 21st-century framework places new emphases on examining multiple kinds of struggles for democratic inclusion and justice over time, both within the United States and elsewhere on the globe. It also recognises the urgency of developing skills derived from engaging with multiple perspectives and deliberating productively across sometimes profound differences. A contemporary framework also requires higher education to be attentive to values as part of the college curriculum, to which some disciplines are particularly averse. Finally, the new conception places more priority on enacting democratic aims publicly in concert with others to address common problems – that is, the doing of democracy, which is leading colleges and universities into unfamiliar but potentially transformative territory.

FIGURE 1: A Framework for Twenty-First-Century Civic Learning and Democratic Engagement

Knowledge

- Familiarity with key democratic texts and universal democratic principles, and with selected debates — in US and other societies — concerning their applications
- Historical and sociological understanding of several democratic movements, both US and abroad
- Understanding one's sources of identity and their influence on civic values, assumptions, and responsibilities to a wider public
- Knowledge of the diverse cultures, histories, values, and contestations that have shaped US and other world societies
- Exposure to multiple religious traditions and to alternative views about the relation between religion and government
- Knowledge of the political systems that frame constitutional democracies and of political levers for influencing change

Skills

- Critical inquiry, analysis, and reasoning
- Quantitative reasoning
- Gathering and evaluating multiple sources of evidence
- Seeking, engaging, and being informed by multiple perspectives
- Written, oral, and multi-media communication
- Deliberation and bridge building across differences
- Collaborative decision making
- Ability to communicate in multiple languages

Values

- Respect for freedom and human dignity
- Empathy
- Open-mindedness
- Tolerance
- Justice
- Equality
- Ethical integrity
- Responsibility to a larger good

Collective Action

- Integration of knowledge, skills, and examined values to inform actions taken in concert with other people
- Moral discernment and behavior
- Navigation of political systems and processes, both formal and informal
- Public problem solving with diverse partners
- Compromise, civility, and mutual respect

Reprinted with permission from *A Crucible Moment: college learning and democracy's future,* © Association of American Colleges and Universities 2012.

Characteristics of civic-minded institutions

With a more comprehensive definition of civic learning and democratic engagement as its goal, *A Crucible Moment* recommends that the academy use as its standard of success the charge laid out in the USA soon after the Second World War by the President's Commission on Higher Education: "The first and most essential charge upon higher education is that at all levels and in all fields of specialization, it shall be the carrier of democratic values, ideals, and process" (President's Commission on Higher Education 1947a: 102). Making clear what was at stake, the commission's report explained: "Only an informed, thoughtful, tolerant people can maintain and develop a free society" (President's Commission on Higher Education 1947b: 3). Achieving such a benchmark of success suggests that everyone at colleges and universities has a role to play, whatever their position or disciplinary training: students, faculty, professional staff and administrators. And that means everyone: no one gets a pass.

A Crucible Moment identifies concrete indicators of just what a civic-minded institution looks like. In doing so, it names four key dimensions: civic ethos, civic literacy, civic inquiry and civic action. The four are elaborated in more detail in the chart below.

FIGURE 2: What Would a Civic-Minded Campus Look Like?

CIVIC ETHOS governing campus life

The infusion of democratic values into the customs and habits of everyday practices, structures, and interactions; the defining character of the institution and those in it that emphasizes open-mindedness, civility, the worth of each person, ethical behaviors, and concern for the well-being of others; a spirit of public-mindedness that influences the goals of the institution and its engagement with local and global communities.

CIVIC LITERACY as a goal for every student

The cultivation of foundational knowledge about fundamental principles and debates about democracy expressed over time, both within the United States and in other countries; familiarity with several key historical struggles, campaigns, and social movements undertaken to achieve the full promise of democracy; the ability to think critically about complex issues and to seek and evaluate information about issues that have public consequences.

CIVIC INQUIRY integrated within the majors and general education

The practice of inquiring about the civic dimensions and public consequences of a subject of study; the exploration of the impact of choices on different constituencies and entities, including the planet; the deliberate consideration of differing points of views; the ability to describe and analyze civic intellectual debates within one's major or areas of study.

CIVIC ACTION as lifelong practice

The capacity and commitment both to participate constructively with diverse others and to work collectively to address common problems; the practice of working in a pluralistic society and world to improve the quality of people's lives and the sustainability of the planet; the ability to analyze systems in order to plan and engage in public action; the moral and political courage to take risks to achieve a greater public good.

Reprinted with permission from *A Crucible Moment: college learning and democracy's future*, © Association of American Colleges and Universities 2012.

While the portrait is an ambitious one, the good news is that a strong foundation of practice has been established at most not-for-profit colleges and universities in the United States, both private and public. The impact on students' civic learning is heartening, as Ashley Finley captured in her review of the literature, "Civic learning and democratic engagements" (Finley 2011). Much is the result of new curricular designs and expectations. Other learning can be attributed to high-impact civic pedagogies. Still more is generated by activities outside the class-room that are centred on student activities and leadership. The last large arena for civic learning and democratic engagement, where some of the most promising impact lodges, is the exciting new campus/community partnerships offered either for academic credit or organised as volunteer commitments. In this latter hybrid territory, which is both academic and community-based, students are knee-deep in collectively addressing with others important social issues of their day. Inevitably, coming to consensus and then taking collective action demands doing democracy at the highest level.

The troubling news about the current state of civic practices is that on most campuses the opportunity for cultivating civic knowledge, skills, values, and action is random rather than planned, optional rather than expected, and without signage to guide students in their choices along the continuum of their undergraduate education. Typically it is available only to some students, which might explain the Eric Dey finding referenced earlier, which revealed that only one third of students strongly agreed that their civic capacities had expanded while in college. Happily, those students who take advantage of multiple key practices at high levels over time do benefit significantly. In a 2010 Campus Compact report of a study of 17 colleges and universities, for example, "students who engaged in more intensive service-learning experiences scored higher on all five measures [retention, academic challenge, academic engagement, interpersonal engagement, and community engagement] than did students who engaged in less intensive service-learning experiences" (Cress et al. 2010: 6).

Foundations that are partly laid

While the agenda for advancing civic learning and democratic engagement is ambitious and a steep hill to climb in the United States, we are buoyed by two factors: 1. trends that have turned campus life into a genuine public commons or public meeting space, and 2. exemplary programmes, pedagogies and partnerships that make clear to everyone that it is possible for higher education to construct innovative, democracy-enhancing academic opportunities for college students. These can be found in a range of locations and disciplines, and typically employ what are referred to as high-impact practices that evidence suggests lead to positive student-learning outcomes. Just as the 2011 Oslo conference asked participants to reimagine democratic societies, so higher education has been asked to reimagine how it organises itself. Innovative practices give testimony to people's willingness to move beyond simply imagining how to do things differently, by implementing a rich array of specific practices.

At this historic juncture, American campuses have great assets that make that transformation all the more possible. The democratisation of higher education by the end of the 20th century contributed to education for democracy in the 21st. Today, trends show that colleges and universities have moved significantly:

- from monocultural space to multicultural space;
- from access for the very few to access for the vast majority;
- from an exclusionary curriculum to a more inclusive one;
- from passive pedagogies to more problem-orientated, hands-on pedagogies;
- from talking about democracy to also doing democracy;
- from reaching out to the community to seeing themselves as part of the community;
- from being sequestered from the globe to engaging with global issues that permeate everyday life locally.

114

Civic literacy across general education

The findings of the research for *A Crucible Moment* unearthed some promising curricular structures that enhance opportunities for students to expand their civic knowledge, skills, values and action. In the United States, students take one third to two fifths of their courses in what we call general education. This is in part what characterises US higher education: its commitment to providing breadth as well as depth. In general education, sometimes referred to as liberal studies or core studies, students must take a wide range of courses in the arts, humanities, social sciences and sciences in addition to whatever major they might specialise in. This combination of expansive exposure and focused study is expected both for four-year baccalaureate degrees and for two-year associate degrees at most US community colleges. Analysing recent institutional changes in what he calls the "second wave of engagement", the historian David Scobey notes that innovations tend to "reframe the discourse of community service into one of collaboration and citizenship, to reconnect community work with systemic issues of policy, power, and justice, and to work for change not only in individual courses, but at the level of the curriculum and the campus as a whole" (Scobey 2010: 191).

Some of those shifts can be detected in the design of new structures and expectations for general education courses. Civic literacy, named in Figure 2 as one of the key characteristics of a civic-minded institution, is often the desired outcome of these restructured general education programmes; in all cases it is defined as a core expectation for all students. To ensure this, Tulane University, a private research university, has created a two-stage developmental civic arc in which all students are required to take both an introductory and an upper-level course. In their first or second year, all students must complete an introductory service-learning course, which refers to a "teaching and learning strategy that integrates meaningful community service with instruction and reflection to enrich the learning experience, teach civic responsibility, and strengthen communities" (Engberg and Fox 2011: 88). Those service-learning courses that carry academic credit incorporate community-based learning that must be completed off-campus, usually working with community-based NGOs in high-need areas. Typically students on such courses must spend at least 25 hours in a community-based setting. In their final two years, every Tulane student must complete one additional public service-approved programme, which can involve a public service research project, public service-based international study-abroad programme, academic service-learning internship or a capstone general education course with a public service component.

St. Edward's University organises its general education across all four years, beginning with a course that introduces students to the struggles for justice in the United States. That is paired with some later courses that focus on global issues and social responsibility. In a senior-level or fourth-year course, referred to in the USA as a capstone course because it is the culmination of learning in specific areas, students are expected to address a social issue connected to their major to strengthen the practice of using knowledge to help solve societal problems.

Civic inquiry within specialised study

Civic inquiry, a second characteristic of a civic-minded institution, is most often embedded in a student's special area of study. As Mary Huber and Pat Hutchings assert in their introduction to *Citizenship across the Curriculum*, every discipline should be able to help students investigate civic questions, dilemmas and consequences rooted in a given field. "To be sure," they explain, "there are some who think citizenship best – and exclusively – addressed as a subject for study in appropriate political science or history courses …. But for those who see preparation for citizenship as a goal of undergraduate education, the possibilities for where it can be taught expand" (Huber and Hutchings 2010: ix).

Worcester Polytechnic Institute (WPI) agrees with Huber and Hutchings. WPI has organised its project-based curriculum for all students in a way that asks students across their years of study to consider the civic consequences of what they are learning. The first-year Great Problems Seminar, for example, focuses on global themes, societal problems and human needs. Seminar options include courses like Feeding the World, Healing the World and Powering the World. After studying a broad swath of related scholarship in their freshmen seminar, students work in small groups, define a specific problem for which they do more research, suggest a public strategy for addressing their issue and then present the results to their peers. During their junior year, WPI students complete interactive qualifying projects, most of which are done outside the USA, typically in collaboration with community partners and always in a team of two to four students. In these upper-level projects, students examine the intersection of science or technology and social issues and human needs. As WPI explains it, their objective is "for WPI graduates to understand, as citizens and as professionals, how their careers will affect the larger society of which they are a part". [31]

Wagner College has initiated an upper-level complement for its civic-infused general education programme that is beginning to define what it calls "civic professionalism" as an outcome for majors. Similarly, the University of Wisconsin-Milwaukee has turned to pre-professional schools as the location for investing in civic inquiry as a routine experience for students. They have created interdisciplinary global course clusters like Global Management, Global Security, Global Cities and Global Communication. Service-learning requirements are integrated within these clusters, as is study abroad, foreign language and overseas internships.

---

31. See www.wpi.edu/academics/Depts/IGSD/iqp.html (accessed on 28 June 2012).

Powerful civic pedagogies

Four especially effective civic pedagogies have been developed in the last few decades in US colleges and universities: 1. diversity and global learning experiences; 2. intergroup and deliberative dialogue; 3. service learning; and 4. collective civic problem-solving. A contemporary framework for civic learning and democratic engagement relies on knowledge of democratic struggles for full inclusion, self-determination and civil rights of varying kinds. It also requires capacities to navigate multiple perspectives and deliberate across differences.

Diversity and global learning experiences

There is evidence that experiences of diversity and global learning can function to accelerate education for democracy. Sylvia Hurtado, director of the Higher Education Research Institute at the University of California, Los Angeles, has overseen a massive research project called *Preparing College Students for a Diverse Democracy* investigating the "links between diversity experiences, learning or cognitive development, and potential skills for civic engagement in a diverse society" (Hurtado 2006: 250). Her study finds that constructive interaction with diverse peers through the many venues in and out of the classroom disrupts students' previously uninterrogated world views and stereotypes, thus influencing cognitive and democracy outcomes. She underscores the importance of "doing democracy" along with "thinking about democracy". She explains: "While the college curriculum may provide the theory and concepts necessary for understanding a multi-racial and multi-ethnic society, students' experience with others of diverse backgrounds (inside and outside the classroom) provides an opportunity to practice living in a pluralist democracy among 'equal status' peers" (ibid: 265).

Intergroup dialogue and deliberative dialogue

These too have been adopted as civic pedagogies in many US colleges and universities. Intergroup dialogue, though sometimes practised outside class, has become an important academic course taught by faculty from a variety of disciplines. Adopted 20 years ago at the University of Michigan as a strong democratic pedagogy of particular value in helping students understand and engage across differences, it has been duplicated by a host of other institutions. In the Michigan model, two dozen or so students from diverse backgrounds spend a semester guided by skilled facilitators, through which they learn discussion skills, investigate social inequalities and explore how to work together. Typically these courses will focus on no more than two major group differences such as race and gender or Black and Jewish relationships.

Michigan intergroup-dialogue scholar Patricia Gurin and her colleagues report that results from 52 parallel field experiments using the Michigan intergroup model reveal that these dialogues help students collaborate across differences, think in a more complex way about others and about larger social issues, and actively commit to working with others to shape the world to be more just (Gurin, Nagda and Sorensen 2011). A number of other studies have shown that, as students engage in interactions across differences, whether in or out of class, they are more likely to challenge prejudice when they see it, listen attentively to other people's views and champion social justice (ASHE 2006).

Deliberative dialogue

California State University, Chico, incorporated deliberative dialogue – a more open mode of speaking and listening thoughtfully to one another – as a central component of its required First-Year Experience course. As a dimension of the course, every student presents on an issue of public importance at an annual town meeting on campus. Before making their argument about a course of action and discussing it with the larger group, each student does extensive research as part of the larger design of the course. Sustained Dialogue programmes, which incorporate deliberative dialogues into campus life rather than in the curriculum, exist on several dozen campuses. They are bolstered by a national Sustained Dialogue Campus Network office. [32] These dialogues are typically student-led, occur weekly and focus on discussing an agreed issue of concern about which there is some controversy. The Olive Tree Initiative, launched in 2007 by students at the University of California, Irvine (UCI), but now spread to other UC campuses, is an interfaith, student-sponsored deliberative dialogue that brings Jewish, Christian, Muslim, Druze and non-religious UCI students together to discuss the conflict in the Middle East. Some of the students also travel to the Middle East to engage in dialogue and explore differing perspectives with a range of community and political leaders, academics and activists. When they return, the students then organise as many as 70 forums for an academic and broader public.

Among the infrastructure for public dialogue that college campuses shelter are centres designed to build bridges between the university and the broader public, identify common problems and organise appropriate groups of citizens and leaders to meet to discuss how to resolve issues collectively. Typically, some of the activities are embedded in courses but the majority involve deeper engagements of the university with community groups as they work together to discuss larger public issues important to both entities. As one study of the effect of these centres reports, they provide space for honing students' and the public's deliberation skills through which they are "listening deeply to other points of view, exploring new ideas and perspectives, searching for points of agreement and bringing unexamined assumptions into the open" (London 2010: 14). The Institute for Civic Discourse and Democracy at Kansas State University, for instance, works in alliance with many groups to bring public voice into issues like immigration, land-use reform and health care. These centres demonstrate the shifting boundaries of the physical campus, expansion of the locus of scholarship and growing

---

32. See www.sdcampusnetwork.org (accessed on 13 July 2012).

efforts to provide ways for students to think, work and participate in deliberative democratic processes.

Service learning

The most widespread civic pedagogy, used on very many campuses, is service learning, described earlier with the Tulane University general education requirements. According to the data collected by the Higher Education Research Institute from entering college freshmen, 85 per cent of US students are arriving at college today saying they "performed volunteer work" "frequently" or "occasionally" as high-school seniors (Pryor et al. 2009: 11). Having arrived at college with a history of voluntary service, students can now deepen their learning through the substantive study of an academic subject that can be illuminated by service in community settings. Service learning has expanded dramatically since its principal national support organisation, Campus Compact, with its 1 100 colleges and universities, was founded in 1985. The estimate is that service learning reaches nearly 60 per cent of graduating college seniors (Finley 2012). Although it is most popularly known as service learning, some people worry that the "service" label might suggest a charity model rather than a reciprocal partnership, and refer to this kind of pedagogy as community-based learning or community-based research.

A Crucible Moment explains: "As the service-learning movement has evolved, many proponents are defining greater nuances between *kinds* of service experiences, *levels* of student responsibility, *scale* of issues addressed, learning *outcomes* sought, and the *impact* of engagement on community partners" (National Task Force 2012: 60). Service learning is one of the most potent pedagogies because it removes students from a familiar environment, asks them to apply their knowledge to unscripted problems and requires them to work across multiple groups with multiple perspectives. It is no surprise, then, that service learning continues to show some of the most positive overall gains in learning for students. The practice is associated with "complexity of understanding, problem analysis, critical thinking, and cognitive development" (Eyler et al. 2001: 4) and also with "personal efficacy, personal identity, spiritual growth, and moral development" (ibid: 1). Another study adds "cultural awareness, tolerance for diversity, altruistic attitudes, moral development, sensitivity and reasoning, and self-esteem" to the list (Finley 2012). Service learning is also linked to positive contributions to global perspective-taking (Engberg and Fox 2011). The list of positive outcomes goes on and on.

The impact of the pedagogy has encouraged more faculty members to incorporate service learning across more disciplines at multiple levels. Identifying placements is particularly time-consuming and often is handled by a campus-wide Community Engagement Centre that liaises with the community. California State University, Monterey Bay (CSUMB), one of the most sophisticated and long-standing of the service-learning models, was so impressed by evidence of the wide range of student outcomes from service learning that it now has a two-tier service-learning requirement in its general education course. Every student must take two courses and the second one, typically taken in the third or fourth year, needs to be rooted in a student's major. At CSUMB, for example, every business student must take a Community Economic Development course, which expects students to give 50 hours of service to a community organisation. The service can come in the form of direct service, research, project responsibilities or other forms negotiated between the student, faculty member and the NGO. But a guiding question overrides the business student's community-based experience: "How can businesses balance the 'triple bottom line' of profit, people, and planet?" (Pollack 2011: 9). They are being urged to think about their public responsibilities and their civic agency.

Collective civic problem-solving

The fourth powerful civic pedagogy that enhances democratic skills, and the newest, is what some are calling collective civic problem-solving. This pedagogy aligns with the larger education reform movement in the United States, which offers evidence that students learn better when they are applying or developing their knowledge in real-world contexts. Such inquiry-based and problem-based approaches have been refined by those who seek to enhance students' civic learning. Most frequently the civic problem-solving pedagogies take place as students are working in the borderland space where universities and communities co-reside. An important new book, *"To Serve a Larger Purpose": engagement for democracy and the transformation of higher education*, makes a case for moving to a democratic engagement paradigm through deep problem-solving partnerships with those outside academia:

> Democratic engagement locates the university within an ecosystem of knowledge production, requiring interaction with other knowledge producers outside the university for the creation of new problem solving knowledge through a multidirectional flow of knowledge and expertise. In this paradigm, students learn co-operative and creative problem solving within learning environments in which faculty, students, and individuals from the community work and deliberate together .... Civic engagement in the democratic-centred paradigm is intentionally political in that students learn about democracy by acting democratically. (Saltmarsh and Hartley 2011: 21)

In a Service Opportunities in Leadership programme at Duke University, students take a two-semester set of interdisciplinary courses that includes summer experience in community-based learning. The first course in the programme is on service leadership and social change, followed by a summer internship focused on social and political change projects, done in concert with organisations in the USA or elsewhere. When students return after the summer, they take a policy research seminar that has as its capstone project what Duke calls a "Social Issue Investigation Portfolio". This comprises an essay on a problem arising from their summer internship, an interview with a practitioner in that arena and a paper focused on policy recommendations addressing their selected issue (Colby et al. 2007: 300).

In an example that layers a series of powerful civic pedagogies and practices that culminate in civic problem-solving, the University of Maryland, College Park, has created what it calls a CIVICUS programme, which requires a two-year interdisciplinary living–learning residential experience where students studying the same five courses, one of which is Leadership in a Multicultural Society, live in the same residence halls. The students jointly plan service activities and their capstone course is community-based, either through an internship or what they refer to as a "discovery"/research project (Colby et al. 2007: 300-301).

Campus–community partnerships

The civic problem-solving pedagogies are finding fertile ground in the territory carved out by the potentially most transformative new enterprise in education for democracy: newly defined partnerships between campus and community. Although "campus outreach to the community" is a familiar label and practice, the evolving partnerships are of a different quality altogether. The values, purposes and methodologies governing collaborations transform the partnerships between the university, community and other public and private partners into innovative, democracy-enhancing alliances. They represent the integration of thinking about and doing democracy. As such, they enact the very forms of democratic engagement endorsed by Saltmarsh and Hartley.

Academic institutions have been moving from a charitable model for these partnerships to a reciprocal model, and are now moving to a generative model where civic prosperity for all, achieved by all, is the goal (Musil 2003). As *A Crucible Moment* describes this dynamic new shared public space: "Interdependency, innovation, multiple perspectives, and a commitment to a long-range investment in the public good define the partnership's core values; higher education no longer sees itself as going out into the community, but as part of the community, whether that community is local, national, or global" (National Task Force 2012: 64). For higher education, this new landscape definitely reimagines the academy's civic mission and in the process reimagines what counts as scholarship, who are considered experts, how disciplines can be taught and how the curriculum itself is organised. As *A Crucible Moment* argues: "In the public space of generative partnerships, democratic values can be tested and civic skills honed; participants challenged to work collectively across differences; and civic aspirations transmuted into collective civic action" (ibid: 65).

Some institutions that are investing in these dramatic new alliances are clustering around common commitments and linking with one another through national networks. One example of this is Community-Campus Partnerships for Health (CCPH), which functions as a non-profit organisation connecting academic institutions, health care delivery systems, community-based organisations, student-service organisations and foundations, and government. [33] The goal of the project

---

33. See http://ccph.info (accessed on 28 June 2012).

as they work together towards systemic change is to "leverage the knowledge, wisdom and experience in communities and in academic institutions to solve pressing health, social, environmental and economic challenges". [34]

Another cluster of increasing influence is found in the Anchor Institutions Task Force, led by the University of Pennsylvania and advised by Marga Incorporated, [35] now numbering more than 170 affiliations. Typically the universities and colleges are in metropolitan areas. Because they see their institutions as important anchors for the communities in which they reside, in much the same way that a large industry or business might be, or a hospital or government agency – all of which they partner with – the Anchor Institutions seek to use their social, political, intellectual and cultural capital to improve the well-being of the overall community including its environment. They describe as their motivating values "collaboration and partnership, equity and social justice, democracy and democratic practice, and commitment to place and community" (National Task Force 2012: 65).

Widener College, in Chester, Pennsylvania, one of the poorest cities in the United States, has used its partnerships to stimulate economic investments, improve the public school system and establish a charter school on its campus. Similarly, through dynamic new alliances, the Barbara and Edward Netter Center for Community Partnership [36] at the University of Pennsylvania has addressed educational, health and economic issues in West Philadelphia, where the university resides. In addition to involving undergraduates in this new academic democratic space, they have been particularly successful in involving their professional graduate schools like dentistry, business and medicine.

Syracuse University in central New York sits amid one of the former manufacturing centres in the state, now beleaguered by abandoned industrial buildings, a school system overwhelmed by the needs of its students, a fragmented community divided by bridges, fences and highways, and a sagging economy. An Anchor Institution, Syracuse University stands as a poster child for reimagined civic partnerships that have the potential to transform lives, communities and institutions of higher learning. Its university president made it a priority to raise funds and political capital that would help jumpstart an entirely unexplored series of alliances between the state and municipal governments, business partners with a stake in the economic and civic recovery of the city, private foundations, community groups, public school systems and, standing alongside not over all of them, Syracuse University itself. The group generated so many projects that they finally decided to form a non-profit organisation to manage them. That neutral entity helped balance the partnership and build common ownership of the overriding civic goals.

---

34. Ibid.
35. See www.margaic.com/initiatives/aitf (accessed on 28 June 2012); see also Maurrasse (Chapter 24, below).
36. See www.upenn.edu/ccp/index.php (accessed on 13 July 2012).

Knowing that one of the fundamental missions of any university, especially a research university like Syracuse, is to advance knowledge and research, Syracuse worked as much on aligning its own internal processes, incentives and values as it did on the broader community partnerships. "Scholarship in Action" is the label Syracuse uses to describe how research can be integrated into robust campus–community partnerships. It describes this new landscape as a place "where students become leaders, scholars become collaborators, and the community is continually energized by new ideas". [37] The University Senate passed new promotion and tenure guidelines acknowledging the value of public scholarship. Some of the most creative faculty were given recognition and time to work on their scholarship in action each year through a new fund, and some departments began to redesign their curriculum to take advantage of the hands-on work in real-work contexts that the citywide alliance offered them. For example, architectural students designed low-income green houses in a neighbourhood, environmental studies students worked with the community to design more beautiful and sustainable pathways to connect formerly divided neighbourhoods, and literature and history majors collaborated with residents from a traditional African-American community to capture in digital forms the historical contribution of that community to democratic racial justice, beginning with its abolitionist activities in the first half of the 19th century.

Syracuse University and its many partners do not merely represent entrepreneurial ventures replete with innovative democratic ideas. They are also seeking to establish democratic ways of working together in this new public space, and they represent constituencies that do not have a history of doing that very well or very often. They are each inventing as they go, negotiating predictable potholes in the road. Moreover, they launched this ambitious venture before the country careered into the worst economic recession since the Great Depression of 1929. Yet, the signs of success can be seen in warehouses in industrial neighbourhoods that now house culinary centres, green technology enterprises and artists' studios. They can be seen in the new housing that is stabilising and revitalising the West Side of Syracuse. They appear in the joint efforts to address the multiple issues for public schools in high-need areas, which include supplementary academic support for teachers and students, health care for families and literacy programmes for parents.

The challenge posed in the 2011 Reimagining Democratic Societies meeting was to explore together what this moment in history required of higher education. In a world of competing democratic principles, fragile new democratic nations and functionally problematic older democracies, what does it mean to educate students to think about democratic matters with discernment and engage in collective action responsibly and democratically? Colleges and universities in the United States are beginning to create some educational experiences for students and some new arenas for scholarship that suggest how, as Sjur Bergan urged, to educate for

---

37. See www.syr.edu (accessed on 17 July 2012).

democratic engagement in diverse democracies. The foundations are partly laid but hardly complete. Possible ways to reinvigorate disciplines, transform how and where teaching is done and advance the knowledge needed to achieve democracy's ends have been sketched out, but not yet fully imagined. Clearly, educating only to promote students' personal gain is no longer a viable moral or societal option for higher education, if it ever was. To quote Gwendolyn Brooks, a Pulitzer Prize winning African-American poet (Brooks 1971: 19),

... we are each other's

harvest:

we are each other's

business:

we are each other's

magnitude and bond.

Thinking and acting democratically helps all of us understand what is at stake in our societies if we fail to recognise this inescapable human reality.

References

ASHE (Association for the Study of Higher Education) (2006), "Research on outcomes and processes of intergroup dialogue", *Higher Education Report*, 32 (4): 59-73.

Brooks G. (1971), "Paul Robeson" in *Family Pictures*, Detroit: Broadside Press.

CCPH (Community–Campus Partnership for Health), "Community–campus partnerships for health: transforming communities and higher education", http://ccph.info (accessed on 28 June 2012).

Colby A., Beaumont E., Ehrlich T. and Corngold J. (2007), *Educating for democracy: preparing undergraduates for responsible political engagement*, San Francisco: Jossey-Bass.

Cress C. M., Burack C., Giles D. E. Jr, Elkins J. and Stevens M. C. (2010), *A promising connection: increasing college access and success through civic engagement*, Boston MA: Campus Compact.

Dewey J. (1916/2008), "The need of an industrial education in an industrial democracy" in J. A. Boydston (ed.), *The Middle Works of John Dewey, Volume 10, 1899-1924: Essays on Philosophy and Education, 1916-1917*, 137-43, Carbondale IL: Southern Illinois University Press.

Dey E. L., Barnhardt C. L., Antonaros M., Ott M. C. and Hopsapple M. A. (2009), *Civic Responsibility: what is the campus climate for learning?*, Washington DC: Association of American Colleges and Universities.

Engberg M. E. and Fox K. (2011), "Exploring the relationship between undergraduate service-learning experiences and global perspective-taking", *Journal of Student Affairs Research and Practice*, 48(1): 85-105.

Eyler J. S., Giles D. E. Jr, Stenson C. M. and Gray C. J. (2001), *At a glance: what we know about the effects of service-learning on college students, faculty, institutions and communities, 1993-2000*, 3rd edn, Nashville TN: Vanderbilt University.

Finley A. (2011), "Civic learning and democratic engagements: a review of the literature on civic engagement in post-secondary education", paper prepared for the US Department of Education as part of Contract: ED-OPE-10-C-0078, 24 May www.aacu.org/civic_learning/index.cfm (accessed on 28 June 2012).

—   (2012), *Making progress? What we know about the achievement of liberal education outcomes*, Washington DC: Association of American Colleges and Universities.

Gurin P., Nagda B. A. and Sorensen N. (2011), "Intergroup dialogue: education for a broad conception of civic engagement", *Liberal Education*, 97 (2): 46-51.

Huber M. T. and Hutchings P. (2010), "Civic learning: intersections and interactions", in M. B. Smith, R. S. Nowacek and J. L. Bernstein (eds), *Citizenship Across the Curriculum*, Bloomington IN: Indiana University Press, pp. IX-XIII.

Hurtado S. (2006), "Diversity and learning for a pluralist democracy" in W. R. Allen, M. Bonous-Hammarth and R. T. Teraniski, *Higher education in a global society: achieving diversity, equity, and excellence*, St Louis MO: Elsevier.

Intercollegiate Studies Institute, National Civic Literacy Board (2007), *Failing Our Students, Failing America: holding colleges accountable for teaching America's history and institutions*, Wilmington DE: Intercollegiate Studies Institute, www.americancivicliteracy.org/2007;summary_summary.html (accessed on 27 June 2012).

London S. (2010) *Doing democracy: how a network of grassroots organizations is strengthening community, building capacity, and shaping a new kind of civic education*, Washington, DC: Kettering Foundation.

McCormick Tribune Foundation (2007), *Civic disengagement in our democracy*, Chicago: McCormick Tribune Foundation.

Musil C. M. (2003), "Educating for citizenship", *Peer Review*, 5 (3): 4-8.

National Task Force on Civic Learning and Democratic Engagement (2012), *A Crucible Moment: college learning and democracy's future*, Washington DC: Association of American Colleges and Universities.

NCES (National Center for Education Statistics (2011), *The nation's report card: civics 2010*, Washington, DC: Institute of Education Sciences, US Department of Education.

Pollack S. (2011), "Civic literacy across the curriculum", *Diversity & Democracy*, 14 (3): 8-9.

President's Commission on Higher Education (1947a), *Higher education for American democracy, Vol. I, Establishing the goals*, Washington DC: Government Printing Office.

— (1947b), *Higher education for American democracy, Vol. II, Equalizing and expanding individual opportunity*, Washington, DC: Government Printing Office.

Pryor J. H., Hurtado S., DeAngelo L., Blake L. P. and Tran S. (2009), *The American freshman: national norms fall 2009*, Los Angeles: Higher Education Research Institute, University of California-Los Angeles.

Saltmarsh J. A. and Hartley M. (eds) (2011), *"To serve a larger purpose": engagement for democracy and the transformation of higher education*, Philadelphia: Temple University Press.

Scobey D. (2010), "Across: the heterogeneity of civic education" in M. B Smith, R. S. Nowacek and J. L. Bernstein (eds), *Citizenship across the curriculum*, Bloomington IN: Indiana University Press, pp. 185-98.

US Census Bureau (2010), "Current population survey, November 2010: civic engagement supplement file," www.census.gov/apsd/techdoc/cps/cpsnov10c.pdf (accessed on 27 June 2012).

13. Educating informed, engaged citizens: AASCU's American Democracy Project

Muriel Howard and Jennifer M. Domagal-Goldman

> I know of no safe depository of the ultimate powers of the society but the people themselves; and if we think them not enlightened enough to exercise their control with a wholesome discretion, the remedy is not to take it from them, but inform their discretion. [38]

In Chapter 12 (above), Caryn McTighe Musil takes a broad look at the civic engagement movement in the United States, what *A Crucible Moment* describes as a national investment in education for civic learning and democratic engagement, which has been gaining momentum over several decades. This chapter takes a detailed look inside a prominent US project in higher education and civic engagement, the American Democracy Project (ADP). [39] It is sponsored by the American Association of State Colleges and Universities (AASCU), [40] a higher education association based in Washington DC with a membership of more than 400 public colleges and universities. AASCU is deeply committed to the concept that public colleges and universities have a public purpose. Creating and sponsoring the American Democracy Project represents a natural expression of that public purpose.

The campuses of AASCU's members are found in all parts of the United States. They and their nearly 4 million students are quite diverse yet, for the most part, they are in the middle of the American higher education system, neither community colleges nor large, well-known research universities. In fact, most AASCU institutions describe themselves as public regional comprehensive colleges and universities, with deep connections to their communities and regions. Most of their students come from nearby and much of their work, in applied research and service, focuses on local and regional issues. Thus AASCU schools share a special sense of obligation to the specific place where they are located. As a means of characterising this obligation and at the same time describing their role, AASCU institutions have defined themselves as "stewards of place" (AASCU 2002). As such, they serve as publicly engaged institutions "fully committed to direct, two-way interaction with communities and other external constituencies through the development, exchange, and application of knowledge, information, and expertise for mutual benefit" (ibid: 7).

---

38. Thomas Jefferson (1820).
39. See www.aascu.org/programs/ADP/ (accessed on 16 July 2012).
40. See www.aascu.org (accessed on 16 July 2012).

As they create and sustain two-way partnerships with public and private entities in their region, AASCU colleges and universities typically focus on one or more of four dimensions of stewardship: 1. community and economic improvement, 2. work with the K-12 schools,[41] 3. community internationalisation, and 4. civic learning and democratic engagement.

In the 21st century, and particularly in the global economic downturn at the end of the first decade, public colleges and universities in the United States face enormous pressures to be engines of economic growth. Part of that economic role involves the expectation that our institutions emphasise career preparation. Yet in a broader, more expansive view of our work, underscored by our role as stewards of place, we believe that our most important responsibility is the obligation to foster sustainable, democratic societies in the communities we serve. The American Democracy Project has been a major vehicle to achieve that civic vision.

In 2003, troubled by research that indicated decreasing engagement in voluntary community groups and organisations, especially Robert Putnam's *Bowling Alone* (2000), AASCU, in partnership with the *New York Times*, created the American Democracy Project, an initiative to help AASCU member institutions improve the civic education of their students. The project, unfunded from its beginning, asked campuses to voluntarily sign up to participate in a series of national and local activities that would increase the likelihood that students would graduate with civic skills and commitments to become engaged and contributing members of their communities. From its inception therefore, the ADP argued that the most significant civic engagement work focuses on student outcomes.

Planning for the American Democracy Project lasted 18 months, conducted by staff members at AASCU and interested chief academic officers. To launch the project, we sent a simple email from the association's president to the 400+ member colleges and universities, inviting participation. Despite no external funding or support, within four weeks 134 campuses had joined up. Clearly there was an enormous interest in this kind of work. That simple email launched a project that has grown into a national initiative; now, 10 years later, it involves more than 250 colleges and universities in 47 states.

AASCU used an existing national conference, the academic affairs summer meeting in July 2003, to launch ADP. For one of the three days of the conference, the focus was exclusively on civic engagement work. Tom Ehrlich, a noted civic engagement scholar at the Carnegie Foundation for the Advancement of Teaching, gave the opening address. Participants, mainly chief academic officers, left the meeting with a series of concrete ideas about how to launch the project on their own campus. They were urged to create a local support structure for the project, to include a local ADP committee and a campus co-ordinator.

---

41. "K-12 schools" means the whole of free primary and secondary education in the USA, from kindergarten (K), for 4- to 6-year-olds, through to twelfth grade (12) for 16- to 19-year-olds.

Almost immediately, the project confronted its first challenge. Campuses were clearly interested in the work, but what exactly would the work be? Initially two national activities were launched: an audit and a shared reading initiative. Each campus was asked to conduct an audit of civic engagement activities already occurring there. Many American colleges and universities have a variety of civic engagement projects, initiatives and programmes under way. Yet on the typical American campus, most of these civic activities are created and directed by individuals, with no connection between the various activities and no direct relationship to the purposes of the institution. Seldom is there an explicit attempt to link a set of activities and projects to create a set of institutional outcomes. The interest, from the beginning, was in trying to create institutional intentionality, a shared, explicit commitment to a goal of civic outcomes for all students. Campuses were asked to form reading groups, primarily with faculty members, to give campus participants a shared understanding of the work to be undertaken. The first shared reading chosen was *Civic Responsibility and Higher Education* (Ehrlich 2000), which describes research at 21 colleges and universities, detailing the various approaches to civic engagement. In retrospect those two activities, the audit and the shared reading, were critical to the launch of the project. They increased the visibility of civic engagement work and the ADP on participating campuses, while giving participants concrete ideas about activities and programmes they could undertake on their own campuses.

The second challenge that the ADP confronted at an early stage was how to define civic engagement. In the United States, the term is used with a great deal of imprecision. For some, it means service learning and volunteerism. For others, it means political engagement. We concluded that, because our participating campuses were so diverse, we should not try to dictate a single definition but instead serve as a large tent of definitions and ideas. Therefore, ADP defined civic engagement as a continuum from volunteerism and service, on the one hand, to political engagement, on the other, with everything in between.

The third challenge was how to go about the work. A lot of people talked about civic engagement but remarkably few frameworks existed to help ADP think about how to create the most powerful civic engagement outcomes. What could and should campuses do to produce thoughtful and engaged citizens for a democracy? After reviewing the literature, ADP concluded that for us civic engagement had four dimensions: knowledge, skills, experience and reflection. A college or university that was serious about creating informed and engaged graduates must address all four elements.

The first few years of the project were a whirlwind of activities. AASCU dispatched the project's founder, George Mehaffy, to a number of campuses to make presentations and meet with ADP participants. Regional meetings were convened in several parts of the United States, sometimes in partnership with other civic groups, notably Campus Compact. A website was launched that chronicled the activities and projects of many ADP participants and produced our first monograph:

Democracy and Civic Engagement: a guide for higher education (2004). That year also saw the first annual American Democracy Project conference, no longer connected directly to the AASCU academic affairs summer meeting.

Yet for all of the enthusiasm and excitement, as well as the outpouring of activities, after several years the project's national leadership began to worry about the impact of the project and its centrality to the work of our institutions. As an unfunded project, ADP was not in a position to dictate precisely what activities any particular institution should undertake. Furthermore, as a membership organisation, AASCU had to acknowledge and honour the unique circumstances and contexts of each institution. Yet the reluctance to dictate activities and provide very precise direction resulted in a lack of focus and often a broad set of sometimes unconnected activities. Indeed, observation of campus programmes and activities revealed that, far too often, the American Democracy Project activities on our member campuses were largely characterised by three features: they were celebratory, episodic and marginal. ADP leaders reluctantly concluded that, far too often, the work that had been encouraged and supported did not reach into the core activities or concerns of our institutions. After some consideration, it was concluded that a different approach was needed. As a result, ADP launched the Civic Engagement in Action Series, designed to drive our civic work deeply into the heart of the institution, by focusing on faculty, courses and specific topics.

The Civic Engagement in Action (CEIA) initiatives are national activities, directed by AASCU; they are designed to provide opportunities for students to become deeply involved in substantive citizenship issues. Each initiative in the CEIA series examines a critical national issue and explores the roles and actions of government agencies, advocacy and educational organisations and citizens in addressing problems and resolving conflicts. Blending national and campus-centred activities, these initiatives design materials and ideas for campuses to use in promoting civic learning and democratic engagement among undergraduates. Each initiative brings together a relatively small group of campuses, which meet to design a set of programmes or activities that they can then launch. Each initiative typically has an organisational partner to provide content expertise and support. The initiatives act as democratic laboratories in which faculty, staff, students and national partners work collectively to create new models for civic learning and democratic engagement, which then can be disseminated to other campuses. Many of the initiatives have created programmes that are now being expanded to other campuses, and some initiatives have produced monographs and other written material. The following initiatives have been created:

- America's Future: Protecting the Fiscal Health of Our Democracy (in conjunction with Public Agenda);
- Democratic Participation: the Political Engagement Project (with the Carnegie Foundation for the Advancement of Teaching);
- Civic Agency (with the Center for Democracy and Citizenship);

- eCitizenship: New Tools, New Strategies, New Spaces (with the Center for the Study of Citizenship and Wayne State University in Michigan);
- Common Ground: The Stewardship of Public Lands (with the Yellowstone Association of Yellowstone National Park); and
- Global Engagement: Educating Globally Competent Citizens (started in conjunction with the Center for Strategic and International Studies).

The Campus and Community Civic Health Initiative is the newest of the CEIA series programmes. ADP and 25 of its campuses have partnered with the National Conference on Citizenship and are working in conjunction with CIRCLE (the Center for Information and Research on Civic Learning and Engagement) and Lyon Software to identify measures of campus and local community civic health and then to take action to collectively assess and improve the civic vitality of these communities.

One of ADP's early and continuing national initiatives is the Political Engagement Project, begun in collaboration with Tom Ehrlich at the Carnegie Foundation for the Advancement of Teaching. Though a non-partisan project, ADP takes seriously its responsibility to educate students for political engagement in our democracy. Through ADP's Political Engagement Project initiative, participating campuses create programmes and activities designed to develop undergraduates' sense of political efficacy and duty. These programmes are also intended to help students develop the political skills needed to engage with the political world, a contribution recognised by scholars John Saltmarsh and Matt Hartley. In their edited volume *To serve a larger purpose*, they write: "The [civic engagement] movement has largely sidestepped the political dimension of civic engagement. With only a few exceptions (the AASCU's American Democracy Project is a good example), institutional (and national) efforts do not explicitly link the work of engagement to our democracy" (Saltmarsh and Hartley 2011: 6). ADP campuses infuse political education and engagement strategies into a variety of disciplines and courses on campus, making them focus on key dimensions of political development such as knowledge and understanding, active involvement, sense of political efficacy and identity, and skills of democratic participation.

Since its inception, ADP has engaged in five broad areas of action: 1. national, regional and local conferences; 2. dissemination and publication; 3. awards and recognition of campuses and individuals; 4. assessment; and 5. campus activities designed to strengthen students' civic learning and engagement.

ADP has hosted 10 national and 16 regional meetings with more than 3 000 participants. These conferences offer participants – faculty, students and administrators – an opportunity to exchange ideas about and successful strategies for strengthening civic learning and engagement on their campuses. Participants also learn from national experts about emerging research and best practices in the civic engagement field.

In an effort to disseminate the work of its national initiatives, ADP has produced 12 monographs, guides or toolkits on topics ranging from *Advancing a Civic*

Engagement Agenda: a guide to marketing, management and money (AASCU 2009) to *Educating Students for Political Engagement: a guide to implementation and assessment for colleges and universities* (AASCU 2010). These monographs give faculty the opportunity to publish their work and other campuses the ability to build on existing ideas and programmes. In 2012 the American Democracy Project worked with Missouri State University, an ADP campus, to establish the *eJournal of Public Affairs*,[42] an open-access, peer-reviewed journal for faculty to publish scholarship related to civic engagement.

As part of ADP's commitment to dissemination of innovative and effective strategies and practices, the project also identifies signature pedagogies and practices of civic engagement – defined as high-impact practices. California State University, Chico, a member of both AASCU and the Association of American Colleges and Universities (AAC&U), was noted in Chapter 12 (above) for its town hall meeting, a powerful civic pedagogy based on deliberative dialogue. The town hall meeting represents just one element of CSU Chico's public-sphere pedagogy – which includes a set of signature civic engagement pedagogies and practices, and was featured in ADP's most recent national meeting in San Antonio, Texas. Faculty from CSU Chico reported that assessment efforts indicate that students participating in the town hall meeting and other public-sphere pedagogies have higher retention and graduation rates than their non-participating peers. Other signature pedagogies and practices of civic engagement include Times Talk,[43] Democracy Plaza[44] and Cafe Demos.[45] In identifying, assessing and promoting various signature pedagogies and practices that originate on ADP member campuses and in other national organisations, ADP hopes to call attention to and spread the adoption of effective ways campuses can advance civic learning and democratic engagement.

In addition to identifying and disseminating specific signature pedagogies and practices, ADP has also sought to spread the focus on civic work to other AASCU mission-relevant arenas. In 2010, AASCU was awarded a Learn and Serve America Higher Education grant of US$433 874 by the Corporation for National and Community Service to design and implement new civic minors[46] in urban education. AASCU selected five urban member campuses to design minor programmes of study that would integrate K-12 service-learning experiences with urban public policy coursework, offering pre-service teachers and

---

42. For the *eJournal of Public Affairs*, see www.ejournal.missouristate.edu/.
43. See www.gcsu.edu/adp/timestalk.htm (accessed on 13 July 2012).
44. See http://life.iupui.edu/osi/civic-engagement/political/dp.html (accessed on 13 July 2012).
45. See http://ww2.ramapo.edu/students/ccec/adp/cafe.aspx (accessed on 13 July 2012).
46. Academic minors are a collection of four to seven courses in a specific subject area. Minors allow a student to explore the offerings in an academic discipline or field, learning subject matter, methodology and skills, but they do not provide the depth of knowledge or experience that an academic major (typically consisting of 10 to 12 courses) does. While all US undergraduates are required to complete a major (their degrees will bear the name of their major), minors are usually undertaken as optional additions to a student's course of study.

other undergraduates a coherent understanding of the larger context of urban education. The Civic Minor in Urban Education will equip future urban teachers to understand the complex context of urban schools, the strengths and capabilities of urban children and the implications of public policy for P-12 public schools. [47] The academic minors are designed to instil in undergraduates a deeper commitment to civic engagement and democratic professionalism, and AASCU's work in this arena and robust framework of existing partnerships and national programmes made it the ideal co-ordinator of this three-year pilot project. Campus design team leaders shared programme specifics and implementation strategies at the 2012 annual American Democracy Project national meeting.

Perhaps the largest dissemination effort ADP has undertaken is to help in the creation of a parallel but closely connected civic project on community college campuses, The Democracy Commitment (TDC). ADP shares office space with the national co-ordinator of TDC, and in 2012 the two organisations participated in an expanded national conference in San Antonio, where more than 500 participants gathered to learn about civic work in the two-year and four-year higher education sectors. ADP has also invited TDC members to participate in many of its national initiatives and programmes.

The American Democracy Project has created two national awards to recognise leadership in civic engagement on AASCU campuses. The William M. Plater Award for Leadership in Civic Engagement is given annually to an AASCU chief academic officer who has made significant contributions in the field. It was named for the chief academic officer who served many years at Indiana University Purdue University Indianapolis (IUPUI), an institution renowned for its civic work. The John Saltmarsh Award for Emerging Leaders in Civic Engagement, honouring another notable contributor to the civic engagement movement, recognises early-career faculty and staff who have made noteworthy contributions to civic learning.

ADP has engaged in a number of efforts to assess civic learning and democratic engagement. A group of ADP schools, along with the ADP national office, worked with the National Survey of Student Engagement (NSSE) to develop a set of civic engagement questions which were then added to the survey for participating campuses. A symposium on assessing student civic outcomes was co-hosted with IUPUI in 2009. Working with colleagues there, ADP developed a set of civic engagement rubrics for curricular and co-curricular assessment of civic learning and engagement outcomes.

In addition to conferences, publications, awards and assessment efforts, ADP campuses have spearheaded innumerable campus activities focused on advancing undergraduate civic engagement. From voter education and registration to

---

47. "P-12" means preparatory to 12th grade, i.e. K-12 without kindergarten. See also note 42, above.

curriculum revision projects, campus inventories of civic engagement work and participation in special days of action and reflection (e.g., annual Constitution Day and Earth Day), speaker series and many recognition and award programmes, the efforts of ADP campuses have been nurtured by the national ADP office. None of these activities, however, fully captures the breadth and depth of the tireless work of ADP students, faculty and staff. From the collective thinking, insights and expertise conveyed through its series of monographs (which serve as snapshots of our ongoing work) to the time participants dedicate to planning meetings, conference calls and webinars, the heart of ADP lies in the spirit of our member institutions and their commitment to preparing the next generation of informed, engaged citizens for our democracy.

Since 2003, AASCU's American Democracy Project and its participating institutions have made an enormous contribution to the capacity of AASCU members to produce informed, engaged graduates for our democracy. What is remarkable about this effort is that it has been undertaken without any external financial support. AASCU often says that the American Democracy Project is the largest unfunded civic engagement effort in the history of American higher education. Yet that is not actually true. It is true that we have not received very much in the way of external support, often the lifeblood of civic projects in the United States. Yet in fact, the American Democracy Project has been richly funded by the enthusiasm and passion of its participants.

The year 2013 marks the 10th anniversary of the American Democracy Project. Despite all that has been accomplished in the project so far, much remains to be done. One key goal for the coming years is to strengthen the ability of colleges and universities to make civic learning and civic outcomes central to the activities and outcomes of an institution, a concept captured in the phrase "institutional intentionality". Another goal is to work with others to create a much more powerful set of civic engagement assessment tools, so that we can identify with more precision those activities, strategies and programmes that make a substantial contribution to the development of civically engaged graduates.

As educators looking at the landscape of American civic and political life, we can see there is still much to do. Deep divisions and polarisation, rising inequality and a growing number of national and global challenges all underscore the critical need for the work that we do. But beyond the civic problems of our country, American higher education also has challenges in its structure and organisation that limit its ability to address civic outcomes for students. First, most of our institutions are a series of silos, disconnected from one another. The concept that all of the different groups and players on a campus could reach consensus and work together to achieve civic outcomes for students is a daunting, indeed almost unimaginable prospect. Even if everyone on one of our campuses could agree on a set of civic outcomes for students, creating the conditions to achieve those outcomes would still be complex. A second challenge is that the work of producing civically capable students is a complex interaction of knowledge and experience. Most ADP institutions, and the majority of our faculty, have little or no training in how to create the optimal current conditions for producing civic outcomes. A third challenge comes from the structure of American higher education, decentralised since our rejection of central authority in the American Revolution. We have no ministry of education that could mandate a civic focus. Given our long history of autonomy and independence as institutions, ministerial decrees would probably have little effect anyway.

Yet perhaps the greatest challenge for the civic engagement movement in the United States is to connect the theoretical and conceptual work with the very difficult, on-the-ground work of educating informed, engaged students that must take place on individual campuses. As noted earlier, one of the areas of enormous weakness is our lack of capacity to adequately assess civic outcomes and the ways that those outcomes were achieved. We have a broad array of civic organisations and groups in higher education, each of which works within its own area of focus and with its own set of institutions. As the civic engagement movement matures, it needs to see more efforts at collaboration between different civic organisations as well as between those who focus on theory and those who focus on practice.

A recent partnership between AASCU and the Association of American Colleges and Universities to create a civic learning working group intended to collect and categorise civic assessments reflects a promising development in collaboration. In 2011 the Lumina Foundation, concerned that far too often degrees do not describe adequately what degree holders can do, created the Degree Qualifications Profile (DQP) (Adelman et al. 2011). The DQP specifies learning outcomes across five key areas of learning for recipients of the associate (two-year) degree, bachelor's degree and master's degree. Civic learning has emerged as one of the five key areas of learning. AAC&U and AASCU have joined together to develop a repository of civic learning assessments at the associate, bachelor's, and master's degree levels. This partnership is an illustration of the kinds of collaboration that need to be fostered, where conceptual frameworks and practical educational efforts are linked to enable colleges and universities to achieve powerful civic learning outcomes for students.

The current focus on civic engagement in higher education in the United States began in the 1980s. Almost 30 years later, as we look back on that work and its successes, there is much to celebrate. Yet looking forward, in the midst of the complex and often divisive politics of the 21st century, it must also be recognised how much is left to do. Above all, ADP is mindful of the critical nature of this work, both for our country and the world. ADP will continue to draw inspiration from our country's founders and their clear and unambiguous understanding of the relationship between education and democracy. As Thomas Jefferson famously observed in 1816, "If a nation expects to be ignorant and free, in a state of civilization, it expects what never was and never will be."

References

AASCU (American Association of State Colleges and Universities) (2002), *Stepping Forward As Stewards of Place*, Washington DC: AASCU. Available at: www.aascu.org/uploadedFiles/AASCU/Content/Root/MediaAndPublications/Free_Publications/02_StewardsofPlace.pdf.

—— (2004), *Democracy and Civic Engagement: a guide to higher education*, Washington DC: AASCU.

—— (2009), *Advancing a Civic Engagement Agenda: a guide to marketing, management and money*, Washington DC: AASCU.

—— (2010), *Educating Students for Political Engagement: a guide to implementation and assessment for colleges and universities*, Washington DC: AASCU.

Adelman C., Ewell P., Gaston P. and Schneider C. G. (2011), *The degree qualifications profile*, Indianapolis: Lumina Foundation. Available at: www.luminafoundation.org/publications/The_Degree_Qualifications_Profile.pdf (accessed on 15 September 2012).

Ehrlich T. (ed.) (2000), *Civic Responsibility and Higher Education*, Phoenix AZ: The American Council on Education and The Oryx Press.

Jefferson T. (1816), "Thomas Jefferson to Charles Yancey", in A. A. Lipscomb and A. E. Bergh (eds), *The Writings of Thomas Jefferson*, Washington DC: Memorial Edition (1903-4), 14: 384.

—— (1820), "Letter to William C. Jarvis 28 September 1820", in A. A. Lipscomb and A. E. Bergh (eds), *Thomas Jefferson on Politics and Government*, Washington DC: Memorial Edition (1903-4), 15: 278.

Putnam R. D. (2000), *Bowling alone: the collapse and revival of American community*, New York: Touchstone.

Saltmarsh J. A. and Hartley M. (eds) (2011), *"To serve a larger purpose": engagement for democracy and the transformation of higher education*, Philadelphia: Temple University Press.

Case studies

14. University of Western Sydney – a case study in equity and diversity

Sev Ozdowski

The University of Western Sydney

The University of Western Sydney (UWS) was created in 1989 from three existing colleges. It operates under the University of Western Sydney Act 1997 and the associated University of Western Sydney By-law 2005. It is a large multi-discipline university with 39 844 students, 1 286 academics and 1 529 general staff. Its net assets are worth over 1 23 billion Australian dollars (A$) and its annual operational revenue is A$558 million. UWS is spread across six campuses in Greater Western Sydney (GWS) and it has a particular responsibility to serve the 2 million people of that region (University of Western Sydney 2011).

The diversity in economic, cultural, social and educational background of the people of GWS is the key to understanding the unique character of the university. The GWS region is the third largest economy in Australia and is expanding rapidly, expected to account for 25 per cent of national population growth over the next 25 years. It includes significant rural areas along with fast-developing cities and urban centres such as Parramatta, Penrith, Liverpool, Bankstown, Blacktown and Campbelltown, each with its own character and identity. As many as 250 000 locally based businesses, small and large, demonstrate its economic diversity.

Cultural and social diversity is a key feature of GWS. It is estimated that the regional population includes people originating from as many as 170 countries. In fact, more than half the population is from culturally and linguistically diverse (CALD) backgrounds. GWS is a home to the highest number of Aboriginal and Torres Strait Islander Australians outside the Northern Territory and to a significant number of Muslim communities.

Historically, the GWS region was underrepresented in higher education and the professions. It has fewer people with post-secondary qualifications than other regions of Sydney, but this is changing. Half the UWS students are of the first generation of their family to attend university and around 70 per cent of these are now drawn from the GWS region.

UWS is well aware of its role as an agent of change in GWS. It aims to ensure that education opportunities are fully open to "first in the family" students and to students from Aboriginal and any other communities where access to education was traditionally discouraged, or even thought to be not possible or appropriate. In other words, UWS acknowledges its important role in advancing Australia as an egalitarian and democratic society.

UWS has a vision to: "Bring knowledge to life in Greater Western Sydney through community and business engagement with our learning and research". *Our Mission* describes the university's aim of being "a vibrant and inclusive intellectual community and being connected locally and internationally". UWS explicitly states that: "Equity of access and inclusiveness and collegiality and participatory decision-making" are values underpinning its operations.[48]

Democracy and equity

The concepts of democracy and equity are interlinked in modern societies. Australian democracy differs from that in the United States and some other Western countries. The principle of "fair go" underpins the Australian political system, its democratic institutions and national culture; individual civil and political liberties appear to have lesser standing.

In fact, Australia has no US-style Bill of Rights guaranteeing civil liberties and the Australian Constitution is silent about many civil rights that are well recognised in the constitutions of other Western democracies. For example, the constitution does not guarantee the fundamental freedoms such as the freedom of association, freedom of movement, freedom of peaceful assembly, freedom of thought, belief and opinion, and freedom from arbitrary arrest or detention, nor the right to a fair trial or due process, and equality of all persons before the law.

Australian democracy is characterised by its egalitarian focus and by reliance on government programmes to deliver equity or "fair go". For example, women's suffrage was introduced as early as 1894 in South Australia and the concept of minimum wages was legislated for in 1904 and sealed by the Harvester Decision of the High Court in 1907. Australia achieved these egalitarian benchmarks well before the Bolshevik revolution in 1917 announced, but never delivered, the supremacy of social equality and economic rights and long before the Covenant on Economic, Social and Cultural Rights was adopted by the United Nations in 1966.

The structure of democracy at academic institutions in Australia relies on this national culture. Australian universities depend more on the underlying egalitarian nature of Australian society and on merit selections and appointments and less on electoral processes to choose their top officials. This allows UWS's charter to declare a commitment to "collegiality and participatory decision making", even

---

48. See www.uws.edu.au/about_uws/uws/mission_goals_strategic_plan – Mission, Goals and Strategic Plan.

though its governing body, the Board of Trustees established under the University of Western Sydney Act 1997, elects only five of its 18 members. The UWS Academic Senate – a peak academic body that decides academic policy and accredits and approves courses – consists of 25 *ex officio* members, three appointed members and 25 members elected by the academic staff, postgraduates and undergraduates. [49] This societal-based participatory democracy brings "Dewey's dream" (Benson, Harkavy and Puckett 2007) closer to fruition at UWS.

Academic democracy and participation in decision-making are more organised around concepts of diversity, equity and inclusion. This egalitarian focus is reflected in federal and state legislation, [50] in academic charters and in implementation of policies and procedures.

The legislation requires that particular attention is paid to ensuring equitable treatment of women, Aboriginals and Torres Strait Islanders, students and staff from CALD backgrounds, people with disabilities (PWD), gay, lesbian, bisexual, transgender and intersex (GLBTI) people and students from a low socio-economic status (LSES) position. The University of Western Sydney regards legislative compliance as being only the baseline for its actions. The UWS official policies and leadership are clear that the university must go further than the minimum standard required by the legislation in the implementation of access and equity principles.

In practical terms it means that UWS is committed to recruiting and retaining students, academics and professional staff from a range of diverse backgrounds and to fostering an environment that celebrates this diversity and draws strength from it. This UWS commitment is focused on fairness for all and creation of a "level playing field" where civility and respect for differences are viewed as enhancing intellectual creativity and innovation, resulting in excellence, productivity and organisational strength. Access and equity measures are here not just to secure enrolments from disadvantaged students, but to ensure that they have every opportunity to complete their studies successfully and gain solid employment.

---

49. See http://policies.uws.edu.au/view.current.php?id=00182 – UWS Academic Governance Policy.
50. The Access and Equity related legislation impacting on academic institutions includes the relevant state legislation (in New South Wales: Anti-Discrimination Act 1977; Anti-Discrimination (Miscellaneous Provisions) Act 2004; Anti-Discrimination Regulation 2004; Disability Services Act 1993) and Federal legislation namely: Age Discrimination Act 2004; Disability Discrimination Act 1992; Disability Standards for Accessible Public Transport 2002; Disability Standards for Education 2005; Education Services for Overseas Students (ESOS) Act 2000; Equal Employment Opportunity (Commonwealth Authorities) Act 1987; Equal Opportunity for Women in the Workplace Act 1999; Sex Discrimination Act 1984; Workplace Relations Act 1996; Higher Education Funding Act 1988; Higher Education Support Act 2003; Higher Education Support (Transitional Provisions and Consequential Amendments) Act 2003; Human Rights and Equal Opportunity Commission Act 1986; Human Rights (Sexual Conduct) Act 1994; Indigenous Education (Targeted Assistance) Act 2000 and Amendment Act 2004; Native Title Act 1993; Racial Hatred Act 1995; Racial Discrimination Act 1975.

Issues to be addressed

In early to mid-2000 the university had been experiencing some difficulties in securing some of its equity objectives. For example, difficulties emerged with accommodating religious and other needs of Muslim students in the broader university framework; bullying in the workforce became recognised as an industrial issue undermining good workplace relations; lack of tolerance and conflict developed between particular student groups, e.g. Muslim and GLBTI students; serious accessibility problems were identified affecting people with disabilities; and a number of issues of sex discrimination and gender equality were identified.

The university decided to undertake a review of its access and equity policies and implementation structures and strategies. As a result a new five-year Access and Equity Plan ("the Plan") was developed, the Equity and Diversity (E&D) Unit was restructured and the former Australian Human Rights Commissioner was appointed to head the E&D Unit.

Advancing democracy through equity and inclusion

The E&D Unit initiated a range of new initiatives to implement the Plan and to address identified problems. It also took measures to advance a culture of democracy, respect and inclusion and to ensure better UWS engagement with its diversity for the future.

Policy development

First, a whole range of existing UWS E&D policies were reviewed and updated, and new policies, procedures and guidelines were developed to support, promote and instil equity and inclusion: for example: Bullying Prevention Policy; Carer's Responsibility in the Workplace Policy; Disability Policy; Discrimination, Harassment, Vilification and Victimisation Prevention Policy;[51] Employee Assistance Program; Equal Opportunity Policy; Indigenous Education Policy; Indigenous Employment Policy; Occupational Health and Safety Policy; Sexual Harassment Prevention Policy; Student Code of Conduct; and the Women's Representation on University Committees Policy.

E&D principles were also incorporated into the all-important *Academic and General Staff Agreements 2009-2012*, including a number of consultation requirements in the agreement about workloads and management of change. The main democratising force of the agreement is in its procedure for misconduct.

---

51. See http://policies.uws.edu.au/view.current.php?id=00265 for Discrimination, Harassment, Vilification and Victimisation Prevention Policy.

Allegations of misconduct are to be determined by an independent committee, which hears evidence and allows the staff member to cross-examine witnesses. This means that academics are free to comment with the knowledge that their job is not on the line should the management of the institution disagree with that comment. [52]

In September 2007, the E&D Unit organised a national conference on Access, Inclusion and Success – Muslim Students at Australian Universities for university administrators and teachers involved with Muslim students. Its aim was to review policies and programmes relating to Muslim students and to explore issues like further advancement of Muslim-friendly culture in academia; effective teaching to Muslim students; participation of Muslim students in university life; local Muslim community educational aspirations and involvement with UWS; the university's role in contributing to an understanding of Islam in Australia; catering for the religious and social needs of a diverse Muslim student community; dealing with cultural tensions, for example, associated with gender, discrimination and promoting respect for difference; and the issue of specific needs and resources.

Valuing and learning to engage with diversity

An institution that values diversity is, by its nature and experience, likely to be more democratic and fair and equitable in its relationships with all its members and other stakeholders. A range of different activities were undertaken over time to build respect, understanding and inclusion among UWS students and staff.

GLBTI people

For example, in 2007 UWS established an Ally Network to educate, inform and provide visible support for GLBTI people, to eliminate discriminatory attitudes and behaviours, and to create a respectful and inclusive organisational environment at UWS. The Allies work with UWS staff and students to forge cultural change, to challenge non-inclusive attitudes and behaviours, and provide support and referrals to GLBTI UWS staff and students. The Ally Network has some 70 members and puts on regular events and seminars. An Ally is a volunteer member of the UWS community (staff or student) who is identified by the display of an official Ally sticker; Allies provide a "safe zone" – a welcoming and confidential environment for GLBTI staff and students – and demonstrate leadership in the areas of respect and inclusion for GBLTI staff and students. In order to become a UWS Ally, they need to complete a training session to develop a better understanding of GLBTI people, issues and culture and of relevant UWS policies and procedures.

---

52. For the academic enterprise agreement 2009-12, see www.uws.edu.au/__data/assets/pdf_file/0016/136051/Academic_Staff_Agreement_2009-2012_26MAY10.pdf.

People with disabilities

Secondly, major initiatives were undertaken to provide students and staff with a disability with a physical, working, learning and social environment that enables and enhances their educational and employment experience. In 2007 UWS undertook a major review of disability policies and practices, which resulted in major improvements to its Disability Policy and additional resources for Reasonable Adjustments. These are administrative, environmental or procedural alterations in the employment or learning situation that remove barriers for people with disabilities so they can perform the inherent requirements of the job or course of study.

The University of Western Sydney has also developed a five-year Disability Action Plan, which among other things provides for centralised funding to purchase equipment for Reasonable Adjustments for staff. Over A$100 000 has been allocated for equipment each year, including special furniture and computer software and hardware. In addition, accessibility of all buildings and grounds was audited by an independent consultant and an implementation schedule adopted to ensure full accessibility to all buildings and transport at university campuses.

Bullying

Thirdly and in addition to the drafting of new Bullying Prevention Policy and Guidelines, it was decided to develop a number of activities and educative programmes to increase awareness among the UWS community of bullying and bring about a necessary cultural shift to combat this adverse behaviour. In 2009 the UWS initiated an Anti-Bullying Awareness Campaign, aimed at both staff and students across all campuses. The campaign activities included messages and letters from the UWS Vice-Chancellor, inclusion of anti-bullying issues on senior and departmental UWS staff meeting agendas, development and distribution of anti-bullying posters, postcards and other materials, creation of a dedicated website with a blog and anti-bullying resources, development of training modules and university-wide consultations on the prevalence of bullying.

Communicating with the broader community

The year 2009 was declared by UWS as The Year of Respect and Inclusion. It targeted the whole university community, staff and students, Greater Sydney's community and ultimately the global community. It was an innovative strategic communication and education initiative designed to celebrate the diversity of UWS and promote respect and inclusion. It also aimed to reaffirm that academic excellence flourishes in a respectful and inclusive environment, where dialogue is possible without discrimination, bullying, harassment and vilification. The Year of Respect and Inclusion project was supported by the university top leadership and officially launched at a highly visible public event by the Honourable Robert McClelland, Federal Attorney General.

In keeping with the multi-faceted nature of the project a variety of communication methods were utilised to ensure that the message reached as wide an audience as possible. The methods included extensive use of print and electronic media, a series of posters aimed at staff and students on identified themes like respect and inclusion, anti-bullying, student and staff conduct, disability, and cultural and religious diversity. There was also series of zines [53] aimed at students to accompany the themed posters. These posters and zines were created by UWS Design students with input from final-year UWS Marketing students. [54]

UWS was proud to initiate a series of international conferences on issues relating to human rights education (HRE), with the involvement of Australian and international speakers from all continents. The first international HRE conference on Human Rights, Peace and Intercultural Dialogue was hosted by UWS in November 2010, the second at KwaZulu Natal University in Durban in November 2011 and the third will be held at the Jagiellonian University in Cracow in December 2012.

The conferences moved the topic of equity and inclusion beyond the university setting. They were organised to explore the role of HRE in the advancement of peace, democracy and multicultural understanding around the world, to highlight HRE international best practice, key trends and achievements, to foster HRE across the world and to build networks and dialogue. In Sydney, there were over 360 participants from 35 countries and every continent, with 150 men and 210 women. There was a broad representation of civil society with a large number of students, activists, human rights advocates, NGO workers, HRE practitioners, government representatives, teachers, academics and others interested in human rights education.

Finally, the E&D Unit continues to organise a series of UWS open fora and seminars. The open fora address topical issues of relevance in globalised world. The fora focus on social justice and "fair go", involve the Greater Sydney community and promote academic excellence, lively discussion and popularisation of knowledge. [55]

---

53. Zines are small-circulation publications of original material.
54. The key events and activities for the year included: Open Forum Seminars – an Equity and Diversity Unit seminar series that is free, open to staff, students and the general public, promoting dialogue about social justice issues; Women's Seminars – seminars focusing on women's issues hosted by the E&D Unit; Indigenous Short Film Festival, 29 May 2009 – an Equity and Diversity initiative promoting cultural exchange and professional development; Queer shorts – lunchtime screening of Queerscreen short films by the Ally Network to provide an opportunity for cultural exchange and increased awareness; Respect and Inclusion Short Film Competition – a Student Support Services initiative to promote creative engagement with the concepts of respect and inclusion; Student Equity Forum – a Student Support Services initiative to promote dialogue about equity issues for students; Multifaith Forum – a Student Support Services initiative to promote dialogue about multifaith issues; Launch of best-practice Equity and Diversity Website – an initiative to promote Equity and Diversity web-based resources; Launch of Student Charter – a Student Support Services initiative to promote respect and inclusive student behaviour at UWS; education and training opportunities – a range of opportunities provided by E&D, National Disability Coordination Officer Program, Professional Development Unit, and other key UWS stakeholders, for staff to actively develop knowledge and skills around the application of respect and inclusion.
55. See www.uws.edu.au/equity_diversity/equity_and_diversity/open_forum.

Conclusion

Dewey's balance between knowledge delivery and the interests and experiences of the students requires a culture of acceptance and inclusion. The post-2006 E&D changes have delivered major and lasting changes to the UWS culture.

In summary, it could be argued that major effort was made to ensure that differences among people are valued; that each person is treated with respect and dignity; that judgments and decisions are based on fairness and merit; and that consultation with people is encouraged, in particular regarding decisions and policies that affect them personally.

At the university level, the concepts of equity and diversity are now well incorporated throughout the university structures, functions and responsibilities. Significant progress has been made to ensure that access, advancement, awards and the recognition of success are firmly based on personal achievement and not on irrelevant characteristics or barriers. Furthermore, the system of monitoring and addressing allegations and incidents of discrimination and harassment has been significantly improved.

At the workplace level, UWS has become a much better place to work in. The number of conflicts and formal complaints or negative media reporting have significantly diminished as new measures made their impact on the university culture and the effect of inappropriate and artificial equity barriers was significantly reduced.

The gender balance has improved across the university employment structure and the UWS was again named in 2011 by the Equal Opportunity for Women Agency (EOWA) as "Employer of Choice for Women". Also progress was made to reduce the gender pay-equity gap.

UWS student satisfaction as measured on the national Course Experience Questionnaire has remained stable at 84 per cent in 2011. Retention of first-year bachelor students has also increased to 80 per cent in 2010-11, compared with 77 per cent in 2004-05. There are increasing numbers of students now nominating UWS as their first preference, retention rates are improving, the number of undergraduates going on to postgraduate studies has doubled, and more mature-age students are being attracted to the university.

Last but not least, UWS engagement and standing in Greater Western Sydney has improved. In particular the Muslim Students conference and other measures improved UWS's standing as a Muslim-friendly university and has improved relations between UWS and the Muslim community of Sydney.

This UWS commitment to equity has been widely acknowledged across Australia. For example, after the new focus was announced in November 2006, the Australian Universities Quality Agency (AUQA) referred to UWS as the "University of the People". The AUQA audit of May 2011 commended UWS for "its clear and strategic focus on advancing its mission for the benefit of the people of GWS". The success of the international conferences on human rights education added to the UWS standing worldwide.

To conclude, a respectful, inclusive environment focus on advances in equity, academic excellence and quality outcomes brought UWS closer to achieving Dewey's dream. The long-term benefits include attraction and retention of a diverse staff and student population that reflects the local community, improved outcomes in teaching, learning and research, engagement of local communities and building more harmonious community environments.

References

Benson L., Harkavy I. and Puckett J. (2007), *Dewey's dream: universities and democracies in an age of education reform*, Philadelphia: Temple University Press.

University of Western Sydney (2011), Annual Report 2011 www.uws.edu.au/__ data/assets/pdf_file/0010/355897/UWS_Annual_Report_2011_Vol1_ FINAL.pdf.

15. MF Norwegian School of Theology and lifelong learning: the role of religious institutions in community development

Vidar L. Haanes and Helene Lund

Introduction

MF Norwegian School of Theology [56] (founded 1908) is a specialised university in Oslo, offering a combination of academic excellence in theology and religious studies and professional relevance for those preparing to serve in churches and religious organisations. The institution offers several bachelor's and master's degree programmes, and has 1 200 students, including 60 PhD students.

MF also offers several master's-level professional degrees for ministers and priests, deacons, catechists and teachers as well as lifelong-learning programmes. The main stakeholder is the (Lutheran) Church of Norway, and the vast majority of the clergy in the Church of Norway are graduates from MF. In addition, there are programmes in the first and second cycle for the Methodist Church, Roman Catholic Church and Pentecostal churches.

For the past five years, MF Norwegian School of Theology has taken social studies into the curriculum in addition to theology and religious studies, offering bachelor programmes in religion, culture and society, focusing on social studies, religious studies and youth culture. At master's level there is a programme in Religion, Society and Global Issues (in English), as well as programmes in Theology, Religious Studies, Diaconal Studies, Religious Education, Psychology of Religion, Sociology of Religion and Practical Theology. At PhD level there is a research school in Religion–Values–Society (http://rvs.mf.no), with partners from universities and schools in Norway as well as two research institutes specialising in social studies and peace and conflict: the Institute for Social Research (ISF) and the International Peace Research Institute, Oslo (PRIO). Partners send PhD students to the school and an exchange of adjunct professors, as well as joint conferences, has been developed.

Especially after the terrible attacks of 22 July 2011 in Oslo and Utøya, there is a need for more work on the main topic of the Oslo conference that gave rise to this publication: Reimagining Democratic Societies: a New Era of Personal and

---

56. See www.mf.no (website in Norwegian and English).

Social Responsibility. The role of religion in society and in the public sphere has been in focus for some time, even in secularised Scandinavia (Beckford 2010). We have found there is a need for information and education in religion, among civil servants and those with responsibility for the development of society; meeting this need is vital for the development of democratic societies in Europe. We believe there is a need for co-operation between higher education institutions and other bodies like religious organisations and churches.

We have seen the importance of focusing on religion and society, due to the growing interest in and need for research and education in that field. Religion is often viewed as a destabilising factor in politics and community life. In Western academia, there has been a tendency to see the worst in religion and its transnational networks, rather than to search for their potential to forge constructive interaction across boundaries. In our judgment, religion can be a positive force for democratisation in society. [57]

In offering an example of best practice, we could have mentioned some of the ordinary study programmes where we focus on democracy and human rights in the learning outcome. Instead we have chosen to focus on a lifelong-learning/community-service programme, Intercultural Methods of Community Development, which exemplifies the importance of involving the different stakeholders – persons, institutions and communities – in furthering democratic citizenship. This programme, like the conference itself, is "part of the co-operation between different partners committed to promoting democracy, human rights and the rule of law as well as social cohesion and intercultural dialogue, and their belief in the key role of education in furthering these goals" (the Conference Outline).

The project: Intercultural Methods of Community Development (IMoCD)

The aim of this project was to generate an intercultural network for community development action, focusing on the role of churches in community development – especially in disadvantaged rural areas. [58] The project started in 2009, financed by the Grundtvig Programme of the European Commission. Th e Grundtvig Programme for Lifelong Learning was started to "provide adults with more ways to improve their knowledge and skills, facilitate their personal development and boost their employment prospects". [59] The programme focuses on people at the

---

57. In October 2009 we hosted, jointly with PRIO, the conference Religious Diversity in the Middle East: Building a Common Good, sponsored by the Norwegian Ministry of Foreign Affairs. We gathered academics from various countries in the Middle East and Europe, as well as from Norway. The conference aimed to redress the balance, exploring the potential role of religious minorities as partners in dialogue, peace building and conflict resolution.

58. See http://teologie.central.ucv.ro/blogs/imcod/about/ for more details of this project.

59. For the Grundtvig programme, see http://ec.europa.eu/education/lifelong-learning-programme/doc86_en.htm.

margins of society, to ensure they have access to adult education. It covers teachers, trainers, staff and organisations working in the sector, as well as networking and partnerships between organisations in different countries.

Our project lasted for two years and involved five European institutions:

- Faculty of Theology, University of Craiova, Romania
- Faculty of Theology, University Sv. Kliment Ohridsky, Sofia, Bulgaria
- EUROPE DIRECT – Carrefour Europeo Emilia, Italy
- Theological Institute of the Estonian Evangelical Lutheran Church, Estonia
- MF Norwegian School of Theology, Oslo, Norway.

The goal was to discuss models of good practice in community development, in the specific five countries and the three churches involved – Orthodox, Catholic and Lutheran churches in Europe. The project also aimed to discuss general theoretical notions about the best ways to initiate community development programmes.

Most of the Norwegian participants were professionals involved in a lifelong-learning programme, but even a few second-cycle (master's) students took the course for credits. Similar groups took part from the other countries, mostly priests, religious sisters and deacons from rural areas.

The first step of the project was to organise courses given in each country. The next step was for the participants to take a course in another country, meeting participants from the four other participating countries, thus meeting clergy (pastors/deacons/religious sisters, etc.) from other churches: Catholic, Orthodox and Lutheran. Methods of community development in rural areas were d iscussed in a multicultural and ecumenical context. The initiative for this project came from Romania. The construction of the project was therefore influenced by challenges in central and eastern Europe. In Romania there is a significant difference, in the levels of development, infrastructure, wealth and so on, between cities and rural areas. In rural areas the church is one of the few institutions providing community development. The Faculty of Theology at the University of Craiova took the initiative to develop a tool as a contribution to educating rural clergy, helping them to develop, build and strengthen local democratic societies. In western European countries like Norway, the challenges are not poverty and lack of infrastructure in rural areas but rather the exclusion of marginalised groups suffering from drugs, loneliness and disabilities from participating adequately in society. However, the idea of the project is to reflect together on the different challenges and the different ways the churches participate in community service, in order to find new solutions to these challenges, inspired by the various practices in the different countries and regions.

The participants in the project did not start with a common, fixed definition of "community development". The partner institutions contributed with their different theoretical notions and approaches, which became an important part of the intercultural exchange and contributed to enriching the dialogues. The project was facilitated in a way that enabled participants in the five countries to exchange experiences and share visions and specific projects that were rooted in their local communities. Community development was understood as improvement in the quality of life, deriving from the mutual benefit and distributed responsibility among the members of the community.

The project could be summarised in three fundamental questions to clergy and members of religious communities engaged in community development:

1. Does the church's mission include a responsibility to take part in building and developing good and democratic communities?

2. How will the various churches support and justify societal work and community service theologically?

3. Is it then possible to make a guideline for *praxis*, to help the local churches to take active responsibility in this field?

MF Norwegian School of Theology organised the project as a lifelong-learning course in the field of religion and society, and the Norwegian participants were given credits (20 ECTS). As teachers we used faculty members responsible for second-cycle study programmes in order to secure input from this special project to our ordinary full-time students: Professor of Ethics, Gunnar Heiene (Lutheran), leader of the master's programme in Religion, Society and Global Issues; assistant professor Tron Fagermoen, leader of the master's programme in Diaconal Studies (Lutheran) and senior researcher Helene Lund (Roman Catholic).

The course syllabus included: 1. theological perspectives on society and social practice, 2. social science, and 3. theory of reflection on practices. The project was constructed so that every participant had to identify a new or ongoing project in his or her own parish that he/she would discuss and develop during the course. The Norwegian participants had to write an essay reflecting on the experiences of their project in their own parish. Thus, the Norwegian participants in the course were theoretically well prepared and stimulated the participants from other countries to apply theoretical perspectives on their projects, which in turn resulted in further development of each project. It was the task of the academic staff to ensure that the participants received appropriate input of theory to promote innovative processes.

Analysis of the experience from the project

There are several aspects that we identified as the strengths of the project and some challenges that we experienced in the process of developing it. First, the strengths of the project:

– The churches were identified as important providers for community development and as places nurturing people to become committed and responsible citizens. Religion is not only a private matter: religious communities are providers of good values, contributing to the development of just and good communities. Even if the churches proclaim the emergence of a heavenly kingdom and the life to come, this project focused on the role of the churches in this world: their responsibility to facilitate and promote development in their local community, their role as providers of values, peace, just societies and development, and their ability to engage lay people in the local community.

– Arranging courses with participants from different countries, belonging to different churches of the main confessions – Orthodox, Catholic and Lutheran – turned out to be a success. We could address common challenges on how to contribute to community development in a group consisting of people from different denominational, political and social contexts. This construction of the project helped the participants to see themselves and their challenges in the light of the experience of others and thereby offered new perspectives for understanding and conducting the participants' own projects. The intercultural and ecumenical frame of the project was a great resource for the quality of the learning process. As Europe is becoming more multicultural and people are moving around for work, there is a need for better knowledge and understanding of society and the different religious traditions. To give one example, in Norway there is a significant number of Romanian immigrant labourers. Many of them are Orthodox Christians. A Romanian exchange student took his master's degree in theology at MF Norwegian School of Theology and after his graduation he became a priest for the Romanian congregation in Oslo. He may be a cultural interpreter between the Romanian immigrants and Norwegian society. In the discussion between Norwegian and Romanian participants in the project, the Romanians explained that the situation back home is difficult: in many rural areas children and elderly people are left alone, while the working population go abroad for work. This should be taken into consideration when we discuss local community development, both in Norway and in Romanian rural areas. The question is whether and how the churches can be resources as providers of values, meaning and responsibility, contributing to good citizenship and a culture of democracy.

– The third strength of the project was also related to the construction of it, in combining five countries and three "church families". In so doing there were participants from each "church family" from at least two different countries (for example, Orthodox participants came from Bulgaria, Estonia and Romania, Catholic participants came from Italy and Norway, and Lutheran participants came from Estonia and Norway). This was useful, helping the participants to exercise self-criticism, in making it easier to discern between elements of religious and cultural aspects in their ways of thinking.

Challenges in implementing the project in a Norwegian context

As we have mentioned, the initiative for this project came from central and eastern Europe. This caused some challenges for the Norwegian participants, as rural areas in Norway do not face the same problems as in Romania. [60] In Norway one is more likely to find people struggling with poverty and loneliness in cities than in rural areas, partly because most immigrants live in the cities.

The Norwegian state has the economic resources to meet contemporary and future financial crises, mainly due to its oil resources. The unemployment rate is about 4.5 per cent and the economy is robust. When it comes to social policy, Norway has a well-developed welfare system and a national insurance system: all who live or work in Norway are compulsory members of the national insurance scheme, and also have rights in relation to the Norwegian welfare state, independent of social status, location or income (Angell 2004).

Further, discussing the church's contribution to community development in Norway needs to address the close relation between the Norwegian state and the (Lutheran) Church of Norway. [61] After the Reformation in 1537, the state (the king) formally took responsibility for the provision of welfare services to the people. The state gained control over the church but continued to use the church as an instrument to provide for the poor and needy. In 1981 Parliament voted to retain the state church system while granting the Church more autonomy. Consequently, in 1984 the General Synod was established and in 1989 the right to appoint ministers was handed over from the government to the diocesan councils. There is a parliamentary agreement to change some passages in the Constitution of Norway in 2012, to loosen the legal ties between the church and state. In the ongoing process to redefine state–church relations there is a need to define the role and responsibility of the Church of Norway in contributing to community development. Although the general welfare of Norwegian citizens, community development included, is a public responsibility, the church contributes significantly to Norwegian welfare provision, not least by its community development work.

The diaconal institutions, being a part of or working in co-operation with the Church of Norway, contribute significantly to community development. They run about 7 per cent of all day-based institutions in the health and social sectors, and in drug care diaconal institutions do 28 per cent of the work (Angell and Selbekk 2005: 23).

Further, the Church of Norway contributes to local community development through its congregations. In a recent study (Angell and Selbekk 2005), four areas of diaconal work in local parish life were identified:

- − One in ten local parishes run institutions like kindergartens or homes for the elderly.

- − Nearly all parishes have some community-developing activities, like visiting services for the sick and the elderly, self-help groups for people in grief, baby song groups, youth groups and so on.

---

60. The presentation of the Norwegian context in this chapter is based on the unpublished paper by Fagermoen (2010). This paper was handed out to the participants from each country.
61. For more details about the Church of Norway, see www.kirken.no/engelsk/engelsk.html.

- Local churches do community-development work through worship and counselling. Special days in the calendar are used to focus on topics related to the diaconal mission of the church, and the worship itself, with its social aspects, contributes to a certain extent to the development of the local community.

- Parishes do community-development work through measures concerning social injustice and environmental protection. In most local parishes, people are involved in activities related to human rights work and development issues. In some parishes there is involvement in activities related to environmental protection. It is interesting to note that most of these activities are directed at human rights work and development issues in other countries, often in other continents. Whether this is due to lack of awareness of the local community's needs, or such needs are hard to find, is an open question (Angell and Selbekk 2005: 9-11).

In a Norwegian study, *Shortcomings of the Welfare State* (Norges Røde Kors/ ECON 2001), the most important challenges were identified as children affected by poverty, young immigrants in a squeeze between two cultures, loneliness (especially among older people), victims of violence, and exclusion from employment and the knowledge society. The conclusion of the study was that these and similar challenges cannot be met by the public welfare system alone and that co-operation between the public welfare system and "civil society" is therefore needed. The welfare society faces major challenges, challenges which cannot be met with financial resources alone. The engagement and obligation to "love your neighbour" – so often preached in the parishes, is a motivation for the members and staff of local congregations to participate in community service.

Conclusion

Five European institutions, among them four higher education institutions, co-operated on a lifelong-learning project: Intercultural Methods of Community Development. The participants were students and ecclesiastical workers from the same five countries and three confessions.

The aim of the study was to reflect on how the churches and local parishes, especially in rural areas, can contribute to community development. An important element of the project was related to the flexibility and ability to adapt to the different challenges facing different local communities. An important lesson to be learnt from this project is the success of multicultural, professional learning environments for discussing common challenges across national, social and religious borders. We may conclude that the programme managed to inspire the participants to see that their engagement in local communities should not focus on religious activities only, but also on inspiring and educating congregations in "personal and social responsibility", reimagining just and democratic societies.

References

Angell O. H. (2004), "Welfare, church and gender in Norway" in N. E. Beckman (ed.), *Welfare, church and gender in eight European countries*, Uppsala: Diakonivetenskapliga institutet, pp. 63-102.

Angell O. H. and Selbekk A. S. (2005), *Kirke og Helse: kartlegging av diakonalt helsearbeid innen Den norske kirke* [Church and health: a survey of diaconal health work in the Church of Norway], Report No. 3/2005 Oslo: Diakonhjemmets Høgskole.

Beckford J. A. (2010), "The return of public religion? A critical assessment of a popular claim", *Nordic Journal of Religion and Society*, 23 (2): 121-36.

Fagermoen T. (2010), "The church's involvement in community development activities: the Norwegian context", unpublished paper.

Norges Røde Kors/ECON (2001), "Sosial puls 2001: Brister i velferdssamfunnet" [Social pulse 2001: Shortcomings in the welfare society].

16. Participatory democracy, neighbourhood revitalisation and the promise of the University at Buffalo

Henry Louis Taylor, Jr

The purpose of this case study is to demonstrate the role that higher education can play in the production of a culture of democracy in distressed central city neighbourhoods. This task is accomplished by examining the use of participatory democracy as an engagement strategy in a neighbourhood planning initiative led by the University at Buffalo (UB) Center for Urban Studies.

This case study is based on four interrelated assumptions. First, participatory democracy is the anchor of truly democratic societies. Second, the revitalisation of distressed neighbourhoods offers a perfect opportunity to ignite the process of inculcating a culture of democracy as part of the quest to transform that community (Taylor and McGlynn 2008). Third, at the community level, involving residents in the challenge of rebuilding and redeveloping their neighbourhood exposes them to societal forces that push back against such development, and this process not only deepens their understanding of the anti-democratic agents operating in society, but also it creates a sense of critical consciousness and bolsters awareness of the importance of participatory democracy (Freire 1970; Krauss 1989). Lastly, unless we imbue distressed neighbourhoods with the spirit of democratic action, we will not succeed in transforming them into communities of opportunity where residents acquire economic self-sufficiency, where children achieve academically and graduate from high school on time, and where all residents reach their full human potential (Buffalo Municipal Housing Authority 2011a and 2011b).

The University at Buffalo: the agent

The University at Buffalo is a public Research One University that is located in Buffalo metropolitan city. UB is a member of the prestigious Association of American Universities and part of the State University at New York (SUNY) public university system, which has 64 member campuses throughout New York State with a total enrolment of just below 370 000. UB is the largest and most comprehensive campus in the SUNY system. It has 29 049 students, including 9 649 graduate and professional students, plus 1 576 full-time and 683 part-time faculty members. The school offers more than 100 bachelor's degrees, 205 master's degrees, 84 doctoral degrees and 10 professional degrees (University at Buffalo 2011).

The University at Buffalo is a central city anchor institution. In the United States, anchor institutions are defined as those organisations rooted in urban areas because of their capital investments and mission. This immobility means that anchor institutions are not likely to move out of the central city. Their rootedness in the central city means that revitalisation of this area is in their enlightened self-interest.

As a major landowner and employer, UB has a significant impact on the local economy. For example, UB's three campuses contain 174 buildings on 1 520 acres (616 ha) scattered across a suburban, central city and a growing downtown campus on the Buffalo Niagara Medical Campus (BNMC). The BNMC is a consortium of the region's premier health care, life sciences research and medical education institutions, all located on 120 acres (48 ha) in a distressed downtown neighbourhood (University at Buffalo 2011). Concurrently, because of its resource base and talented faculty, students and staff, the university is ideally situated to drive the redevelopment of distressed neighbourhoods and to imbue them with a culture of democracy (Benson, Harkavy and Puckett 2007).

The context: the city of Buffalo

The University at Buffalo is vital to the socioeconomic development and stability of the central city. Situated on the Canadian border in the Great Lakes region, in New York state, Buffalo is a transcontinental city that is seeking to redefine and recreate itself, while grappling with a shrinking population, a sluggish economy and a hostile suburban hinterland. An old industrial city, Buffalo's population dropped by more than 55 per cent between 1950 and 2010, falling from 580 000 to 259 000. Many of those Buffalonians leaving the central city moved to the suburbs, but others left the region altogether. This population shift had a racial and class dimension. Many of those leaving the city were higher-income whites, while blacks and Latinos were overrepresented among those staying behind. For example, less than 25 per cent of whites living in Buffalo's metropolitan city reside in the central city. Moreover, over the last 20 years, increasingly, higher-income blacks and Latinos have also started to leave the central city for the suburban region (US Census 2005-09).

A change in the regional economy from heavy industry to service, high technology, education and the health sciences greatly complicated these demographic changes (Goldman 2007). This new Buffalo economy re shuffled the workforce, spawning structural joblessness and poverty, with numerous workers living on the economic edge (Taylor 1990). The restructured economy combined with emigration of higher-income residents and a decline in federal fiscal support of the central city to create much hardship in Buffalo. Its 30 per cent poverty and 37 per cent jobless rates made it one of the poorest cities in the United States (US Census 2005-09).

Between 1940 and 1980, the rise of a new metropolitan city also contributed to the growth of poverty and hardship in Buffalo. The metropolitan city was composed of a central city and suburb. Policy makers believed that lack of planning and land-use regulation had hopelessly scarred the central city. As a consequence, they decided that the city should be the primary living place for blacks and other low-income groups, and the suburbs should become a residential area mostly for whites and middle- and upper-income residents (Taylor 2011). The emigration of higher-income groups, along with business and industry, combined with the growth of neo-liberal urban policies to worsen conditions in the city (Hackworth 2007).

The situation was particularly dire among African Americans. For example, the proportion of married couples among African Americans is only 18 per cent. This means that many single parents, mostly women, are raising children with little or no help from a partner. In this setting, making ends meet and bolstering one's quality of life is more difficult for one wage earner, especially when those wages are low. Single-parent family statistics, then, are surrogate figures for hard times among African Americans. The socioeconomic status of black males helps to explain why the percentage of married couples in the black community is so low. A staggering 26 per cent of black males do not have a high school degree, while the black male jobless rate is 50 per cent and the poverty rate is 37 per cent (US Census 2005-09). Given their dismal economic state, many black men simply do not qualify as marriageable in a society dominated by neo-liberal capitalism, where men are expected to be the primary wage earner or at least be a major contributor to household income (Fox 1986).

In the United States, distressed populations typically live clustered together as a racial or ethnic group, residing in the most undesirable neighbourhoods. This is especially true of African Americans. Buffalo is one of the most racially segregated cities in the United States, and African Americans are overrepresented on the eastern side of the city, where conditions have worsened over time. Main Street divides Buffalo into eastern and western sections, and in 1970 blacks comprised 31 per cent of the East Side population, but only 2.7 per cent of West Siders, while whites comprised 69 per cent of the East Side population, but 96 per cent of West Siders. In 1970, blacks comprised 20 per cent (N = 94 262) of Buffalo's population, whereas whites constituted 78 per cent (N= 364 367); therefore, most of these African Americans were clustered in the predominantly black East Side neighbourhood. Thirty years later, in 2000, the percentage of blacks on the East Side had grown. Now, East Side blacks comprised 52 per cent of the population, but only 16 per cent of the West Side population. However, whites now formed 70 per cent of the West Side population and 43 per cent of the East Side residents. Even though a significant number of whites still lived on the lower East Side, they mostly resided in segregated neighbourhoods (Yin 2009).

What is significant about this snapshot is how much the East Side economically declined in contrast to the West Side over the second half of the 20th century. This East Side/West Side disparity took place even though a significant number of higher-income whites were leaving the central city. For example, from 1951 to 1980, the median housing sale price in dollars per square foot was US$10.00 on the East Side and US$12.00 on the West Side, a negligible difference.

The decline in the East Side community accelerated after the reduction of federal involvement in cities following the election of Ronald Reagan as President of the United States. In the 1970s and 1980s, the city's economy plummeted and efforts to revive it focused on downtown development, construction of a light-rail transit system along Main Street and expansion of the Buffalo–Niagara Medical Corridor. East Side neighbourhoods, in contrast, were the site of an intensive demolition campaign, as hundreds of housing units were torn down to make way for institutional expansion and road widening/construction. As a result, between 1980 and 2000-04, a significant differential developed between East Side and West Side housing prices. Now, the median housing sale price in dollars per square foot is US$18.15 on the East Side and US$28.27 on the West, a differential of US$10.12. Concurrently, the average family income of East Siders declined in relationship to West Siders. In 1970, the average family income among East Siders was US$8 879 and US$9 600 for West Siders, a difference of less than US$1 000. By 2000, the average family income was US$32 899 for East Siders and US$42 887 for West Siders, a difference of almost US$10 000 a year (Yin 2009).

Declining economic conditions in Buffalo were matched by intensifying neighbourhood decay caused by the hyper-aggressive East Side demolition programme. These developments were part of a broader strategy to create a transport system to serve Buffalo new metropolitan city. The result was a metropolitan building strategy that triggered the rapid decline of the East Side. By 2000, the East Side of Buffalo had turned into a declining, distressed neighbourhood characterised by tracts of vacant land and rundown, decaying housing units. This physical decay created a distressed inner-city residential environment, which reinforced the socioeconomic problems of residents and constrained the socioeconomic development of the central city and the suburbs, albeit to a much lesser degree (Taylor 1991; Ihenko 2003).

The case study

The problem of distressed neighbourhoods is not only a big problem in Buffalo, but one of the most urgent domestic problems in the United States. The reason is that neighbourhood distress creates havoc particularly in the lives of blacks and people of colour, holds back the socioeconomic development of the central city, contributes to urban sprawl and threatens the democratic promise of the United States. The distressed neighbourhood problem will persist as long as suburbanites view the central city as a dangerous place and a socioeconomic drag on the metropolitan city (Ferguson and Dickens 1999). As long as they view the central city as an urban nightmare, suburbanites will residentially distance themselves from the core and will support public policies that steer investments away from the central city and that reduce government spending on social issues (Macek 2006). Moreover, as neighbourhood distress intensifies, higher-income groups from across the racial divide progressively leave the city, thereby worsening the distressed neighbourhood problem, making it increasingly complex and difficult to solve (Logan and Schneider 1984). Therefore, solving Buffalo's distressed neighbourhood problem is an urgent task.

This is where the University at Buffalo comes in. As an anchor institution, which is not likely to leave the central city, the university has a special stake in solving this complex problem. UB's Center for Urban Studies (CENTER) was founded in 1987 to play a role in solving the problem of neighbourhood distress. It engages in interdisciplinary studies on neighbourhood distress and works with troubled communities on planning and neighbourhood development issues. Since its inception, the CENTER has been working on the construction of a model for revitalising distressed neighbourhoods, a model which integrates the physical redevelopment of distressed areas with the redesign of supportive services and the reform of public schools. Towards this end, in 2010, the CENTER in partnership with the Buffalo Municipal Housing Authority (BMHA), obtained a Choice Neighborhood two-year planning grant funded by the US Department of Housing and Urban Development to create a transformative plan for a distressed Buffalo neighbourhood.

The goal is to develop a strategy for turning this distressed neighbourhood, Perry Choice, into a community of opportunity where residents become economically self-sufficient and their children do well in school, graduate from high school on time and go on to college and/or get a job tied to a career ladder. When the planning period ends, the BMHA will have the opportunity to compete for a US$30 million implementation grant. Perry Choice is a demonstration project, which the Obama Administration believes will produce a replicable approach to neighbourhood development.

The participatory democracy model

The Choice Neighborhood strategy developed by the UB Center for Urban Studies and the Buffalo Municipal Housing Authority is based on the premise that participatory democracy lies at the core of the struggle to transform and recreate any distressed neighbourhood. If residents can take an active role in the struggle to rebuild and develop their community, their engagement in fighting for their vision of neighbourhood development to triumph will lead to a deeper, richer understanding of the importance of participatory democracy in community-building (Krauss 1989; Arnstein 1969; Forrester 1999; Healey 2006). In this way, residents will anchor the recreation of their community with the value of participatory democracy. Thus, the more deeply residents are involved in neighbourhood planning and development, the greater will be their understanding and appreciation of the value of democracy.

This approach to neighbourhood revitalisation is based on the premise that reimagining democratic society starts by enabling residents to become involved in those community-level decision-making activities that affect their lives (Benson, Harkavy and Puckett 2007). To this end, to place the logic of democracy at the core of the Choice Neighborhood planning initiative, a citizen participation strategy was developed that maximised the involvement of residents in the planning process.

The approach

To optimise the participation of residents in the Choice Neighborhood planning initiative, a multi-level citizen engagement model was designed. It should be stressed that the various levels in this model are highly interactive, reinforcing each other. At the top level, residents were appointed to the project's Steering Committee and Advisory Board, thereby giving them representation on the initiative's two main governing bodies. The Steering Committee sets policy and makes decisions that guide the initiative's development. Three of the seven seats on the committee are filled by residents. Although the residents do not control this committee, they have a significant voice on it. This is important because the committee works on a consensus model, and votes are taken only when a consensus cannot be reached. The project is still in its early stages, but thus far no votes have been required (Taylor 2011).

The residents also have membership on the Advisory Board. This is a non-voting body composed of stakeholders, including representatives of organisations that are making investments in the Choice Neighborhood initiative. Therefore, membership on this body gives residents the ability to speak directly to those individuals on whom the project depends for its success. In this democratic model of citizen participation, to increase the capacity of residents, they were given an opportunity to be directly involved in the neighbourhood planning process. To this end, the project planning team formed three working groups, People, Housing and Neighborhoods, and appointed residents to each one, thereby creating an opportunity for them to work directly with professional members of the planning team. This approach enabled the residents to learn about plan making, especially the role played by research in the neighbourhood plan-making process (Buffalo Municipal Housing Authority 2011).

To prepare residents for this more advanced level of participation, educational workshops were held on housing design and neighbourhood development. On this point, a decision was made to involve the project architects and developers at later stages in the planning process, so the residents would be better positioned to drive the process. In addition, whenever possible, residents are hired to do specific tasks. For example, when conducting the community asset and needs assessment, rather than hire outside interviewers, local residents were hired to conduct the survey. At this capacity-building level, the project team is still establishing a neighbourhood-based planning and information centre (P&I) to more deeply involve residents in the planning process.[62]

---

62. This centre is now opened and is staffed by three residents, two graduate students in urban planning and one recent graduate of the University at Buffalo planning department.

Conveniently located, the centre is designed to optimise community participation. For example, the project's communication hub, which features a website, Facebook and Twitter pages along with a newsletter, is going to be housed in the P&I centre. Resident volunteers will be recruited to work on the website, newsletter and social media pages. The P&I centre will provide the planning team with an opportunity to teach residents website-management skills and the use of more advanced computer software, such as Photoshop. Moreover, the P&I centre will make it possible for residents to drop by, at their convenience, to find out about the Choice Neighborhood planning initiative and how they can become involved (Kretzmann and McKnight 1993).

At the final level, the residents are the prime source of information about community needs and assets. This information is gathered from them through focus groups, public meetings, informal needs interviews, community workshops and a needs survey. One innovative method of gathering information about community needs and assets was Resident Neighborhood Walking Tours, a novel approach to data gathering that was inspired by a resident. Based on a visual assessment methodology, in the walking tours the residents take members of the planning team on a journey through the neighbourhood, showing them the things they like or dislike, the places they fear and the places where they feel safe, and the places and events that should be remembered.

During the tour, the residents are encouraged to talk about their neighbourhood experiences and share special moments or memories, some good and some bad. Thus far, the planning team has conducted about 86 walking tours with residents from across the spectrums of age and race. These tours have deepened our understanding of the neighbourhood as a place and will inform the site planning process. Moreover, the residents will work closely with the planning team to find ways to incorporate historical memories and events into the design of the revitalised neighbourhood.

The project team members are designing a Geographic Information Systems (GIS) map that will convey the spatial dimensions of this work and illustrate to the residents how their walking tours are to be used to inform the site development process. Students in the UB Center for Urban Studies will produce a baseline GIS map that contains five different layers: like, dislike, safe, unsafe and places to be remembered (Craig, Harris and Weiner 2002). The goal is to show the residents how their input is used and why it is so important.

Summary and conclusion

Participatory democracy lies at the core of the problem of reimagining democratic societies and recreating societies anchored by an ideology of authentic democracy. It also lies at the core of our ability to recreate and redevelop distressed central city neighbourhoods. Within this scheme of conceptualisation, the litmus test of any democratically based society is the involvement of those at the bottom of the socioeconomic order in the governing process. The secret to solving this problem is to create a culture of democracy in neighbourhoods and communities. By a culture of democracy, I mean the establishment of a way of life in distressed neighbourhoods where participatory democracy is normalised and made part of the routine of life in that community. The university is an ideal institution to play the lead in this process. Its scholars possess the time to study and reflect on conditions inside neighbourhoods and then formulate strategies for forging redevelopment, in partnership with the residents, which are rooted in the ideology of participatory democracy. The project discussed in the case study, although still in its early stages, provides one example of how participatory democracy can be linked to the quest to involve residents in the neighbourhood planning and development process. This project provides a case study of one way in which the university can use its resources to create a culture of democracy in distressed neighbourhoods.

References

Anderson G. L. (1998), "Toward authentic participation: deconstructing the discourses of participatory reforms in education", *American Educational Research Journal*, 35 (4): 571-603.

Arnstein S. R. (1969), "A ladder of citizen participation", *Journal of the American Institute of Planners*, 35 (4): 216-24.

Benson L., Harkavy I. and Puckett J. (2007), *Dewey's dream: universities and democracies in an age of education reform*, Philadelphia: Temple University Press.

Buffalo Municipal Housing Authority (2011a), *Choice Neighborhood Planning Initiative*, Buffalo NY: Office of Housing and Urban Development.

—   (2011b), *Quarterly Report to the U.S. Department of Housing and Urban Development, Choice Neighborhood Planning Initiative*, Buffalo: Buffalo Municipal Housing Authority.

Craig W. J., Harris T. M. and Weiner D. (2002), *Community participation and geographic information systems*, London: Taylor & Francis.

Ferguson R. F. and Dickens W. T. (eds) (1999), *Urban problems and community development*, Washington DC: Brookings Institution.

Forrester J. (1999), *The deliberative practitioner: encouraging participatory planning processes*, Boston MA: M.I.T. Press.

Fox K. (1986), *Metropolitan America: urban life and urban policy in the United States, 1940–1980*, Jackson, MI: University Press of Mississippi.

Freire P. (1970), *Pedagogy of the oppressed*, revd 20th Anniversary edn, New York: Continuum.

Goldman M. (2007), *City on the edge: Buffalo, New York*, Amherst: Prometheus Books.

Hackworth J. (2007), *The Neoliberal City: governance, ideology and development in American urbanism*, Ithaca NY: Cornell University Press.

Healey P. (2006), *Collaborative planning: shaping places in fragmented societies*, New York: Palgrave.

Ihenko U. E. (2003), *Constructive approaches with contradictory results: community development and the dynamics of housing demolition in the inner city of Buffalo, New York, 1960-1997*, Buffalo NY: State University of New York at Buffalo.

Krauss C. (1989), "Community struggles and the shaping of democratic consciousness", *Sociological Forum*, 4 (2): 227-39.

Kretzmann J. P. and McKnight J. L. (1993), *Building communities from the inside out: a path toward finding and mobilizing a community's assets*, Chicago: ACTA.

Logan J. R. and Schneider M. (1984), "Racial segregation and racial change in American suburbs, 1970-1980", *American Journal of Sociology*, 89 (4): 874-88.

Macek S. (2006), *Urban Nightmares*, Minneapolis: University of Minnesota Press.

Taylor H. L. Jr (1990), *African Americans and the Rise of Buffalo's Post-Industrial City, 1940 to Present*, Buffalo NY: Buffalo Urban League.

—   (1991), "Social transformation theory, African Americans and the rise of Buffalo's post-industrial city", *Buffalo Law Journal*, 39 (2): 569-606.

—   (2011), *Project Management File*, Buffalo NY: UB Center for Urban Studies.

Taylor H. L. Jr and McGlynn L. (2008), "Solving the Dewey Problem: where do we go from here?", *The Good Society*, 17 (2): 56-62.

University at Buffalo (2011), *UB at a Glance, 2011*. Available at www.buffalo.edu.

US Census Bureau (2005-09), *American Fact Finder, American Community Survey 5-Year Estimates, Detailed Tables*.

Waddock S. A. and Post J. E. (1991), "Social entrepreneurs and catalytic change", *Public Administration Review*, 51 (5): 393-401.

Yin L. (2009), "The dynamics of residential segregation in Buffalo: an agent-based simulation", *Urban Studies*, 46 (13): 2749-70.

17. We believe we are called to serve our neighbour: tragedy and community engagement

Paul C. Pribbenow

The institution

Augsburg College, a private, liberal arts university founded in 1869 and affiliated with the Evangelical Lutheran Church in America, is located in a diverse, urban neighbourhood in Minneapolis, a city of 300 000 residents. Augsburg serves 4 000 students in a wide range of academic programmes, including traditional undergraduates, adult learners and graduate students. More than 40 per cent of Augsburg's intake each year comes from communities of colour (which, in the US context, includes African immigrants, African-Americans, Asian-Americans, Hispanic Americans and Native Americans). This case study is focused on the college's community engagement efforts in its immediate neighbourhood – known as Cedar-Riverside – whose residents are primarily East African immigrants (Somali and Ethiopian) and whose children more and more see Augsburg as their college.

The case

In the autumn of 2008, an Augsburg undergraduate student, Ahmednur (Nur) Ali, was murdered in the Cedar-Riverside area near our campus. Nur, who had grown up in the neighbourhood, was tutoring children at a local community centre as part of his campus work assignment and apparently had an altercation with some young men inside the centre. When he came out of the centre after completing his assignment, the young men shot and killed him. Nur was the first member of the Augsburg community to be murdered in our vicinity in our more than 140-year history. The case has never been solved because potential witnesses were frightened to come forward and offer evidence. It was a time of great fear and anxiety for our campus community, a time that called into question Augsburg's deep commitment to being in the neighbourhood and with our neighbours, a time that challenged our calling as a college, articulated as: "We believe we are called to serve our neighbour."

But I saw first-hand the seeds of healthy engagement at a community meeting after the murder to address safety concerns in the aftermath of the shooting. At the meeting, we all experienced together the wrenching emotional impact of this shooting on our lives. Though we intended to talk about security cameras and safety patrols, instead we listened to urgent longing for community. When an imam stood to speak, his first words were "God is good" and, though we were a roomful of people of very different faith traditions, we could whisper, "Yes, God is good, and this is not what our God wants for us". In that spirit, our community came together to rededicate itself to the well-being of our neighbours – yes, to more security cameras and personnel, but even more urgently to finding common purpose in the health, safety and well-being of our neighbours and neighbourhood (Pribbenow 2009). We are a stronger – and safer – neighbourhood today because we lived in the tensions of that painful moment and found our way forward together. It is what we did together in the days and months thereafter to make our local community stronger and safer that serves as the lesson I want to share about the relationships between higher education institutions and their neighbours.

What we did together in the aftermath of this tragic incident

I want to focus on three initiatives that were undertaken in the days and months after Nur's murder that helped to heal and strengthen our community.

First, we accompanied each other in our fear and mistrust. Faculty, staff and students joined with local residents, religious and civic leaders and others from around the city to navigate the tensions occasioned by the murder. This work took very concrete forms. We admitted that we were frightened and that we did not know whether we could be assured of our safety and well-being, and then we did something about it. We came together in open meetings to discuss our fears and concerns. We participated in safety walks to create a presence on the streets at night and to show solidarity with each other. Our students learned from local imams about Muslim practices concerning the recently deceased and we honoured those practices in our own Christian rituals on campus. We engaged with Nur's family – prominent members of the local Somali community – to support them in navigating the local police and court systems.

Second, we renewed our commitment to the community service and service-learning programmes that were at the core of our relationships in the neighbourhood. An after-school tutoring programme at a local church, in which Augsburg students helped Somali youth every afternoon with homework, allowed for personal relationship-building and showed that we were committed to their success in American schools. Our Campus Kitchen programme, which uses left-over food from the college cafeteria to prepare meals for local children and seniors, redoubled its efforts to use food as a community-building tool. This work led to an expansion of our community garden and the creation of a weekly Farmer's Market that is jointly sponsored by the college and neighbours. Service-learning courses did not pull back from their forays into the community – despite needing to allow for and address the very real fears of students (and their parents) about being in the neighbourhood.

Finally, we joined together with our local institutional friends, business owners and resident organisations to focus the work of a new organisation – the Cedar-Riverside Partnership – which had recently been created to help leverage resources to serve the region's needs and interests. Though the murder could have been a distraction from the broader concerns of the partnership, it actually served to bring focus and clarity to the partnership's work in its first six months. The local police department saw the partnership meetings as constructive places to come and build trust with neighbours. Institutions stepped up and made contributions to the community centre to help support added security forces. The various police and security forces in the neighbourhood began to do joint patrols and work towards a more collaborative effort to ensuring safety. Augsburg's leadership of the partnership was particularly significant and showed our students and the wider community how an institution could overcome its own fears and narrow self-interest to serve the good of the entire neighbourhood.

Perhaps the most poignant outcome of these various initiatives was the remark of a Somali elder, a year or so after the murder, to a local newspaper that the Augsburg community – from its president to faculty and students – was with us in this time of deep need and that will never be forgotten by the neighbours. Four years later, the neighbourhood is safer and stronger than ever before. Students and faculty are ubiquitous in the neighbourhood, building community, meeting needs, learning from neighbours. The work of the Cedar-Riverside Partnership is now focused on a complex set of important economic development and local infrastructure needs. But this progress is all grounded in what we believe we are called to be and do as a university dedicated to community engagement and civic education – an abiding commitment that was tested and strengthened by a terrible tragedy. This important commitment to both being and doing – to the links between our identity as a university and our actions in the community – is at the heart of the lessons we have learned in the aftermath of Nur's murder.

What have we learned?

The lessons of our response to the death of Nur Ali bring us back to our academic and civic missions.

For those of us who have the privilege to be part of an academic community like Augsburg, dedicated at its core to the liberal arts academic tradition, there is much to celebrate about the promise of our education. At its best and most faithful, the liberal arts tradition claims that genuine learning, grounded in humility and openness, must experience and embrace difference and otherness, must seek to hold the tension of opposites and conflicting perspectives without falling apart. In fact, I might argue that we are most learned and faithful when we give up attempting to control our world, when we recognise that the gifts and ideas and experiences of others are at the heart of any community that is healthy, just and compassionate and when we lift up the ways in which our learning and lives are enhanced by living with the tension of opposites, by seeking to comprehend all sides of an issue, to be comfortable with complexity and ambiguity, to honour paradox in thought, speech and action. For those educated in the liberal arts, the ideal outcome is that our hearts – the intersection of mind, spirit and community – are formed by living in the tensions that define human life.

That said, we are not always at our best in our academic communities. How easy it is once we have been educated to believe that we have learned enough, that we have found the right way to the truth, that our ways of seeing the world and acting in it give us a leg up on those who do not share our superior learning. And often, when we do engage with those who do not share our beliefs and education, those we count as less learned, our behaviour at best leans towards finding ways to help "correct" their deficiencies, or marginalising and ignoring them at worst.

This, then, is the abiding tension in our lives – the tension between our aspiration to embrace the other, the stranger, in our educational journeys and the arrogance that too often creeps in when we believe that our education privileges us and allows us to stigmatise and ignore the other. It was by living with this tension in the days and months after Nur's murder that I believe Augsburg came to a clearer sense of its role as an anchor institution[63] in our neighbourhood, living out its academic mission in genuine partnership and mutual service in its diverse context. And it is in our ability to navigate this tension that our hearts are forged.

American educator Parker Palmer has written compellingly of this challenge for our hearts. He has firmly in mind Alexis de Tocqueville's idea of habits of the heart when he suggests that "we are at a heartbreaking moment in American history ... the conflicts and contradictions of twenty-first-century life are breaking the American heart and threatening to compromise our democratic values" (Palmer 2010: 231). He argues that this heartbreak is both a personal and a political condition, and that our ability to navigate the tensions of our lives in a life-giving (and not death-dealing) way is at the core of the future of democracy.

Palmer describes two ways in which our heart can respond in the midst of this heartbreak (ibid: 232). The conventional image of a broken heart is that the tension grows unbearable because of stress and divisiveness and hardness and there is no outcome possible except that our hearts break into a thousand shards, falling apart and spreading pain in ourselves and to those around us. In this scenario, the broken heart becomes an unresolved wound, inflicted on ourselves and others. All we can do is try to pick up the pieces.

The second image of a broken heart imagines the "small clenched fist of a heart broken open into largeness of life, into greater capacity to hold one's own and the

---

63. For the concept and role of anchor institutions, see David Maurrasse's contribution (Chapter 24, below).

world's pain and joy" (ibid: 232). This heart broken open is in evidence all around us, Palmer argues, in the examples of those who have learnt compassion and grace as the fruits of suffering. "Here, heartbreak becomes a source of healing, enlarging our empathy and extending our ability to reach out" (ibid: 232).

There are two ways in which our hearts are forged in our world. The first – the heart broken apart – is shaped by our impatient and control-obsessed culture and does not allow us to hold social and political tensions in ways that open us to the world. Our hearts are hardened, shut down, either withdrawn from the world or lashing out at the other whom we see as threat and never as (even potential) friend.

The second – the heart broken open – does not deny the realities and tensions of the world but does not allow those realities and tensions to define what is possible. In fact, the heart broken open holds the tensions creatively – living in love, seeking the balance between private and public goods, believing that peace – even a glimpse of peace – is possible between peoples and nations.

And here, Palmer claims, is the choice we all must face: "Will we hold our hearts open and keep trying to love, even as love makes us more vulnerable to the losses that break our hearts? Or will we shut down or lash out, refusing to risk love again and seeking refuge in withdrawal or hostility?" (Palmer 2010: 232).

So, our response to Nur Ali's senseless murder could be seen as a way of forging the habits of our hearts in ways that promote openness to the stranger and common purpose in our neighbourhood. We challenge our students (and ourselves) to cultivate habits of the heart that will make them (and us) good and informed citizens. We come to teach and learn, to cajole and inspire, to puzzle and rejoice, to live with and through our students, with the wild hope that their hearts will break open to love the world. We come to live out the call powerfully articulated by the poet William Wordsworth when he wrote: "What you have loved, others will love, and you will teach them how" (Wordsworth 1805).

At the same time, though, we are not naïve enough to believe that simply being educated in our college, with our deep commitment to the liberal arts, will cultivate in students' hearts that love of the world. They must make that choice. They must decide whether this education that seeks to embrace the tensions, to welcome the strangers, that believes in the promise of human significance and community, will form their hearts to choose life-giving instead of death-dealing ways in the world. They must choose whether their hearts will harden and break into pieces useless to them and the world – or break open to offer a way of healing and grace that serves the needs of the world and their fellow travellers therein.

We trust they will choose well and we believe that our institutional responses to tragic situations such as the murder of a student serve a critically important role in modelling how to be neighbourly in the world.

Lessons for others

From our perspective, the question is not whether our experiences are replicable for other higher education institutions – with their diverse missions and contexts. We do believe, however, that there are themes to our experience that are relevant for other institutions.

The first theme is how an institutional response to a situation such as we faced can be an occasion for reflection on academic mission. If our response had simply focused on volunteer service to neighbours, it might have made a difference but it would not necessarily have accomplished what we exist to do – to educate students to be informed citizens, thoughtful stewards, critical thinkers and responsible leaders. Universities with a strong civic identity must ground that identity in academic mission.

Second, our responses to Nur Ali's murder challenged us to overcome the institutional hubris (even arrogance) that often characterises higher education reactions to challenges. We tend to think we know best, that we are the experts, that we have the right answers. Nur's murder humbled Augsburg. We did not keep our students safe. But instead of responding by building fences and trying to keep out the danger, we said that we could not keep our community safe unless we joined together with neighbours and asked each other for help. In that spirit, Augsburg and its various community engagement efforts reframed our work as genuine neighbourliness, an abiding commitment to shared values and partnership. Mutuality is the centrepiece of our work in the neighbourhood.

Finally, we believe that we have learned important and relevant lessons around the need for a comprehensive and integrated institutional approach to civic education. It is sometimes easy for colleges and universities to fall into the trap of creating wonderful community-service and service-learning programmes that are ad hoc and disconnected from other institutional priorities – perhaps doing fine work, but not necessarily considering all of the ways in which the institution and neighbourhood will benefit from a more integrated and planned approach to this important work. For Augsburg, Nur Ali's murder was the occasion for exploring all aspects of our common lives – curriculum, outreach, campus life, neighbourhood development and relations – and the result is a sophisticated institutional model for pursuing our mission-based commitment to educate students to be informed, engaged and effective citizens of neighbourhoods and cities and the world.

Summary and conclusions

All of us at Augsburg remember vividly – even four years later – the sad and difficult days and weeks following Nur's death. That said, we are convinced that our responses to the tragedy have made both Augsburg College and its surrounding Cedar-Riverside neighbourhood safer, more vibrant and more focused on our future together. That, it seems to us, is the "stuff" of civic education, which we all have the privilege and responsibility to pursue on our campuses and in our communities.

References

Palmer P. J. (2010), "The politics of the brokenhearted: on holding the tensions of democracy" in *Essays on deepening the American dream*, Kalamazoo MI: Fetzer Institute.

—   (2012), *Healing the heart of democracy: the courage to create a politics worthy of the human spirit*, San Francisco: Jossey-Bass.

Pribbenow P. C. (2009), "To serve our neighbor" in *We believe we are called to serve our neighbor*, Minneapolis MN: Augsburg College.

Tocqueville A. de (1835/1840), *Democracy in America*, vols 1 and 2.

Wordsworth W. (1805/1850), "The Prelude".

18. The university as a factor in a democratic society: Mykolas Romeris University, Lithuania

Giedrius Viliūnas

A university that has grown up with society

Today Mykolas Romeris University (MRU) in Vilnius, the capital of Lithuania, is the second largest university in the country. It has over 1 500 academic and support staff and more than 20 000 students studying law, economics, public administration, political science, education, public security, social informatics and related subjects. It is the largest social sciences higher education institution in the country and the dominant one in areas like public administration. MRU was the first educational institution to register joint programmes with partners from Finland, Austria and France; it was one of the first to perform an audit organised by the European University Association; and at present it is striving to transform all its second-cycle (master's) studies into joint or double degrees. It has gained the greatest favour with students due to its exceptional facilities and has become a top-ranked national university.

MRU is the only large national higher education institution without a pre-history in the period of Soviet occupation lasting until 1990. To be precise, it was established by the Reconstituent Parliament of the Republic of Lithuania in 1990 as a higher education institution preparing public security officers for the independent state. Each year since then, MRU has expanded on average by another 1 000 students, and every five years or so it has undergone a significant qualitative change. It represents an exceptional case of interplay between the development of a university and development of a democratic society. [64]

Overture

The most dramatic moment in the history of modern Lithuania was 13 January 1990 when the government of the collapsing Soviet Union, using military force, tried to curb the attempts of reviving Lithuania to disengage itself from Soviet

---

64. The author is grateful to Professor Alvydas Pumputis, MRU rector, Professor Vytautas Pakalniškis, Chairman of the Senate, and professors Vidmantas Egidijus Kurapka, Justinas Sigitas Pečkaitis, Tadas Sudnickas and Vainius Smalskys for inspiring conversations and explanation of some aspects of the university's history that are unrecorded in any sources.

occupation. During the night of 12-13 January, columns of tanks and armour-clad vehicles moved from the military base in the North Town in Vilnius towards the main state institutions. The army and troops specially sent from Moscow attacked the crowd gathered around the Radio and TV buildings and seized them, killing 13 and injuring more than 600 unarmed people. An attack on Parliament was imminent. As Professor Alvydas Pumputis, now rector of MRU, remembers:

> That night clearly separated our past from future. A group of people from the old staff joined the Soviet occupational structures and became collaborators of Makutinovich[65] and Jedinstvo,[66] while the majority of the university staff and students were determined to protect the reviving democratic Republic of Lithuania.

The differentiation was more than explicit: during that night the storm troopers of a special unit (OMON) loyal to the Soviet-orientated staff of the Ministry of the Interior seized one of the then buildings of the Police Academy of Vilnius and turned it into their headquarters while the majority of 500 first-year students and the teachers, all wearing uniforms, moved towards Parliament to defend it. Soviet armour-clad vehicles were approaching the central part of the school whose premises housed several dozen armed teachers at the academy.

Transformation of public security: from repression to public service

The establishment of its own forces maintaining public order was one of the most urgent tasks of the Republic of Lithuania. The state inherited the Soviet militia apparatus, which in the emergency supported the new government of the country and thus considerably contributed to the peaceful liberation from Soviet totalitarianism, but it was created according to the model of a totalitarian state. It was urgent not only to adopt Western democratic police models but also to change the values of police officers and train a new generation of officers.

Therefore, one of the first decisions of the government and parliament of the independent state was to establish its own police academy, based on the four inherited Soviet militia schools. The first political leaders of the independent state – Chairman of the Supreme Council Vytautas Landsbergis, Prime Minister Gediminas Vagnorius, the ministers of the Interior and Justice Marijonas Misiukonis, Vidmantas Žiemelis and Vytautas Pakalniškis and President Algirdas Brazauskas – were personally in charge of establishing that school. On 27 April 1990 in accordance with a decision of the Government of Lithuania, the Vilnius Militia (Police) Academy was established. It was the first educational institution taken over from the Ministry of the Interior of the collapsing Soviet Union to be placed at the disposal of the restored state. On

---

65. Boleslav Makutinovich was commander in Vilnius of a special militia unit (OMON) of the Ministry of the Interior; he was in charge of armed Soviet actions against the Republic of Lithuania.
66. Jedinstvo was a Soviet-inspired political group in Lithuania opposing independence in 1989-91.

14 May 1990 the Seimas (Parliament) of the Republic of Lithuania approved the statute of the Police Academy of Lithuania (Lietuvos policijos akademija: LPA) and the LPA became a fully autonomous higher education institution not subordinate even to the Ministry of the Interior.

The teaching staff of the new higher education school immediately embarked on an essential reorganisation of law enforcement. They supervised the drafting of the new Law on the Police of Lithuania (1991), prepared the concept of the police reform pursuant to the Universal Declaration of Human Rights and the United Nations Code of Conduct for Law Enforcement Officials and contributed to drafting the Criminal Code, the Criminal Procedure Code and other legislation (Liubertas 2004: 22-7; Pumputis 1995). The provisions of the European Charter of Police Officers adopted in Strasbourg in 1993 became the basis of further activities of the academy and its drafts of legal instruments. It was an institution funded by taxpayers and obliged to protect their rights (Pumputis 1996: 70). Initially, this idea was revolutionary in the law enforcement system liberating itself from totalitarianism. Even the first version of the Law on Police Activities did not omit the provision by which law enforcement was a part of the executive whose main function was to ensure law and order.

In articles published during the first decade of independence, the academic scholars of the academy severely criticised the shortcomings of the police and the whole system of law enforcement. The state police were acting with wider powers than those in Western countries; the administrative apparatus was too large and too centralised, so it did not co-operate with the general public; most low-ranking police officers were not properly educated; police activities were too concentrated on criminal investigation instead of crime prevention and on protecting the accused person's rights but not the victim's rights.

During the first years of independence the police still formed a repressive institution rather than one protecting citizens; the Ministry of the Interior was the institution that waited longest before undergoing any reforms, being a real hangover from the Soviet type of state control over society, unlike the courts and prosecutor's offices, which had been reformed earlier. With the general commissioner of the police being *ex officio* deputy Minister of the Interior, the police became dangerously politicised and their activities were being destabilised. Owing to inefficient division of activities among the Ministry of the Interior, the Customs Department, the State Security Department and the Prosecutor's Office, as many as 20 or 30 per cent of police activities were being duplicated and separate departmental police systems were being established. It was evident that those problems of the police were structural and could not be solved at departmental level; structural reform of the law enforcement system at the highest level was urgently needed (Pumputis 1996; Pumputis 1997).

The academy itself was developing and spreading a different police culture. It introduced a three-cycle study system encompassing the training of low-ranking and high-ranking officers. From the very beginning, higher studies were orientated towards university education, and on completion students gained the qualifications to become a lawyer. The orientation of the authority of the academy and the staff was purely Western: from the very first year, visiting teachers transferred the principles of the police systems of Germany, Sweden, Denmark, France and the Netherlands (Liubertas 2004: 38-9). As early as 1994, a system of credits was implemented, working towards bachelor's and master's degrees. Specialised research works were published. It was one of the first pre-Bologna reforms of higher education in the country. The 200 international experts who visited the academy in its first five years contended that the LPA was an exemplary institution in central and eastern Europe and commended it as an example for other countries of the region (Meištaitė 1997: 13). Exceptionally significant was a very positive evaluation by the Research Council of Norway, which in 1995 conducted a systematic overview of Lithuanian research and higher education at the request of the Ministry of Education and Science (Research Council of Norway 1996).

The practical implementation of this transformation was not effortless. The fact that the academy was no longer subordinate to a government department and became an autonomous higher education institution caused great dissatisfaction in the Ministry of the Interior. Senior officials were irritated by officers trained at the academy who thought critically but were not unconditionally obedient. For several years, conservative forces in the Ministry of the Interior boycotted the decisions of the Seimas to transfer first-cycle police schools to the academy and made efforts to establish an alternative departmental system of police training and to enforce subordination of the academy (Liubertas 2004: 34-6). Progressive ideas for reorganisation of the law enforcement system were frequently stifled and graduates of the academy were hindered from being promoted.

These circumstances demonstrated the shrewdness of the decisions by the academy and the political authorities concerning entrenchment of the autonomy of the LPA: they guaranteed an independent, professional critical discourse and a counterbalance against the intentions of its past. While annually training almost 500 police officers, the LPA was slowly altering the values and the concept of the role of the system of internal order.

Law studies for a democratic state

In 1996 the Minister of Justice of the Republic of Lithuania wrote to the main Lithuanian higher education institution training lawyers – Vilnius University (VU) – requesting a considerable increase in the number of trained lawyers, who were necessary for the state apparatus and market economy. However, the Faculty of Law of Vilnius University and its professors were deeply involved in extensive legal practice for the independent state and market economy, and so they could not increase student numbers sufficiently.

Therefore the government's request was re-addressed to the only other higher education institution in the country with the ability to train lawyers – the LPA (Ramonas 1997). On 8 May 1997 the Government of the Republic of Lithuania adopted the decision "On the Formation of Academic Groups in Management and Law Studies in the Police Academy of Lithuania" and decided on an additional enrolment of 150 students from 1 September of the same year. In a week the government accepted, and in several months the Seimas approved, the LPA Senate's request to change the name of the LPA to the Law Academy of Lithuania (Lietuvos teisės akademija, or LTA).

From the start the new higher education institution began expanding the doctrine of democratic law, contrary to the legislative heritage of the totalitarian state. The provisions for human rights and the state providing service to society became its nucleus. The subjects of constitutional law, civil, private and administrative law, international law and business law – all of which were analysing and modelling a new democratic society – became the foundation of the study programme. Alongside traditional but expanded criminal law and criminology, penitentiary law was developed, which was eventually supplemented by the subjects of social work, psychology and adult education. Thus the transition from a "statist system of legal regulation to the doctrine of natural rights declared in the Constitution" became evident (Pumputis 2000: 14).

As with the reform of public security, with the help of different programmes a Western law tradition was being revived and academic partnerships were being developed. One of the crucial steps was the TEMPUS-PHARE project Training Officials for the Reform of the Legal System, which was co-ordinated by the LPA in 1996-97. Thanks to the project, partners from well-established higher education institutions in Germany and France were found, the teaching staff of the academy was involved in the international university community and the foundations were laid for independent doctoral law studies and consolidation of the academy's position as one of the leading centres of social sciences. Even in the European context of legal studies, the multi-cycle system of LTA studies seemed innovative, with the first cycle laying a comprehensive basis for legal education and the second one focusing on specialisation.

The conservative legal establishment of the country did not welcome these innovations, which received the same critical reactions as the reorganisation of public security; however, at that time the reaction came not so much from state departments but from the academic sphere, which felt fierce competition. According to national and international assessments, from the mid-1990s the LTA law school began to compete with that of Vilnius University; soon various insinuations were spread about the quality of training of lawyers at the LTA. The national audit of law studies organised in 2004 became the climax of this competitive struggle; it could have brought about the funeral of the new law school. Instead, it turned into an affirmation of LTA's endeavour with a touch of irony to jealous rivals. The Minister of Education and Science intended to close study programmes of doubtful quality but, in accordance with the conclusions of the international experts, the LTA programmes were unconditionally acknowledged to correspond to standards while the VU programmes contained considerable shortcomings and their accreditation was suspended for a period of correction. Evidently, no one wanted to close the programmes of the old school. Since then, the provision to apply not to national but international agencies of assessment whenever possible has become one of the strongest factors in the growth of quality and international integration of the LTA.

Training of officials and public administration

The young democratic society of Lithuania was faced with a major lack of specialists in public administration and management. Older higher education institutions and the new sector of private higher education promptly reacted to commercial interests in training professionals for business, economics and marketing, but for several years public administration found an almost complete vacuum of educational offers (Pumputis 2000: 13). In this respect, the LTA, a strong and state-orientated school of social sciences, was in a favourable position.

From the very beginning, the training of lawyers was connected to the needs of public administration. Even the LPA, alongside the first pure law study programme, launched a law and governance study programme designed for training competent public officials. In 1998 the LTA established a separate faculty of Public Administration which eventually split into three independent faculties: the Faculty of Public Administration, the Faculty of Strategic Governance and the Faculty of Economics and Finance Management, though the first two were later merged again into the Faculty of Politics and Management. In the national register of study programmes, alongside law, programmes of public administration and social work were registered. The training of police officers was supplemented with border security, customs activities and other more profiled study programmes.

Governance studies started from the traditional legal concept of training public officials. However, the breakthrough in this field of study occurred with the beginning of independent studies of public administration based on competences of political science and management. Having contemplated the ideas of new public management in the 1990s, the scholars of LTA later began to base their activities on next-wave theories of public governance and public policy centred around the categories of polycentric civil society (Patapas and Smalskys 2010; Smalskys 2010). New ideas and the determination to co-operate corresponded to the interests of the main state institutions responsible for the civil service. The university worked together with the Civil Service Department and the Committee of Local Government, organising training courses for civil servants of ministries and local government. It also provided opportunities to gain second-cycle higher education directly related to the positions of its students. LTA scholars conducting research in the fields of public administration, political science and management have contributed to very significant reforms of public administration since 2000. They participated in drafting the Law on Public Service and in creating the concepts of the reforms of local government, regional administration and assessment of the activities of the civil service.

This new niche underpinned the growth of the school. In the first ten years of LPA–LTA, the number of students increased from 700 to 4 300, and in 2004 in the Faculty of Public Administration alone there were almost 5 500 students. In view of the increased student numbers and expanding research activities, the status of an academy became inadequate to the actual position and in 2000 the LTA became the Law University of Lithuania (Lietuvos teisės universitetas, LTU).

The LTU soon became the leading school of public administration in the country. Today its successor, Mykolas Romeris University (MRU), trains about 80 per cent of the specialists in public administration studying in all higher education institutions. Despite the youth of the institution, graduates of MRU comprise almost 22 per cent of graduates in public service in Lithuania, which means MRU is the second largest after the oldest and largest university in the country – Vilnius University (Mykolo Romerio Universitetas 2010: 52). It has gained a similar position in training professionals in the field of social work, which together with law and public administration has become the third pillar of this young institution.

While implementing its social mission of educating society, the academy (now the university) was not strictly confined to higher education studies, research and provision of commissioned services for the state. As early as the 1990s, the Legal Aid Centre was opened and together with the local government of Vilnius it provided help for socially supported people free of charge. Furthermore, the Crime Victims' Care Association of Lithuania was established. Its aim was to compensate for the disproportion in law enforcement between the accused person's rights and protection of the victim and compensation for damage. People who could not afford to hire a lawyer were not only consulted but also represented in court; amendments of laws protecting their interests were proposed.

The market of education and services for society

Far exceeding the boundaries of a law school, at the end of 2004 the LTU changed its name once again and became Mykolas Romeris University. Mykolas Romeris was one of the most prominent statesmen of the first Republic of Lithuania of 1918-40, a lawyer and the first rector of the University of Lithuania established in Kaunas in 1922. Thus, with the help of this name the university has retained links with its history and the identity of a higher school training lawyers. At the same time it marked a new stage – it became a university with a wide spectrum of social sciences. The core of its identity became the concept of a service university orientated towards all kinds of needs of society (Kurapka and Mačiuikaitė-Žvinienė 2010: 741).

Having established itself in the market of training lawyers and officials of public administration, the university opted for openness to the needs of a free society and the importance of education for democracy as further guidelines for its activities. The authorities of the LTU and MRU emphasised that education as the main prerequisite for the implementation of human rights was inseparable from an independent state, a democratic political system and independent courts (Pumputis 1996: 70). In 2004-05 alongside the faculties of Law, Law Enforcement, Public Administration and Police, the Faculty of Social Work and the Faculty of Economics and Finance Management were established; later the Faculty of Social Informatics and the Institute of Humanities were opened. Alongside firmly established fields of studies of law, law enforcement and public administration, popular new ones were introduced: psychology, economics, management, political sciences, education and informatics. The university began to function not only for the public sector but also for non-governmental spheres and the free market, and became guided by more diverse purposes and interests, not just those of public service but also of private enterprise.

The change in the university's income structure illustrates how this new orientation responded to the needs of society. Having been a higher education institution completely dependent on the state's commission of specialists, by the turn of the millennium the university received almost half of its income from students who paid for their education themselves. More than half of those students were already employed and determined to invest in updating their skills. In 2010 as many as 66 per cent of the master's degree graduates had gained their bachelor's degree at other universities but chose MRU for their second-cycle studies to meet the competition in the labour market. The income of the university from private sources now amounts to 76 per cent of its budget and in 2008 the number of students exceeded 22 000. Thus, the university proved its potential to provide competitive education in practical terms as "it is impossible that universities train economists, lawyers and other specialists without being participants in the market themselves" (Jaunius 2008: 65).

As in its earlier stages of development, changes in the institution's profile were controversial. The university has had to withstand a public polemic with national education policy and much of the business world dominated by technocratic discourse. With the growth in popularity of social studies, the public sphere was flooded with arguments to the effect that the country's higher education institutions were training "too many" lawyers and master's graduates of public administration and education science. The leadership of the national higher education system was urged to restrict enrolment to those studies, to annul "excess" study programmes and even to close "surplus" higher education institutions and direct youth to engineering studies or jobs requiring technical and manual skills that were supposed to be necessary for the economy of the country.

In this debate, one of the essential counter-arguments of the university became the proof of the transformation of the national and international community into a service society. In line with trends in the global economy and labour market, the university was constantly drawing its opponents' attention to the irrevocable change in the structure of the economy as the industrial society was becoming post-industrial and the industrial and agricultural parts of the GDP were being overtaken by services. At the beginning of the 21st century, in the structure of the GDP of Lithuania, services exceeded 60 per cent and now they are approaching 70 to 80 per cent, a share typical of developed countries. In modern society an essential factor in the economy and labour market turns out to be not functional professional specialisation but flexibility of education, universality and personal generic competences such as initiative, responsibility and the ability to learn and change, which are all covered by the concept of entrepreneurship. Therefore, the general social competences provided by MRU have become more promising and attractive than the tuition provided by engineering schools, which may be of high quality but are also niche-like and therefore not a very safe choice under conditions of changing economic activities.

In the case of the popularity of social studies, the second argument of the university was the abovementioned fundamental provision that education is a natural right of an individual, and any kind of administrative restrictions violate the principle of the decision of a free person. This aspect of the mission of the university, which has still not received adequate resonance in public discussions, will be tackled later.

The university has been guided by satisfying public needs and educating society not only in teaching but also in research. Since the very beginning its research programmes have been orientated towards regional and national social problems, the nurture of civil and cultural identity, the development of effective governance and democratic principles. The programmes were designed on the basis of categories of new public management and social innovation. During the second decade of its development, the university became the largest centre of doctoral studies in innovation in the business sector. In 2008 the national analysis of research resources acknowledged the exceptional standard of the university's research in the fields of the rule of law, constitutionalism, social security, family policy and psychology. At the end of the last decade the university took the initiative to create a national platform for innovations in the service sector (Kurapka and Mačiuikaitė-Žvinienė 2010: 739-55). While reflecting the most problematic issues of the development of the state, MRU is now capable of performing systematic reviews of the status of the country and formulating a vision of its development (Mesonis 2008; Katuoka 2008; Mesonis 2010).

Bridge of internationalisation

Throughout both decades of the university's existence, internationalisation has been one of the most significant pillars and prerequisites of its successful development and its contribution to the development of democratic society. During its initial period, this higher education institution took over, adapted and creatively developed the experience of those Western schools of public security and law whose profile was close to its own. The university essentially relied on co-operation with Western partners in order to develop the fields of study of law enforcement and law, to create a progressive system of studies, to expand scientific research and to launch doctoral studies. With involvement in more extensive academic links, it became evident that it was impossible to ensure both the quality of studies and the progress of research without stable and universal academic ties. In its strategic documents the university has contended that contemporary science is gradually acquiring the nature of a network; it is possible to withstand international competition only by being involved in the network of global partnership.

Internationalisation has become a separate service to a society that was joining international political and economic communities. During its very first years, the university introduced the study of international law and European Union law; after a short time it launched programmes of comparative international law, international trade, comparative social policy and welfare and other similar ones. When Lithuania was preparing to accede to the European Union (in 2004), the Institute of EU Politics and Management, headed by future member of the European Parliament Professor Laima Andrikienė, was established; seminars on the structure of the EU, energy, negotiations, agricultural policy, Lithuania's prospects and other issues were held at the institute and it co-ordinated scientific research programmes of the university. The academic staff worked in numerous integration work groups and institutions.

Being guided by the ideals of the international democratic community, in 2005 the university gave shelter to the European Humanities University (EHU) from Belarus, whose activities in Minsk had been terminated by Lukashenka's totalitarian regime. Before an international platform of donors for this university was formed and administrative staff for its activities in exile were organised, the MRU supplied the democratic flagship of the neighbouring country with classrooms, library resources, teachers and administrative support for its integration into new social and legal surroundings.

Even before the beginning of the official Bologna Process, the university unconditionally adhered to the culture of the quality of international studies. It was among the very first universities in the country to invite international assessors of study programmes and institutions, design international study programmes and encourage student exchange. In 2003 the university signed the Magna Charta Universitatum. Thus following the trend of European integration the university joined the European family of higher education and committed itself to its values of academic freedom, openness to society and responsibility for its progress. In 2002 the LTU became a full member of the European University Association; it was one of the first Lithuanian universities to perform the EUA institutional audit (2006) and was the first to publicly announce its conclusions. In 2004 MRU became a member of the International Association of Universities; in 2008 the rector of the university became one of the six full members from Europe of the Administrative Committee of the IAU and in 2010 MRU hosted the General Conference of the IAU. At present, MRU has more than 200 academic partners throughout the world and participates in the Agence Universitaire de la Francophonie (AUF), the European Association for International Education (EAIE), the Global University Network for Innovation (GUNI), the Asia-Europe Foundation (ASEF), the Euro-Mediterranean University (EMUNI), the Association of Arab and European Universities (AEUA), the University Network of European Capitals of Culture (UNeECC) and the Talloires Network among others. [67]

Involvement in these global fora of higher education accelerated the interception of the latest ideas of academic management and social mission of the university. After the IAU conference on Globalisation: What Issues are at Stake for Universities? in Quebec in 2002, the university launched open distance-learning studies. The Barcelona forum on The Social Commitment of Universities in 2004 facilitated an extensive definition of the mission of universities teaching social sciences; the priorities of technologies of distance learning and entrepreneurship were brought from the IAU Penang Forum. Having foreseen that Lithuanian society was on the threshold of becoming part of global society and that present-day students will have to work in a multicultural labour market, surrounded by global mobility of ideas and intellect, the university set out to change all its second-cycle study programmes into joint programmes in co-operation with universities of other countries.

International openness and becoming part of the global academic community mean not only the adoption of new international ideas but also their generation. In the abovementioned General Conference of the IAU in 2010, MRU suggested establishing a *bona fide* university network based on the values of tolerance and humanism as well as responsibility to society. The idea of drafting the guidelines for global university ethics crystallised from discussion of this suggestion; at present this idea is being discussed in the International Ad hoc Group of Experts working on Re-thinking Internationalisation. [68]

"Their main vocation is a social mission"

The rapid development of MRU throughout the two decades was based on the same set of values. The parameters of the identity of this higher education school have always been autonomy, openness to society and competition. Its strategy has never been restricted by the internal interests of the institution but has relied on a view of its social mission. "Everyone agrees that the main activities of universities are studies, research and services to society but their main vocation is a social mission,"

---

67. See www.mruni.eu/en/university/naryste/membership_in_organizations_and_networks.php.
68. See www.iau-aiu.net/content/re-thinking-internationalization.

stated Professor Alvydas Pumputis in his address to the university after his election as the rector of MRU in December 2004 (Pumputis 2004b: 1). Universities are not just centres for accumulating and conveying knowledge, and generating innovations based on that, because the basis of their activities is their values and humanism. Universities must educate and nurture each person as a unique individual possessing an unequalled and absolute value. This value should not be overshadowed by other tasks of higher education or subordinated to other values.

The leadership of the university linked this social mission with constitutional doctrine. Article 18 of the Constitution of Lithuania stipulates that human rights and freedoms shall be innate. It is implied in this fundamental provision that a person, a citizen, empowers the state to perform certain tasks but not the contrary – the state does not make use of a person. Therefore, while using certain prerequisites of "the demand for specialists" it is not correct and lawful to restrict a person's quest for education. This idea is echoed by Article 41 of the Constitution of Lithuania, which stipulates that higher education shall be accessible to everyone according to his or her individual abilities (Pumputis 2003: 2).

These provisions have made the university extremely responsive to the needs of society and sensitive to any manifestation of discrimination. Study programmes of the university are designed in direct interaction with various stakeholders and are open to everyone without any a priori quota or barriers to enrolment. About half of the students have chosen part-time studies and the majority of full-time and part-time students are employed. Therefore, the timetable is flexible and allows students to study in the evenings and choose modules or sessions of examinations. Possibilities for additional studies or bridging courses for college graduates create links between different cycles of studies, fields of studies, vocational and university education. There also are open studies in which students can study separate subjects that can later provide a basis for earning a degree. It is also possible to recognise the competences acquired in non-formal and informal learning, to evaluate them by credits and include them among achievements in degree studies. One of the priorities of the university is distance and electronic studies, as traditional attendance of lectures in full-time studies may be too complicated for employed or socially disadvantaged students.

In the rector's opinion, a likely future of the university is its deinstitutionalisation, dissolution in society, becoming a network of widely spread learners and teachers (Pumputis 2004a, Pumputis 2004b). The accessibility of the university is enhanced by an efficient tuition fee policy. Owing to reasoned management, the MRU has succeeded in having some of the lowest tuition fees among Lithuanian universities. Therefore, higher education for young people, who cannot pay for much more expensive studies like medicine or technological sciences in other universities, is accessible in this university.

Thus MRU has most clearly said "yes" to mass higher education in Lithuania and at present it consistently defends the position that higher education is a public good and, in a certain sense, a public property. Its expansion corresponds to the aspiration of society to attain higher levels of competence and cannot be regarded as a "market failure" or evaluated as "inflation of education". The fact that, disregarding the open-door policy, this higher education institution is the most favourably assessed by students in national ratings and employment of its graduates fluctuates around 95 per cent even during a global economic recession proves that the proclaimed values are not merely marketing tricks.

The university's social obligation is understood as a direct duty to take care of socially vulnerable people. The university is implementing its programme of social support for students. Every year a certain number of students who are in a difficult financial situation get a reduction of tuition fees or are exempted from paying them at all. Part of the university's income is redistributed in order to substantially subsidise the students' canteen so that students from indigent families can board there. Students' hostels are subsidised for the same reason.

Coda

On 29 September 2011 a working group formed by the Prime Minister of the Republic of Lithuania announced proposals for optimisation of the country's network of public higher education institutions. The suggestion was to reduce the network of 14 state universities to four or five by merging them. The working group noted the exceptional achievements of MRU among other national universities, its successful management and independence from public funding. The academic community of the university was recommended to consider the prospects of even greater independence from budget assignments and to look for strategic investors in the country and abroad.

Conclusion

The development of MRU between 1990 and 2010 is almost a laboratory case of mutual links between higher education and a democratic society. A university educates necessary catalysts for the democratic transformation of a society – the people who are able to develop independent opinions, to move away from institutional thinking and the inertia of the past and to draft alternative scenarios for the development of different spheres of society. A university also accumulates and adapts the experience of other countries in establishing democratic institutions and practices in a faster and more qualified way than any other institution.

During the two decades of its existence, MRU has made a deep impact on several essential areas of its country: it has contributed to law reform, the establishment of a system of social security and professionalisation of the environment of public administration. It has also made a contribution to establishing new practices in penitentiary activities and social work, to the international integration of the country, to integration of best international practice in various areas of the public sector and to the support of democratic voices in neighbouring countries.

On the other hand, the development of democracy and the market opens new possibilities for the university, new areas in which the academic community is able to meaningfully apply its competences, creativity and critical thinking. The case of MRU shows how important it is for a university not to confine itself to its academic tradition but to be susceptible to the needs of emerging social practices. This university has grown by listening to the voices of new institutions in society and anticipating the needs of big new markets for higher education.

It is vital that the development of a university should be based on explicit and consistent values. From its origins, MRU has developed as an institution relying on the categories of supremacy of the rule of law, an open society and human rights. Therefore, the university has retained a consistent distance from the concepts of an authoritarian state, which it faced at the beginning of its existence, and has taken a specific position with respect to the discourse of technocratic governance of society, which sees higher education institutions as mere machines producing a skilled labour force. The university holds that it is individuals who have to make a decision about the type of education and what he or she needs. While disagreeing with a priori restrictions of the right to education, the university educates informed citizens as the prerequisite of a democratic society and the guarantee of its efficiency.

The academic identity of MRU is based on a combination of academic autonomy, openness to society, institutional competitiveness and commitment to the social mission of the university. It offers a tested recipe for universities striving to redefine their role in changing democratic societies.

References

Jaunius V. (2008), "Netrukdymas reiškia paramą", pokalbis su M. Romerio universiteto rektoriumi A. Pumpučiu [Non-interference means support: a talk with the Rector of Mykolas Romeris University, A. Pumputis], *Veidas*, 38: 64-5.

Katuoka S. (ed.) (2008), *Teisė Besikeičiančioje Europoje/ Law in the Changing Europe/ Le droit dans une Europe en changement: Liber amicorum for Pranas Kūris*, Vilnius: Mykolo Romerio universiteto Leidybos centras, 945 pp.

Kurapka V. and Mačiuikaitė-Žvinienė S. (2010), "Universiteto mokslas Lietuvai – per Europą" [University scientific research for Lithuania – through Europe] in G. Mesonis (ed.), *Regnum Est: 1990 m. Kovo 11-osios Nepriklausomybės Aktui – 20. Liber amicorum Vytautui Landsbergiui*, Vilnius: Mykolo Romerio universiteto leidybos centras, pp. 739-60.

Liubertas P. (2004), "Lietuvos policija atkūrus nepriklausomybę (1990-1996)" [The police of Lithuania after the restoration of independence, 1990-96] in P. Liubertas and Č. Mančinskas, *Lietuvos Teisės Universitetas*, Vilnius: Lietuvos teisės universiteto leidybos centras, 322 pp.

Meištaitė L. (1997), "Lietuvos policijos akademija: ateities policininkas ir dabartinė netvarka" [The Police Academy of Lithuania: a future police officer and present day disorder], *Justitia*, 2: 12-14.

Mesonis G. (ed.) (2008), *Parlamentas ir valstybinės valdžios institucijų sąranga. Liber amicorum Česlovui Juršėnui* [Parliament and the structure of state institutions. Liber amicorum for Česlovas Juršėnas], Vilnius: Mykolo Romerio universiteto Leidybos centras, 593 pp.

—   (ed.) (2010), *Regnum Est: 1990 m. Kovo 11-osios Nepriklausomybės Aktui – 20. Liber amicorum Vytautui Landsbergiui* [*Regnum Est:* Act of Independence of 11 March 1990, 20th anniversary: *liber amicorum* for Vytautas Landsbergis], Vilnius: Mykolo Romerio universiteto leidybos centras, 1060 pp.

Mykolas Romeris University (2009), *Mykolo Romerio Universitetas, 2004-2009*, Vilnius: Mykolo Romerio universiteto leidybos centras, 144 pp.

—   (2010), *Mykolo Romerio Universitetas, 2010 m.*, Vilnius: Mykolo Romerio universiteto leidybos centras, 152 pp.

Patapas A. and Smalskys V. (2010), "Viešojo administravimo studijų krypties savarankiškumo problema" [The problem of independence of the field of studies of public administration], *Viešoji politika ir administravimas*, 32: 85-93.

Pumputis A. (1995), "Establishment of the Police Academy of Lithuania and its development 1990-1995", *Kriminalinė justicija*, 4: 13-22.

—   (1996), "Policija kaip paslauga" [Police as a service], *Politologija*, 1: 68-80.

—   (1997), "Teisėsaugos funkcijų sistemos klausimu" [On the functions of the system of law enforcement], *Kriminalinė justicija*, 7/8: 183-7.

—   (2000), "Lietuvos teisės universiteto raida (1990-2000 m.)" [Development of the Law University of Lithuania, 1990-2000], *Jurisprudencija*, 15 (7): 13-15.

—   (2003), "Didžioji Universitetų Chartija: atsakomybė už ateities intelektą" [Magna Charta Universitatum: responsibility for future intellect], *Mokslo Lietuva*, 17 (2): 20.

—   (2004a), "Socialinis universitetų vaidmuo XXI amžiuje" [Social role of universities in the 21st century], *Mykolo Romerio universitetas*, 8 (76): 6.

—   (2004b), "Autonomija įpareigoja atsakomybei ir susitelkimui" [Autonomy obliges responsibility and concentration], *Mykolo Romerio universitetas*, 9 (77): 1-2.

Ramonas A. (1997), "Policijos ar teisės akademija?" [Police or Law Academy?], *Mokslo Lietuva* (28 May): 2.

Research Council of Norway (1996), *Evaluation of Research in Lithuania*. Vol. 1: *General Observations and Recommendations prepared by the Advisory Board, and Summaries of the Panel Reports*, Vol. 2: *Panel Reports*, Oslo: Research Council of Norway.

Smalskys V. (ed.) (2010), *Viešasis valdymas. Vadovėlis* [Public administration textbook], Vilnius: Mykolo Romerio universitetas, 388 pp.

19. Act as though you live in a free society

Sondra Myers

"Act as though you live in a free society" was Adam Michnik's admonition to his fellow Poles when they were suffering under oppressive Communist rule in the 1980s. Easier said than done. But Michnik, co-founder of the Solidarity Movement, now editor-in-chief of *Gazeta Wyborcza*, Poland's largest newspaper, had it right. So right – and so counter-cultural in Communist Poland – that he spent a number of his youthful years in prison. It was no accident that the title of his first book was *Letters from Prison and Other Essays* (Michnik 1985).

Michnik knew that awakening citizens to their rights and responsibilities is at the very heart of democratic transformation. It is revolution at its best, clear and focused in its aims and peaceful in its application. His words stand as a simple and eloquent truth about democracy's essence – and in my view, they suggest a syllabus for what we in higher education need to put at the very core of what we teach about civics in and outside the classroom. Students in both old and new democracies need to understand what a free democratic society is, what a citizen is and the essential – not marginal – role that citizens play in making and keeping a free society free. They need to realise that being a good citizen is not a pastime or a feel-good activity, but rather a necessary element in the evolution and sustainability of a democracy.

So perhaps we should begin by asking ourselves and our students how to act as though we live in a free society.

How do we do that?

Michnik's credo has been at the core of my own work since I happened upon *Letters from Prison* in the mid-1980s. Indeed it changed my life. I moved from a career that travelled on parallel tracks in the arts and humanities to one that has led me on a global journey – involving writing, editing, publishing, speaking and directing projects that focus on the central role that citizens play in making democracy work around the world. Citizens ignite democracy. Without their active and informed participation democracy is inanimate – a good idea, an unrealised dream. We must give students the intellectual grounding as well as the emotional fervour to do what they need to do – act as though they live in a free society. Those in democracies of long standing, along with those that are only now emerging, share the need for this vital civic lesson.

We in higher education, particularly those of us who have committed ourselves to strengthening civil society and preparing students for global as well as local and national citizenship, need to be at once bolder and more finely tuned in doing that. I have found many academic institutions to be resistant to adopting an academic strategy for this important project. We are sold on community service and volunteering and, in my view, seriously lacking in persuading students in the way we usually persuade them – through learning – that the role of the citizen goes far beyond the good deeds they perform. We have a responsibility to teach, through the various disciplines and across disciplines, both the architecture and the dynamic of democracy – and the inherent civic imperative. Such knowledge is not only illuminating but it is also empowering – and more often than not, it is inspiring – even exhilarating. That knowledge, I would argue, must be gained in the classroom as well as in the public square: it is a matter of thinking and acting. History and philosophy, literature and other art forms, economics, sociology, psychology, political science – and, indeed, all disciplines – should be called into service.

The ways in which higher education can approach this challenge are only limited by our imagination. Here are several strategies that I have selected from a variety of sources.

The hard drive

This came from a roundtable discussion at the University of Scranton in 2007, focusing on The Role of the Jesuit University in Strengthening Democracy and the Culture of Interdependence. Educators from 13 American Jesuit institutions concurred that the topic of civic engagement belongs in the hard drive – the academic heart – rather than the softer co-curricular and extra-curricular components of the institution. That is not to dismiss the essential work that goes on through volunteering and service-based learning, but students need to grasp the philosophical and historical roots of citizenship intellectually if it is to become an integral part of their individual identities and their commitment to society. According to the late US Supreme Court Justice Louis Brandeis, "The most important political office is that of private citizen" (Dissenting opinion, *Olmstead v. US*, 1928). Preparing for that "office" cannot be delegated to the sidelines.

An interdisciplinary approach

This example came from the American University in Paris, which went through a process of curricular adaptation to ensure that its students were armed with the will and the skills for global citizenship upon graduation. Here is a course that did not require curricular change, but rather some imaginative collaborative thinking and doing. A professor of comparative literature, Celeste Schenck, now president of AUP, co-taught a course on human rights with a sociologist. She took for her assignment Michael Ondaatje's *Anil's Ghost* (Ondaatje 2000) while her sociologist colleague taught the Universal Declaration of Human Rights. To put this human rights learning into action the students were charged with creating a non-governmental organisation and presenting it to UNESCO. There is no limit to the opportunities for creative collaboration along these lines.

The sustainability workshop model

At the University of Scranton we have a sustainability workshop. Although its focus is on sustainability of the physical environment, civic and political sustainability inevitably seep into the curriculum. Faculty members from all disciplines are invited to join the workshop, read suggested texts, take part in seminars and prepare a syllabus to be incorporated into the curriculum, use it and report on it. Participants receive an honorarium for their engagement. It is an approach that permits faculty members to expand their own knowledge of sustainability and bring it directly to their students. It is an effective approach that does not upend the institution by calling for radical curricular reform; rather, it expands the purview of faculty and students, offering new knowledge and perspectives that enable the students to understand and perform more effectively as citizens, whatever their major or professional calling is. What I like about the model is that it is dynamic and directed; within a relatively short time the faculty members' new knowledge and new perspective is transmitted to the students.

Some topics that would make for interesting study

Ratifying a constitution

On 17 September 2011, Constitution Day, Akhil Amar, professor at the Yale Law School and one of the United States' leading constitutional scholars, spoke at the University of Scranton. He called to our attention that while our constitution was not the first in the world, it was the first that required the ratification of citizens. I am amazed at both the wisdom and the courage of our founders who risked the serious possibility of rejection of the whole enterprise of becoming a nation rather than remaining a string of former colonies by putting it "out there" for the people to decide. Shall we say the risk paid off?

The US Constitution has been in place for over 224 years with very few changes, and the document has been crucial to the United States in its effort to evolve as a pluralistic and powerful democracy. I would argue that this grand project succeeded because it required citizens' approval and that it was amended according to the people's will. We know that the present holds daunting challenges for us – as will the future – but I believe that it is essential for those of us who are engaged in education to let students know what the characteristics and demands of democracy are, so that they can continue the endless but essential search for social justice and freedom.

Globalisation and interdependence

As the revolution in information and communications technologies has given increased prominence to globalisation – economically and politically – we have been forced to acknowledge our interconnectedness – our interdependence, which changes the purview of our civic responsibility. The emergence of the environmental movement has shown us that our actions in our homes, schools, communities and workplaces have implications for others in the world and, indeed, for the generations that come after us. The rights and responsibilities of citizenship are in our hands. We need to learn the moral consequences of our actions in an interdependent world.

Action in the present tense

Behold the Arab Spring! It can be the new laboratory for our civic deliberations. Beginning in January 2011 we witnessed a string of peaceful demonstrations in North Africa and the Middle East that have been dubbed the Arab Spring. They have moved pandemically across a region and ultimately across oceans. At the same time, those demonstrations have spawned violence: in Libya, an elongated struggle that resulted in regime change; in Syria, a battle between government and insurgents that continues. Does this suggest a teaching moment? I think it does. It is likely that Occupy Wall Street has more in common with the Arab Spring than with another prominent American uprising, the Tea Party. But does it? If so, why? If not, what bias of my own causes me to think that it does? The Arab Spring brings a demand for freedom and democracy. Occupy Wall Street is about the 99 per cent of Americans who are not benefiting from, but rather punished by, legislation and loopholes that benefit the richest Americans.

Let us make this period, still far from settled with regard to outcomes, a case study for our students. In an increasingly globalised world, we all have a stake in the phenomenon and it would be an opportunity for students of history, politics, sociology, philosophy, geography and economics, to mention a few, to delve into the origins of this extraordinary set of events and its capacity to inspire others. There are more questions than answers about this phenomenon, but the study of them, combined with the study of democracy and its basic components, could make for a lively educational experience in the classroom.

A message from the Arab Spring

Most of my examples and comments refer to my American experience and I recognise that the American educational experience is significantly different from the European one. And yet we talk and learn together, not just about the big picture and grand schemes but about the stories and programmes, successes and failures that we know. We live at a time when boundaries are crossed but not necessarily obliterated.

The Arab Spring and what it might yield in democratic transformation, religious freedom, civil liberties, gender equality or rights of assembly and speech, is still unknown. But we can and should observe it as an important equation-changing phenomenon for the entire world. The Council of Europe higher education programme could conceivably design a conference on "The Arab Spring: its origins, its consequences, its future". Such a project could help us to learn from each other about the diversity of our opinions, perspectives and pedagogical practices and about the impact of the Arab Spring on our respective nations. We are working together to infuse the lives of our institutions and our students with the civic sensibility, to impart to them the will and the skills to enjoy the rights and embrace the responsibilities that old and new democracies require. The Arab Spring calls to mind a mega-situation of global concern that echoes and enlarges the condition that Adam Michnik encountered and addressed in Poland in the 1980s. The voices that informed the Arab Spring came from within and outside the region through face-to-face discussions and through the social media. Was the message the media? Was it the 21st-century version of Michnik's advice to act as though you live in a free society?

The message, however it is described or interpreted, has resonated in oppressive regimes everywhere; as the growing gap between rich and poor sweeps through and corrupts our older democracies, it has also resonated with young people and disenfranchised people of all ages in all nations. Let us take advantage of challenging times, which call for action to teach our students that they are the citizens who will preserve democracy for posterity by improving it in their time.

The American sociologist Robert Bellah and his co-authors had this to say about the state of the world in their internationally acclaimed book, *The Good Society*:

> Accepting the tragedies of the 20th century and the toll they took on all the world's people is the beginning of wisdom. Paradise on this earth, we have learned, is beyond our capacity. But we can, if we are modest and hopeful, possibly establish a reasonably liveable purgatory and escape the inferno. (Bellah 1991: 51)

And, in an act of poetic justice, let me return to Adam Michnik and his most recent book, *In Search of Lost Meaning: the new eastern Europe* and the wisdom of an idealist who labours in the real world with its disappointments and setbacks:

> The idealist devoid of illusions has always followed one rule: do not succumb to despair. After my Hungarian friend Janos Kis, I shall therefore repeat: democracy is not only about free elections, though democracy is impossible without them. Democracy is also about a permanent dialogue that is a dispute between values and the methods by which they are realized. It is also a debate about the past, historical truth, and the valuing of the freedom to search for that truth. Only thus do we pay true homage to those who fought for that truth and died for it. (Michnik 2011: 72)

It is our job to prepare our students for that dialogue, that debate, and the actions that derive from it. We are the citizens of our separate but increasingly and inevitably interconnected and interdependent worlds – and that is our challenging and sacred responsibility.

References

Bellah R. (1991), *The Good Society*, New York: Albert A. Knopf.

Michnik A. (1985), *Letters from Prison and Other Essays*, Berkeley: University of California Press.

— (2011), *In Search of Lost Meaning: the new eastern Europe*, Berkeley: University of California Press.

Ondaatje M. (2000), *Anil's Ghost*, Toronto: McClelland & Stewart.

20. Democracy and education: the Tuskegee University governance model

Gilbert L. Rochon and Thierno Thiam

In the United States, institutions of higher learning are, by history and design, primary bedrocks of democratic governance. As self-governing communities of teachers and scholars, they were created to foster an environment for free thinking. By virtue of the circumstances that created them, by virtue of their governance structure and by virtue of their projection of the democratic ideal locally, nationally and even globally, some higher educational institutions hold a particularly powerful place in the historical narrative of the USA.

Tuskegee University, formerly Tuskegee Normal School for Colored Teachers, later Tuskegee Normal and Industrial Institute, and then Tuskegee Institute, holds such a place. Tuskegee University embodies the practice of democratic governance in a way that warrants chronicling and reflection. This exercise could not be any timelier as recent developments both nationally and on the world stage [69] have led to calls for more academic engagement in the quest to reimagine democratic societies.

Background: land-grant institutions

On 2 July 1862, by signing into law what came to be known as the Land Grant Act, or the Morrill Act, President Abraham Lincoln sought to champion the establishment of a new kind of college that would "promote the liberal and practical education of the industrial classes in the several pursuits and professions in life" (1st Morrill Act 1862). The Land Grant Act offered grants of federal land to states for that purpose. By the very language of the Act and by its very mode of operation, it became clear that the institutions that would be born out of this Act would quintessentially be educational institutions designed to fulfil the promise of citizen participation. Land-grant institutions are therefore, by design, institutions of democracy.

This idea is perhaps captured best by the noted historian of the land-grant system, Earle D. Ross. He explains:

---

69. At the national level, the debate around voting identification laws, or the rather selective nature of such laws, is currently one of the thorniest issues in the democracy debate in the USA. At the global level, few recent events have brought to the fore the debate about democracy more than what is generically dubbed the Arab Spring, an experiment in democracy in a region of the world long deemed to be unprepared for participatory democracy.

> The land-grant college is a peculiarly American institution … Whatever the name, the real test of all the land-grant institutions was their ability and disposition to fulfil their peculiar mission in the new era, and it was in ministering to the technical, social, and political needs of the nation come of age that they attained measurably to the vision of the true prophets of the industrial movement in becoming real people's colleges with all their limitations a distinct native product and the fullest expression of democracy in higher education. (Ross 1942: 181-2; 1969)

Today there are 109 land-grant institutions located in all 50 states, several US territories and the District of Columbia. Land-grant institutions are members of the Association of Public and Land-grant Universities (APLU), formerly known as the National Association of State Universities and Land Grant Colleges (NASULGC). The APLU is a research and advocacy organisation of public research universities, land-grant institutions and state university systems.

Land-grant institutions are also referred to and categorised as 1862, 1890 and 1994 institutions, based upon the date of the legislation that designated most of them with land-grant status. Broadly, a land-grant institution is defined as one that has been designated by its state legislature and by Congress to receive the benefits of the Land Grant Acts.

Tuskegee University, in the heart of the South, occupies a pivotal place in this system not only historically and geographically, but also for other reasons chronicled below. The creation of Tuskegee Normal and Industrial Institute was in itself an act of faith, an act of democratic inclusion and democratic revolution. [70] The 1st Morrill Act (1862), which gave birth to land-grant institutions, revolutionary as it was, did not go far enough in its attempt to effectively include key segments of the disenfranchised US population. The passage of the 2nd Morrill Act (1890) should be understood within such a context as an attempt to move towards more inclusivity and more democracy in higher education. The 2nd Act made special provisions for the then-segregated Southern States to receive funds with the aim of making higher education accessible to a significant portion of their population, specifically the black population. The institutions that were founded out of this Act, such as Tuskegee Institute, came to be known as "the 1890 land-grant universities and Tuskegee University" (2nd Morrill Act 1890; Mayberry 1991).

Moreover, the fact that Tuskegee, Cornell and the Massachusetts Institute of Technology are the only private land-grant universities in the USA has notable implications for democratic governance, both in the way Tuskegee University is organised and in Tuskegee's projection of the ideal of democracy as measured by its contributions to democratic governance at the local, state and national levels.

---

70. Tuskegee Institute was created to give access to education to a segment of the USA, the black population, that otherwise would be left out. The institution of Tuskegee, when many were hostile or thought it could not be done, was a meaningful step for the black population in its quest for full citizenship.

The notion of democracy in higher education is quite often synonymous with a commitment to creating the conditions for more equality, more political rights and more civil liberties. It is also understood as a process that leads to the establishment of political relations between the state and its citizens that feature broad, equal, protected and mutually binding consultation (Tilly 2007). But none of the above will matter in the end without a conscious, informed and well-prepared citizenry. At its core, democracy is empty without the full participation of educated and informed citizens.

Booker T. Washington, the founder of Tuskegee University, understood this at an intimate level. In his 1896 address before the Institute of Arts and Sciences in Brooklyn, New York, he brought the point home in simple, yet very powerful terms. "Character, not circumstances," he argued, "makes the man" (Washington 1896). He well understood, especially in the context in which he operated, that a pragmatic, quiet and diplomatic approach could be more effective if he were to achieve his goal of training his disenfranchised people.

Booker T. Washington's approach at first sight might have seemed to run counter to the very idea that the African-American, the population which his institution was targeting, was primed for social and political participation. The argument against him is well known, especially in the aftermath of his Atlanta Compromise Speech. [71] Specifically, his argument, which was structured around the idea that "in all things that are purely social we can be as separate as the fingers, yet one as the hand in all things essential to mutual progress" (Washington 1895) was deemed to be all too accommodating. W. E. B. Du Bois, [72] on the other hand, made a counter-argument that carried the day in African-American intellectual circles. In hindsight, given that the economic progress of African-Americans has essentially failed to keep pace with the political enfranchisement and societal access afforded by the Civil Rights Movement, it is evident that the sustainable economic development of African-Americans should have been pursued with as much vigour as the voting rights and desegregation campaigns. It is also evident that the dichotomy between the institution building of Booker T. Washington and the Pan-Africanism of Du Bois has been misrepresented and exaggerated in the literature.

However, even if one disagrees with the essence of Booker T. Washington's Atlanta Compromise, it is useful, indeed important, to re-examine his practice with the Tuskegee Institute and the institute's contributions to strengthening democracy in the United States and the world. These internal and external dynamics in the field of democracy are especially important in light of the fact that Tuskegee is part of a restricted group of three institutions of higher learning that are both land-grant and private institutions.

---

71. Booker T. Washington's Atlanta Compromise Speech is online at http://historymatters.gmu. edu/d/39/.
72. W. E. B. Du Bois, an eminent American sociologist and civil rights activist, is often cited as the most influential critic of Booker T. Washington's views and policies of racial accommodation and gradualism.

Tuskegee University's governance structure

The democratic element of Tuskegee University's governance structure was forged when Lewis Adams, a former slave, tinsmith, harness-maker, shoemaker, community organiser and autodidact, was able to secure a US$2 000 state appropriation, through negotiations with a Democratic candidate for re-election to the Alabama Senate, W. F. Foster, in exchange for solidifying the African-American vote. The appropriation's intent was to cover teacher salaries at a school (yet to be established) for recently emancipated slaves. A Hampton Institute graduate and former slave himself, Booker T. Washington was assigned the *ab initio* role of establishing such a school, without land, faculty, books or students.

From its humble beginnings in one room near Butler Chapel AME Zion Church in Tuskegee, Alabama, later expanded to 100 acres (40 ha) and a brick kiln, Tuskegee University's campus now covers 5 000 contiguous acres (200 ha) with over a hundred buildings. Several of the original buildings were designed by the first African-American graduate of the Massachusetts Institute of Technology, Robert R. Taylor, an architect retained by Booker T. Washington, and in whose honour Tuskegee University's School of Architecture was recently renamed.

There have only been six presidents of Tuskegee University since its founding in 1881 by Booker T. Washington. The founder served for 34 years, Major Robert Russa Moton for 20 years (Hughes and Patterson 1956), Frederick Douglass Patterson for 24 years and both Luther Hilton Foster and Benjamin Franklin Payton each served for 28 years. The incumbent president, Gilbert L. Rochon, began his tenure on 1 November 2010. This degree of administrative stability, though not so uncommon among Historically Black Colleges and Universities (HBCU), is rare in the United States. The two longest-serving presidents among all colleges and universities in America are both at HBCUs: Dr Norman C Francis has been president at Xavier University of Louisiana since 1968 and Dr William R. Harvey has been president of Hampton University since 1978.

The Board of Trustees of Tuskegee University appoints the president, who is the chief executive officer, and approves the annual budget, oversees the endowment, major land sales and acquisitions, approves honorary degrees, and is the ultimate governance and control entity for the university. It comprises no more than 25 members, 20 of them self-perpetuating and five appointed by the Governor of the State of Alabama, by virtue of Tuskegee University's land-grant status. The 20 members serve a three-year term, renewable; the gubernatorial appointees serve until they are replaced by the governor. Thus Tuskegee University is a private university that is also state-related. To foster inclusivity, one seat is reserved for a recent graduate of the university (within the past three years). Senior administrative staff are invited to attend board meetings, as are the President of the Faculty Senate, the President of the Staff Senate and the President of the Student Government Association.

The position of Chairman of the Board of Trustees, in reality and symbolically, is an indicator of institutional gravitas, stability and sustainability. The previous chairman, Dr Andrew F. Brimmer, served for 45 years on the Board of Trustees, 28 years in the chair. He was also the first black Governor of the US Federal Reserve Board, serving a 14-year term. The current chairman, Major General Charles E. Williams (ret.), is the first alumnus of Tuskegee University to become Chair of the Board of Trustees and was the first African-American to become a general in the US Army Corps of Engineers; he later became Director of the Bureau of Overseas Building Operations for the US Department of State, overseeing construction of over 50 US embassies and consular offices throughout the world.

In addition to the usual array of vice presidents (fiscal affairs, student affairs, legal affairs, development, federal affairs, capital projects and facility services, information technology) and the chief of staff, the Provost/Vice President of Academic Affairs reports directly to the president. Each of the deans in turn reports directly to the Provost. At Tuskegee University, academic programmes are divided between the:

- Andrew F. Brimmer College of Business and Information Science,
- College of Agriculture, Environment and Nutrition Science,
- College of Arts and Sciences,
- College of Engineering,
- College of Veterinary Medicine, Nursing and Allied Health,
- Robert R. Taylor School of Architecture and Construction Science,
- School of Education.

Tuskegee University has conferred the Doctor of Veterinary Medicine degree upon 75 per cent of all African-American veterinarians in the USA. It is the sole HBCU with a School of Veterinary Medicine, an accredited Department of Aerospace Engineering and the only HBCU with PhD programmes in materials science and engineering, in integrative biosciences, in pathobiology and in agricultural and environmental engineering. Tuskegee University has, *inter alia*, been designated by the NAS (National Academy of Science) as a National Centre of Academic Excellence in Information Assurance for the period 2012-17; by the National Science Foundation as a Centre of Research Excellence in Nanobiomaterials as derived from Biorenewable and Waste Resources; as a Centre of Excellence in Agricultural Sustainability and by NASA as a Centre for Food and Environmental Systems for Human Exploration and Development of Space.

In June 2012, the APLU celebrated the 150th anniversary of the 1st Morrill Act of 1862, which established land-grant universities in every state and territory. The 2nd Morrill Act of 1890 provided funding to designate separate institutions of higher learning for blacks in those states that did not open the doors of their universities to black students. The Council of 1890 Universities is composed of the presidents of Historically Black Colleges and Universities that were designated land-grant institutions by the 2nd Morrill Act. This group of 18 HBCUs is chaired by the current president of Tuskegee University.

From their inception and in light of their history, HBCUs have always been conscious of issues related to funding for their students, who tend to come from low-income households. Faced with such prospects, Tuskegee University's third president, Frederick Douglass Patterson, realised that there could be greater strength in collectivity among the private HBCUs with respect to fundraising. Accordingly, he founded the United Negro College Fund (UNCF), the largest, oldest, most successful and most comprehensive higher education assistance organisation for minority and underrepresented groups in the United States. The UNCF continues to raise funds for HBCU capacity-building and for scholarships for minority students, under the slogan "A mind is a terrible thing to waste!" Patterson's successor, Luther H. Foster, also served on the board of directors of the UNCF, and Foster's successor, Benjamin Payton, was a member of the Council of Presidents of the UNCF. This tradition lives on, as Tuskegee's new president, Gilbert Rochon, is also a member of the Council of Presidents of the UNCF, representing private member institutions.

As is the case with the Council of 1890 Universities, the Council of Presidents of the UNCF Member Institutions each exercise one vote, notwithstanding the size of their university or college. A complete list of UNCF member institutions appears at the end of this chapter.

Tuskegee University and the democratic principle

The idea, the mission and the goals of Tuskegee University at their very heart have the same basis as Jeffersonian democracy, [73] which rests on a fundamental belief in the common man. For Jefferson, the very essence of democracy was a system that guaranteed equal political opportunity to all, including the "yeoman farmer" and the "plain folk". The yeoman farmer, Jefferson insisted, was the main pillar of republican democratic government (Wood 2011: 220).

Tuskegee University was indeed designed to train the "plain folk" and the "yeoman farmer" to be people who added value to society, a *sine qua non* for informed democratic participation. This tradition in training the hands, heart and mind of an informed, skilled citizenry to carry on the task of nourishing the ideal of a government by the people, of the people and for the people, had significant consequences over the course of the 20th century. Such consequences on advancing democracy are multi-faceted and can be measured specifically at two essential levels: the local, state, national, on the one hand, and the global, on the other.

---

73. Jeffersonian democracy takes its name from Thomas Jefferson (1743-1826), an author of the US Declaration of Independence, third President of the United States and founder of the University of Virginia.

Tuskegee University and civil rights: local, state and national implications

First, Tuskegee's contributions in advancing democracy can be measured in terms of its critical role in the civil right movements. This awareness would not have been possible but for the strategic initial steps that made this institution a reality in the first place. Never was Tuskegee University's transformation into a leader in the struggle to achieve civil rights and political liberties more evident than when it mattered most, in the 1960s. The institution became an organising ground as well as a hub of student action. There is perhaps no greater tragic symbol of sacrifices made on the altar of democratic inclusiveness than the martyrdom of Sammy Younge, Tuskegee University student and member of the Student Nonviolent Coordination Committee, on 4 January 1966. He was gunned down in a petrol station in Tuskegee because he defied one of the ultimate symbols of political, social and economic exclusion in the South. He would not use a toilet shamefully marked "For Colored". He was only 22 years of age.

Second, Tuskegee's involvement, contributions and commitment to the democratic ideal can also be measured in the landmark *Gomillion v. Lightfoot* case, which went to the heart of one of the central tenets of democracy, voting rights. In 1957, the State of Alabama passed Act 140, which changed the boundaries of the City of Tuskegee. This was intended to exclude significant portions of the electorate on the sole basis of race and to ensure that white candidates were elected. Tuskegee's boundaries had previously been a square but the legislature decided to redraw them as a 28-sided figure, thus excluding all but a handful of potential African-American votes.

Faced with this prospect, Charles A. Gomillion, a professor of Political Science at Tuskegee Normal and Industrial Institute, represented by Attorney Fred Gray (Gray 2002),[74] led the charge against Tuskegee mayor Philip M. Lightfoot and other city officials. The case went to the US Supreme Court, which faced one of the most defining issues of that period, that is, whether or not Act 140 of the Alabama legislature violated the 15th Amendment.

The Supreme Court's decision came in no uncertain terms in favour of Charles Gomillion. The court's decision was issued by Justice Felix Frankfurter,[75] who

---

74. Fred Gray, a lawyer in Alabama, came to prominence during the civil rights movement for his work with the leader of the civil rights movement, Martin Luther King Jr, Rosa Parks and the Montgomery Improvement Association. He also represented the survivors of the infamous US Public Health Service Syphilis Study that withheld treatment from poor black sharecroppers in Tuskegee and surrounding communities.

75. The fact that the court's decision was issued by Justice Felix Frankfurter – one of the most important justices in US history – was both significant and ironic. Justice Frankfurter was known for his philosophy of judicial restraint, believing that courts should not interpret the constitution

argued that the Act did indeed violate the provision of the 15th Amendment prohibiting states from denying anyone their right to vote on basis of race, colour or previous condition of servitude. Beyond Gomillion, the Supreme Court decision signalled that the march towards inclusivity, the protection of civil rights and political liberties, in short the march towards a more perfect democracy, would not be stopped. Tuskegee has played an important part in that march.

The *Gomillion v. Lightfoot* case was a highly significant event that, along with several others, in the context of a heated debate on the future of democracy in the United States, would lay the foundation for the 1965 Voting Rights Act, which outlawed discriminatory voting practices. Tuskegee University alumna Amelia Platts Boynton Robinson, now aged 101, was a survivor of the brutal attack on the Edmond Pettus Bridge Voting Rights Demonstration and continues to engage youth on the necessity of exercising their right to vote, which had been won with such sacrifice and determination.

Today this tradition in civic engagement and the fight to perfect democracy is captured best by two major organisations on the Tuskegee University campus, notably the Tuskegee University College Chapter of the National Association for the Advancement of Colored People (NAACP) and the Tuskegee University Chapter of College Democrats of America (CDA).

These two organisations are known for their engagement to further the ideal of democracy. Their engagement is not merely a matter of socio-political rhetoric; it is an everyday boots-on-the-ground commitment to the democratic ideal. Their level of activity, which is designed to improve levels of democratic inclusion and participation, can be measured by the wide range of political activities, including voter-registration drives and awareness workshops on the significance of issues as important as voting, income disparities and health disparities.

The NAACP was co-founded in 1909 by W. E. B. Du Bois and is today the oldest, largest and most widely recognised grassroots-based civil rights organisation in the USA. [76] The Tuskegee University chapter is particularly active. As for the College Democrats of America, it was founded in 1932 to promote the ideas of presidential nominee Franklin Delano Roosevelt and has since become the formidable youth outreach arm of the Democratic Party. Today, it consists of over 100 000 US college and university students. Tuskegee has played no small role in the CDA. The dynamism of the Tuskegee Chapter of the CDA is attested by the ascent to its presidency in 1998 of a Tuskegee graduate, Harold Powell, the first African-American to hold this prestigious position.

---

in such a way as to impose limits on the authority of the legislative and executive branches, and being reluctant to apply the federal constitution to states.

76. See the NAACP home page at www.naacp.org/pages/naacp-history (accessed on 8 April 2012).

Tuskegee University and the fight for democracy: the global implications

It is important to note that Tuskegee University's commitment to the democratic principle transcends the bounds of the United States. Perhaps the most dramatic demonstration of such commitment was evidenced during the Second World War. When the Third Reich trampled on the democratic principle by seeking to impose tyranny over Europe, an all-African-American 332nd Fighter Group, trained at Tuskegee Institute, fought for the democracies of Europe and the world, against all odds and against all bets. Most strikingly, the Tuskegee Airmen did so at a time when they did not enjoy all the benefits of democracy at home. The rationale for the imperative of winning the war was put forward, in simple yet very powerful terms, by a Tuskegee airman himself, John Gray:

> Our attitude was, if the Germans or the Japanese won the war, the white folk would get on their side and we'd have to fight both the Germans, the Japanese, and the white folk. So what we did was go over there and win the war and then come back up and pick up the gauntlet where we tried to get our civil rights. (Gray 2007)

These words sum up the Tuskegee spirit. The choice was stark: on the one hand, there was the vision of the Allied forces fighting for freedom and democracy; on the other was the vision of the Third Reich, which sought to remake the world to fit its tyrannical and oppressive desires. Tuskegee University, through its airmen, wanted to help reclaim democracy for the world (Caver, Ennels and Haulmann 2011).

Building upon that tradition, largely through its Reserve Officers Training Corps programmes, Tuskegee University has educated more African-Americans who attained the rank of general or admiral than any other college or university, including the US Military Service Academies. This indicator of "service to the nation" was one of several criteria, including the volume of research and "social mobility" (defined as the capacity of an academic institution to propel low-income students through the ranks of bachelor's, master's and doctoral degrees) that led to Tuskegee University's No. 1 ranking among all 309 baccalaureate colleges in the USA, as reported in the September/October 2011 National College Rankings issue of *Washington Monthly*.

Finally, it is also worth noting that Tuskegee has educated, and continues to educate, citizens who have gone on to affirm democracy not only at home but also abroad. This is especially significant in the context of the centennial of the African National Congress (ANC), one of the most significant political parties in Africa. Tuskegee was a crucible for the early leadership of the ANC, which ultimately ushered in democracy to South Africa. For instance, Dr John Langalibalele Dube (1871-1946), co-founder and first president-general of the South African Native National Congress (1912-17), which became the ANC in 1923, was highly influenced by Booker T. Washington during one of his visits to the USA (1887-89). Upon Dr Dube's return to South Africa in 1900, he founded the Zulu Christian Industrial Institute (whose name he changed one year later to the Ohlange Institute) on 200 acres (80 ha) of land, closely modelling it after Tuskegee Institute. Dr Dube also established a newspaper in Zulu and English, the *Sun of Natal (Ilanga lase Natal)*, which became a voice of opposition to the policies and practices of the Natal colonial establishment (Marable 1976). Dr Alfred Bitini Xuma (1893-1962) began his studies at Tuskegee Institute in 1913, and he graduated from Tuskegee as one of the top three students. At the institute's commencement ceremony, Xuma gave a speech entitled "Problems in poultry raising". In 1920, Xuma graduated with honours in Science from the University of Minnesota and in 1926 he received an MD from Northwestern University. In 1938, Xuma became the first black South African to receive the Diploma in Public Health from the London University School of Hygiene and Tropical Medicine. Xuma was elected to serve two terms as President of the African National Congress (1940-49), drafting the ANC's new constitution in 1943, which opened membership to all races, enfranchised women with equal rights and eliminated the House of Chiefs. Xuma later strongly opposed the Pass Laws, land restrictions against Africans and other apartheid policies, and supported solidarity with the oppressed populations in Rhodesia and Namibia, then South West Africa (Gish 2000).

Summary and conclusions

The very idea of Tuskegee is at the heart of democracy, especially Jeffersonian democracy. If Jefferson is credited as an exceptional theoretician of democracy, Booker T. Washington and the institute that he founded are, without a doubt, among the foremost examples of democracy in practice. The Tuskegee experiment was and continues to be a model in the practice of democratic governance. From its beginnings as the Tuskegee Normal School for Colored Teachers, and its transformation into the Tuskegee Normal and Industrial Institute, Tuskegee Institute and now, Tuskegee University, the institution has positioned itself as a champion of democratic governance.

As shown by the case of *Gomillion v. Lightfoot* and the involvement of students and faculty in the civil rights movement, Tuskegee has contributed significantly to the democratic cause nationally. Tuskegee University's commitment to the ideal of democracy, however, transcends the national bounds of the United States of America, for it also has a global reach. When the Third Reich imposed a regime of tyranny and denial of democracy, Tuskegee sided decisively with democracy over tyranny by training and sending its airmen to participate in the restoration of democracy and the rule of law in Europe. The airmen chose democracy for the world at a time when it was denied to them. Today, the fight for a more perfect democracy is still central as the activism of the Tuskegee University College Chapter of the National Association for the Advancement of Colored People (NAACP) and the Tuskegee University Chapter of College Democrats of America (CDA) shows. Democracy, after all, is anything but a finished product. Rather, it is a process towards a more perfect system of governance and society.

References

1st Morrill Act (1862), online at www.csrees.usda.gov/about/offices/legis/morrill. html (accessed on 10 March 2012).

2nd Morrill Act (1890), online at www.csrees.usda.gov/about/offices/legis/ secondmorrill.html (accessed on 10 March 2012).

Caver J., Ennels J. and Haulman D. (2011), *The Tuskegee Airmen: an illustrated history: 1939-1949*, Montgomery AL: New South Books.

Gish S. D. (2000), *Alfred B. Xuma: African, American, South African*, London: MacMillan.

Gray F. (2002), *Bus ride to justice: the life and works of Fred Gray*, Montgomery AL: New South Books.

Gray J. (2007), "Fighting for democracy: a PBS documentary", online at www. pbs.org/thewar/at_war_democracy_african_american.htm (accessed on 9 March 2012).

Hughes W. H. and Patterson F. D. (1956), *Robert Russa Moton of Hampton and Tuskegee*, Chapel Hill: University of North Carolina Press.

Marable W. M. (1976), *African nationalist: the life of John Langalibalele Dube*, Michigan: UMI Dissertation Services [PhD thesis, University of Maryland].

Mayberry B. D. (1991), *A century of agriculture in the 1890 Land-Grant Institutions and Tuskegee University, 1890-1990*, New York: Vantage Press.

Ross E. D. (1942), *A history of Iowa State College*, Ames IA: Iowa State College Press.

—   (1969), *Democracy's college: the land-grant movement in the formative state*, New York: Arno Press/New York Times.

Smith J. (2004), *Climbing Jacob's Ladder: a trial lawyer's journey on behalf of "the least of these"*, Montgomery AL: New South Books.

Tilly C. (2007), *Democracy*, New York: Cambridge University Press.

Tutu D. (1999), *No future without forgiveness*, New York: Doubleday.

Washington B. T. (1895), "Atlanta compromise speech" (Atlanta GA), online at www.pbs.org/wnet/jimcrow/historical_docs/hist_doc_altantacomp1.html (accessed on 25 April 2012).

—   (1896), "Education and democracy: address before the Institute of Arts and Sciences" (Brooklyn, New York) online at http://teachingamericanhistory. org/library/index.asp?document=57 (accessed on 25 April 2012).

Williams C. (2011), *My road: from a trail to a super highway – only in America*, Atlanta GA: Publishing Associates.
Wood G. (2011), *The idea of America: reflections on the birth of the United States*, New York: Penguin.

UNCF (United Negro College Fund) member institutions

Alabama

Miles College, Birmingham
Oakwood University, Huntsville
Talladega College, Talladega
Stillman College, Tuscaloosa
Tuskegee University, Tuskegee

Arkansas

Philander Smith College, Little Rock

Ethiopia

Addis Ababa University, Addis Ababa, Ethiopia

Florida

Bethune-Cookman University, Daytona Beach
Edward Waters College, Jacksonville
Florida Memorial University, Miami Gardens

Georgia

Clark Atlanta University, Atlanta
Interdenominational Theological Center, Atlanta
Morehouse College, Atlanta
Spelman College, Atlanta
Paine College, Augusta

Louisiana

Dillard University, New Orleans
Xavier University of Louisiana, New Orleans

Mississippi

Rust College, Holly Springs
Tougaloo College, Tougaloo

North Carolina

Johnson C. Smith University, Charlotte
Bennett College, Greensboro
Saint Augustine's College, Raleigh
Shaw University, Raleigh
Livingstone College, Salisbury

Ohio

Wilberforce University, Wilberforce

South Carolina

Allen University, Columbia
Benedict College, Columbia
Voorhees College, Denmark
Claflin University, Orangeburg
Morris College, Sumter

Tennessee

Lane College, Jackson
LeMoyne-Owen College, Memphis
Fisk University, Nashville

Texas

Huston-Tillotson University, Austin
Paul Quinn College, Dallas
Jarvis Christian College, Hawkins
Wiley College, Marshall
Texas College, Tyler

Virginia

Saint Paul's College, Lawrenceville
Virginia Union University, Richmond

21. Building partnerships between universities and communities to strengthen university autonomy and democratic citizenship: the *Artes liberales* movement at the University of Warsaw[77]

Piotr Wilczek

The independent Republic of Poland emerged in 1989 after the fall of Communism. The new republic inherited the old, inefficient system of higher education, which was state-owned and state-controlled with one exception: the Catholic University of Lublin – a private institution established and fully financed by the Roman Catholic Church. All other universities, technical universities and teacher training colleges were controlled by the state. The new regulations after 1989 cleared the way to establishing non-state (non-public) higher education institutions. This non-public system now comprises 338 higher education institutions with about 660 000 students – more than one third of the 1 927 762 students in Poland; there are still 132 public universities and colleges. The University of Warsaw, founded in 1816, is the largest, with 57 000 students and 3 500 employees, and among the leading universities in Poland.

The structure of the 40 Polish public universities is rather anachronistic when compared to universities in the United States and most western European countries. The system of management is based on ostensibly democratic rules, established after the fall of Communism without changing other major aspects of the way the universities function. This democratic system is, paradoxically, now very inefficient. Rectors and deans are elected by large groups of professors and other members of the community, and all major decisions must be approved by large senates or councils and boards of various kinds. The new Law of Higher Education of 2011 introduced a number of minor changes aiming to strengthen the role of top management. Attempts to improve or rationalise the structure of university management are perceived in academic circles as attacks on university freedom and self-government; but there are more important dangers to the public university system, especially the small number of creative research and educational programmes and almost non-existent mobility of faculty.

---

77. This chapter is based on working materials prepared with Jerzy Axer and others from the University of Warsaw on various occasions in 2008-12. The author would like to thank Jerzy Axer, Donald W. Harward, Mark O'Connor and Andrzej Waśkiewicz for many inspirational conversations on liberal education in that period.

Since 1989 higher education in Poland has been changing rapidly. The three most important aspects of the new system are:

- the unprecedented development of private schools, enabling thousands of new students to receive academic degrees;
- the introduction of three levels of study (BA, MA and PhD), making the system more flexible;
- the introduction of large-scale co-operation with the European higher education system.

Artes liberales

In Poland there is still a need for educational experiments, which can emerge from the public universities and are sources of new educational ideas promoting democratic values. I would like to present a few examples of this kind, all from one unique educational and research centre, the Artes Liberales Institute for Interdisciplinary Studies at the University of Warsaw (www.obta.uw.edu.pl/en). This institute, together with a non-governmental organisation, the Artes Liberales Institute Foundation, has set up new institutions and organised a number of conferences, seminars, summer schools, meetings and public debates over the past 20 years.

The principal originator and founder of the initiatives and institutions, Professor Jerzy Axer, explained his ideas recently in the following way:

> What guided us was the idea of universities free from any government political pressure, concentrated mainly on their mission to liberate individuals from the totalitarian system's legacy, encouraging them to be active and responsible and to reveal instead of conceal their desires and needs. Our aim was to break free of imposed restraints in favour of restraints intentionally chosen and accepted by teachers and students in their desire to renew the university community protected by its autonomy from future claims by authorities. (Axer 2012: 243)

The following initiatives are examples of how higher education can support democratic citizenship and democratic society by engaging local and regional communities in promoting democratic commitments and cultures.

Interdepartmental Individual Studies in the Humanities *(Międzywydziałowe Indywidualne Studia Humanistyczne* – MISH)

The first MISH initiative was described by its founder as:

> a system of learning and not a university unit. Within a few years, all the University of Warsaw's humanities and social sciences departments joined the project, forming a kind of confederation. It enabled a group of students, those who passed a special qualification procedure, to obtain BA- and MA-level degrees in a mode hitherto unknown in Poland. They were guaranteed tutor supervision, and with their tutors could

design individual curricula ...; they were held jointly responsible for their choices; and apart from professional training, they were obligated to obtain a broad, general and interdisciplinary education. (Axer 2012: 244)

This model would not look revolutionary for a reader in western Europe, still less in America, but in Poland in the early 1990s this was a real revolution and many MISH graduates have become leaders – scholars, journalists, politicians, business people – responsible for many positive changes in Polish society in the last 20 years.

The Warsaw centre co-ordinates a network of similar educational initiatives in major Polish universities and has helped in establishing such a network in Ukraine (Lviv and Kiev) and Russia (Rostov). There is also a national programme of this kind, Academia Artes Liberales, encouraging students' mobility within Poland. The eight major universities in Poland established this network, which plans to expand the existing system of interdepartmental individual studies in the humanities to the dimension of inter-university studies.

The East European School in the Humanities *(Międzynarodowa Szkoła Humanistyczna Europy Wschodniej)*

This was founded in 1996 in the framework of Polish-Ukrainian university co-operation. The purpose of the school is to disseminate modern theories and methodologies in the humanities and, primarily, to support the development of a new generation of scholars in disciplines particularly neglected in central and eastern Europe under communist rule. The essential goal is to create an international, interdisciplinary community capable of effective scholarly co-operation and thus to eliminate the existing vacuum that risks being filled with an ideology of primitive nationalism and ethnocentrism. Numerous workshops, seminars, conferences and summer schools have been organised, devoted to various issues in the humanities and social sciences that are essential for the development of democracy. To date, over 4 000 Russians, Belarusians, Ukrainians and Poles have actively participated in these sessions.

Academia in Public Discourse

This programme is a continuation of the experience of reforming the system of higher education in Poland and, more broadly, central and eastern Europe, building relationships and jointly exploring the place of academia in the contemporary world. In particular, the project aims to build lasting bridges between the Polish and Russian academic communities in the course of intensive dialogue with other participants in the public debate. The project began with the pilot programme Opening the Window: Poland–Russia, involving three Polish-Russian meetings, held in turn in Poland and Russia. Each meeting comprises a three day debate, featuring leading specialists from both countries, and workshops enabling the participants to hold discussions and share their reflections inspired by the two nations' historical and cultural experience. Between the meetings, seminars on the topics of successive debates are held at the Artes Liberales Institute for Interdisciplinary Studies at the University of Warsaw (IBI AL), the hosts being from Poland and Russia.

All these debates are held either in Poland or in Russia, but participants who are not present in the conference halls, including students and scholars from Ukraine, are also included through the system of videoconferencing.

Siberian Challenges

There has been a series of intensive contacts with Russian academics within the Siberian Challenges programme, including a major conference on The Borderland as a Framework of Civilisational Identification.

Collegium Artes Liberales

This is an experiment in interdisciplinary teaching in the spirit of liberal education. Its establishment and development is a result of co-operation between Poles and Americans, inspired by the experience of the US liberal arts college, but introducing new elements based on local traditions and experiences. As Jerzy Axer wisely observed:

> In view of the lack of a local tradition of the Humboldtian university, there was a chance to develop a model looking to the future and combining the local republican tradition with the best experience of the Western European and U.S. education systems .... We can set up colleges in the spirit of *artes liberales* at the best universities. This should not mean mechanical transplanting of the American model. We need to find our own formula, compatible with the experience and tradition of the country we live in, maintaining a constant dialogue with our American colleagues but also with other academic cultures – from the West and East of Europe. (Axer 2011: 27)

The Collegium Artes Liberales is a department at the University of Warsaw established jointly by the university and two foundations: the Christian A. Johnson Endeavor Foundation and the Artes Liberales Institute Foundation.

The Collegium is not an American-style liberal arts college. It is deeply rooted in the Polish original, "intuitional" liberal arts tradition – represented by MISH (Interdepartmental Individual Studies in the Humanities) – and also in the wider European tradition (Collège de France and Oxford).

It offers an interdisciplinary programme of studies in social sciences, humanities and natural sciences designed for the students of the University of Warsaw. The goals of the Collegium are: to provide students with an environment favourable to expanding their knowledge, understanding and skills and to develop their thinking and judgment through interactive forms of teaching and study, as well as through close interaction with their lecturers and tutors. The methodology used to accomplish these goals relies on individual curricula suited to students' interests; it is aligned with the liberal arts formula tested at universities recognised for their excellence. The formula requires that the students are guided towards a full awareness of their needs and talents. It centres on a core curriculum covering a body of knowledge judged necessary to an understanding of the social world, seen as a world of culture rooted in a natural environment.

It took several years and co-operation with lecturers and experts from the United States to develop the Collegium's curriculum. The core curriculum was inspired by the curriculum of the College at the University of Chicago. The goal of the Collegium is not only to provide the students with a certain body of knowledge from various academic disciplines but also to equip them with skills they could use both within and outside academia. Among these are: the ability to read texts critically, in depth; to make contributions to a debate; to deliver a cogent, complex but clear argument; and the ability to write texts of various length-essays, reviews and academic papers. Students practise these skills throughout the semester. This course of study requires that the student work more outside class than is usually the case. After most of the courses a public conference or debate is organised and the students offer their presentations to their colleagues and a wider public. The Collegium Artes Liberales welcomes students who upon graduation are willing to serve the public interest with the comprehensive knowledge, understanding and skills acquired in the course of their studies.

The Collegium has been making several attempts to introduce elements of civic education and civic engagement, which are practically absent from Polish higher education. It regularly organises workshops on these and many other issues for the faculty and students – for example, in April 2012 there was a series of workshops conducted by Dr Donald W. Harward, former President of Bates College and currently Senior Fellow at the American Association of Colleges and Universities.

The April 2012 workshops for the Collegium students were devoted to multiple perspectives on the nature of liberal education and – above all – the civic mission of the university. The workshops for faculty members were devoted to the following issues:

- multiple understandings of the nature and extent of objectives of liberal education;
- how we understand the "civic mission" of the university, of higher education in Poland;
- what constitutes, and what could result from, privileging student learning.

Conclusions

All the above-mentioned Polish initiatives aim at:

- bringing academic voices into public discourse;
- encouraging researchers to come out of their ivory tower as a group and as individuals;
- promoting the dialogue of Polish and Russian academic communities with Belarusian and Ukrainian partners;
- overcoming the isolation of individuals and marginalised groups by allowing their voices to be heard in insufficiently democratic milieux;
- building a space for a more universal dialogue, also through the Internet;
- creating productive relationships between academics and policy professionals;
- developing and sustaining EU and non-EU countries' academic networks;
- promoting more intense and substantive dialogue between representatives of various academic communities: American and European, including EU and non-EU countries.

All these examples of educational programmes prove that – in a country that has gone in 23 years through an unprecedented political, social and economic transformation and is now one of the most prosperous members of the European Union – there has been an urgent need, and space has been found, for unique activities aiming at transforming the public university system, which had remained one of the most conservative elements in the country, unchanged in its attitudes to the needs of democratic society and the expectations of new generations of students. All the above-mentioned projects have concentrated on transforming a traditional public institution and encouraging students and employees to create space for educational experiments that can improve the whole system and be models for educational change.

In 2012 the Artes Liberales Institute for Interdisciplinary Studies achieved a great success: it was selected in a nationwide competition as a partner of the Polish Ministry of Science and Higher Education in a project devoted to creating and implementing a new system of interdisciplinary and transdisciplinary studies at Polish higher education institutions. The projects discussed here – especially Interdepartmental Individual Studies in the Humanities, Collegium Artes Liberales and the East European School in the Humanities – will serve as case studies for further development of a new system that combines interdisciplinary education with a civic mission of the university. I believe that these programmes and projects may also be of interest to other countries in Europe and elsewhere that undergo transformation from an old-fashioned, inefficient higher education system to a democratic, up-to-date model of higher education. The co-operation of the Artes Liberales centre with Belarus, Ukraine and Russia proves that such exchanges of ideas can be useful for all partners of co-operation.

References

Axer J. (2011), "From the humanist Respublica Litteraria to the Collegium Artes Liberales" in M. O'Connor and P. Wilczek (eds), *Collegium/ College/ Kolegium: College and the Academic Community in the European and the American tradition*, Boston MA/Warsaw: Sub Lupa, pp. 22-7.

— (2012), "International perspectives on liberal education: Polish case example" in D. W. Harward (ed.), *Transforming Undergraduate Education: theory that compels and practices that succeed*, Lanham MD: Rowman & Littlefield, pp. 239-52.

22. Democracy at De Anza College

Brian Murphy

Almost half of all undergraduates in the United States attend two-year community colleges. These 13 million students are extraordinarily diverse. They are largely working-class with a range of ages, often employed full or part time; many are immigrants. The community colleges are open-access institutions and students come for many reasons. Many seek transfer to university, others to vocational and technical training; some are acquiring English-language skills, others are pursuing lifelong learning. All too often, community college students have been ignored in discussions of civic engagement – an omission that, at long last, is being rectified. A new movement is emerging in American community colleges, insisting that our students must be engaged in the political process and must learn civic and democratic skills.

Students or employees-in-training?

This flies in the face of conventional political dialogue. The dominant language in American higher education is economic, despite a counter-movement for civic learning in universities. But the public rationale for investment and reform is the revival of the American economy, and the purposes of education are too often limited to preparation for careers. Nowhere is this more true than for the community colleges, which President Obama calls "career centres". Virtually every recent national report on community colleges calls for more "alignment" with the needs of industry. Our students become, in this argument, employees-in-training and there is silence about their civic and social roles.

No one disputes the need for employable skills in an advanced economy, least of all students seeking employment. But the purely economic rationale ignores the larger civic dimension of our students' lives and offers little guidance for what preparation and engagement are required for our students to take their place at democracy's table. What skills and capacities will they need to be citizens, how will they assume leadership in their communities, how might they work in the non-profit independent sector so critical to the nation's civic life? More broadly, how will they engage each other across the multiple divisions of the society to both protect themselves and build a sustainable future? These are questions asked by more and more community college students and by the colleges themselves.

The Democracy Commitment [78] is a new national coalition of American community colleges committed to developing our students' democratic capacity. Many

---

78.   See www.thedemocracycommitment.org.

of the United States' leading community colleges are engaged in this work: Miami Dade, the Maricopa Colleges, LaGuardia, Moraine Valley, Lane, Los Rios, Kingsborough, Valencia, Broome and some 80 more. Together we enrol almost two million students.

De Anza College is among these colleges. Our work illustrates what can happen in community colleges and how community college students can engage in public work as an essential element of their education. The college also asks a critical question of its own practice: how can we democratise the college itself as we build an education in democracy for our students?

The college

De Anza College[79] is a Californian public community college, one of 112 in the state. The college offers exemplary lower-division courses for transfer to university, Associate of Arts and Associate of Science[80] degree programmes in 60 fields, 125 certificate programmes and career/technical education in specialised areas. The college has a national reputation for its transfer rates to universities, particularly to the University of California and the California State Universities. The college has been devoted to issues of equity and social justice for many years and has taken a public role in advancing the work of democratic engagement for students.

De Anza is large and diverse, with more than 24 000 students from across Silicon Valley. Our students are often immigrants or the children of immigrants, from Mexico, Vietnam, China, the Philippines, India and Korea. These students, and their African-American and European-American classmates, represent a wide range of socioeconomic backgrounds: 80 per cent work full time or part time; 65 per cent speak another language in addition to English. Most are the first in their family to attend college. More than 80 per cent of them come to college without the academic preparation required for college or university work, due to poor high schools, recent immigration or the instability of poverty. As a result, the college offers a wide set of courses in basic skills, offering students a second chance at university access.

De Anza's academic reputation rests on its history of transferring students from all backgrounds to some of the finest universities in America. De Anza students are not the stereotypical college students at elite or traditional universities, yet they are multi-talented, with enormous drive and commitment.

---

79. The college website is at www.deanza.edu.
80. Associate degrees are two-year collegiate degrees conferred in the United States for students completing a course of study at a community college, often leading to transfer to a four-year university. The degree can also be conferred for vocational and career technical programmes.

Students who come to De Anza College are now finding that California is dramatically reducing its commitment to higher education and the national economy remains sluggish. Our students are not among those for whom the American Dream is guaranteed by birth or privilege. Too many come from communities blighted by racism, poverty and unemployment. And those who come from middle-class communities join a college community that integrates all, seeks the talents of everyone. For our students, democracy is not an abstraction but a path to engagement and power. They need more than vocational or academic training for employment; they need the skills and competences of democratic citizenship – even if they are not all citizens [81] – if they are going to lead their communities and work across the boundaries of race, class and language to build a more just nation.

What, then, does a college like De Anza do to develop the democratic capacities of its students? What have we learned from our experience? How well are we doing?

Campus culture

De Anza is clear: we care about the development of democratic skills, we offer courses and programmes that engage public issues and bring students into local communities to work, we have staff and faculty dedicated to democratic engagement and we have crafted democratic practices in the operation of the college itself. The Institutional Core Competencies (ICCs) identified by the faculty, and now incorporated into the college mission statement, include awareness of and sensitivity to environmental and social issues, and the college strategic plan cites "community engagement" as one of the college's four principal goals.

These declarations send a broader signal to students and the community that issues of social and political change matter here. This message is reinforced by myriad public events, speakers, films and debates and annual demonstrations. The college leadership is consistent in its messages about the importance of public work and the central role of the college in preparing students for a public life; and the faculty leadership is equally vocal in its support of student engagement.

The college supports a campus culture of engagement and dialogue by a wide range of student clubs and organisations, all of them autonomously developed by students and funded through student government. There is a public and cultural life on campus, even though we have no residence halls – everyone is a commuter. Indeed, many commute long distances past other colleges to attend De Anza, in no small part because of our reputation for engagement. This has included direct

---

81. Many immigrant students may not yet be legal citizens, and several hundred De Anza students do not even have legal documentation establishing their immigration status. Yet these "undocumented" students are among the college's most active and engaged students, often working on immigration reform. When speaking of the skills of citizenship, then, the college seeks to develop these capacities in all students regardless of legal status.

political engagement, as De Anza students have consistently been state leaders in annual mobilisations to support public education. Each year hundreds of our students march in the state capital in support of education. Indeed, it is an anomaly in California that both the leadership and the mass of student activists have often come from among community college students, more so than from university students.

Courses and programmes

De Anza offers multiple course avenues into democratic work through our Institute for Community and Civic Engagement. [82] The college offers community service learning (CSL) courses that assign students work, through non-profit and government agencies, in local communities. These courses are formally designated in the catalogue and schedule, and are noted on student transcripts. [83] The college offers training for faculty members seeking to integrate service-learning methodologies into their classes. Many faculty members also integrate civic issues into courses not officially designated as CSL.

The college offers a certificate programme in Leadership and Social Change, a course sequence that introduces students to the history and methodologies of community organising and leadership. [84] This certificate course is closely tied to our student development work and many of De Anza's elected student government leadership complete the programme. This programme also features in a national coalition of community colleges aiming to develop the next generation of community organisers and community leadership in low-income communities. The Community Learning Partnership [85] has projects in several US cities, and De Anza faculty and staff serve on its national co-ordinating bodies.

There are several other course-based projects that provide both substantive learning and opportunities for public work. APALI (Asian Pacific American Leadership Institute) has a long history of summer courses and year-long projects aiming to develop leadership capacity. APALI also sponsors a joint Asian/Latino leadership series for elected and community leaders who come together at the college to discuss common issues and problems. [86]

LEAD (Latina/o Empowerment At De Anza) is a course sequence that introduces students to Latino and Mexican-American history and literature as well as providing service and work opportunities in local migrant farm-worker communities.

---

82. For the institute, visit www.deanza.edu/communityengagement.
83. For community service learning, see http://deanza.edu/communityengagement/csl.html.
84. For details of the certificate, see www.deanza.edu/communityengagement/LeadershipandSocial-Change.html.
85. See www.communitylearningpartnership.org.
86. Silicon Valley APALI, www.svapali.org.

Students enrolled in LEAD courses are expected to participate in public projects, and each class (of 30 or 40) is organised in 10-student *familias*, each of which takes on projects of their own. Each member also assumes responsibility for the participation and attendance of all other *familia* members, thus creating a powerful community. LEAD has provided critical public leadership on immigration, among other key issues, sponsoring public dialogues and staff training on documentation and deportation issues. These courses now enrol more than 450 students each year, Latinos and non-Latinos, in a model of cross-cultural dialogue and action.[87]

The college also offers degree coursework in speech/communication, in which students learn both rhetoric and facilitation. It is quite common for public gatherings at the college to have student facilitators who manage debate, lead discussion groups and learn the dynamics of public discussion on tough issues.

Beyond coursework, the college has institutionalised programmes that sponsor and provide training for student democratic action and faculty development. This includes the Institute for Community and Civic Engagement, which sponsors public events, co-ordinates the service learning programme, works co-operatively with the college Office of Staff and Organisational Development to provide faculty and staff training, and liaises with state and national networks. The college's Office of Equity, Social Justice and Multicultural Education (previously the Diversity Office), in addition to collaborating on staff training, sponsors public events on issues of diversity and community.[88] Finally, the college has an academic division –Intercultural and International Studies – devoted to ethnic studies programmes and international or world languages. The college teaches 13 world languages, including Spanish, Mandarin, Vietnamese, French, Arabic, Russian, Urdu and Farsi, and co-sponsors public programmes on issues of race, ethnicity, language and culture.

Student life

The college is committed to the idea that student leadership develops when there is autonomous student action, and the space and time to organise it. The college has staff who support student clubs and student government, with "support" being the operative word. These staff do not lead. Students themselves define the purpose and parameters of their own organisations and manage their work. Student government at De Anza has an annual budget of more than 1 million US dollars, entirely generated from self-imposed student fees and entrepreneurial activities. The student senate is elected under a modified parliamentary system of opposing slates and has a rich history of leadership. Under the recent regime of state budget cuts, students at De Anza have voted three times to tax themselves to support

---

87. LEAD is at www.deanza.edu/communityengagement/LEAD.html.
88. Office of Equity, Social Justice and Multicultural Education, www.deanza.edu/equityoffice.

programmes otherwise at risk. This has included tutoring services, community outreach, the arts and political action.

The students have a deep commitment to environmental sustainability and have worked with the college to ensure that the college – from dining services to grounds and maintenance – operates in a sustainable fashion. The students voted independently to assess a quarterly transit fee on themselves to pay for the Eco Pass, which students can use for unlimited rides on public transit – an environmental boon that has the complementary effect of easing travel to the college for students without a car and/or those who live further away across the valley. More than 6 000 students used the passes in the first year of the programme. De Anza students have worked for years to develop a broad coalition supporting a local biodiversity and wildlife corridor and our Environmental Studies programme insists on public work as an element of students' degree programmes.

All this has been achieved by students who go to classes, work for pay, commute and/or have families. They destroy the stereotype that working-class and low-income students do not have the time to do public work. They report to us that what makes a difference is knowing that the college supports them and honours their achievements and the fact that they are building their own culture of social practice. They actively recruit each generation of leadership; they teach each other; they support each other. They also report that the physical space of the campus matters: De Anza is designed with many small and large free spaces, where students can meet, organise and create. Campus buildings and landscaping are designed with this very interaction in mind.

Our student leadership has now had national impact, appearing in regional and state-wide organising meetings, national conferences and at the White House. They have built their own networks. They keep in touch. They inspire the college. Marlo Alvarado Custodio, Ze-Kun Li, Neesha Tambe, Emily Kinner, Thomasina Russaw, Shaela Ramos – these are just a few among the student leaders who built a public culture for the campus.

Democratising the institution

With all the focus on student engagement, De Anza has also developed its own democratic practice. The college is, on the one hand, institutionally structured in fairly traditional ways: there are faculty, classified professionals, administrators. There is an Academic Senate and a Classified Senate, elected bodies through which the academic faculty and the classified (non-instructional) staff are represented. There are unions and collective bargaining. There is a sister college, a district administrative office, a chancellor and an elected board of trustees. There is a blizzard of state regulations, the overlay of federal law and the standards of accreditation.

All of this is relatively conventional. On the other hand, the college has a history of using its structures and organisations for robust public dialogue and debate. Its shared governance processes are more than words in a manual; they form a structure of involvement and representation through which a democratic practice is developed. Faculty and staff elect their own leaders and seek these leadership positions.

This has been heightened during the last four years of fiscal crisis. The college now deliberates its annual budget through a decentralised representative system in which faculty, staff, administrators and students openly discuss all budget choices, do analyses and comparative reviews of programmes and projects, and make recommendations to the campus-wide representative body, the College Council. Each step of this process generates data, all of it entirely public. An ever-widening world of faculty and staff better understand the budget, its programmatic implications and the often harsh choices forced on us by state reductions.

The result of this process is not uniform consensus, but transparency and knowledge. Each department and programme is brought into dialogue with others and therefore must understand itself as part of the whole and articulate its purpose and outcomes. But there is a deeper result: a campus culture in which debate is encouraged, in which developing the public skills of genuine listening, dialogue and critique are tied to real and significant outcomes for the community.

The Democracy Commitment

De Anza College was among the initial organisers and signatories of The Democracy Commitment, the coalition of American community colleges publicly declaring that the development of democratic capacity among our students is one of our principal goals. The commitment is that every graduate of our colleges will have had an opportunity to participate in public work, to develop civic knowledge and to develop the skills of active citizenship.

What this means varies in each college, according to the setting and context of each. But The Democracy Commitment signals an important development in the landscape of American higher education: that the community colleges will regain their traditional role as democracy's colleges, that we will not be limited by a functionalist language that reduces us to trade schools. Of course it is true that we prepare students for employment, and we are proud of it. Not a single student at De Anza College is confused that they need employable skills and that they will need good work for their futures. But they deserve more: that we help them prepare for a world of political and civic work, not just employment.

But the commitment to democracy is more than a preparation. It involves young people doing the actual work, both on their campus and in their communities. It means having multiple movements, different ideological and political and social perspectives in play all at once. It means robust debate and protected spaces in which difference is encouraged. It means argument and sometimes conflict. But these are expected when the college actually engages real issues right in front of us: the budget, state revenues, educational priorities, immigration, the rights of workers, electoral choices and public policies.

What we have learned

The claims of democratic practice are among many claims in the modern college. The curriculum is rooted in a Germanic tradition of disciplines and driven by the necessity that our courses align with university requirements; the job market deeply affects the choices of our students; a consumer culture dominates popular language and images of success; academic rigour and the search for the truth have their own rhythms; each member of the community balances between private lives and public demands.

In this De Anza is like all colleges and universities: complex, not uniform, dynamic and sometimes contradictory. But we have learned a few things about how to develop a democratic culture on campus.

1. Leadership matters. The faculty and administrative leadership must be clear about their commitment to student engagement and support it.

2. Resources matter. A college or university that cares about both student and faculty/staff engagement must devote staff time, budgets and institutional space to the work. It cannot remain on the margins.

3. Architecture matters. A college or university must devote space to the autonomy of student life, must develop places where students and faculty can gather, deliberate, plan and act.

4. Action matters. A college must support the independent actions of its students. They may work on the environment, immigration, local issues, education itself. Their leadership will vary year-to-year; their strategies will change. But they must know that the college supports this element of their lives.

5. Democratic practice matters. No college or university is free from bureaucracy and hierarchy; all are bound by law and tradition. But all colleges and universities honour the full diversity of opinion and practice among the faculty and have traditions of debate and dialogue. Beyond these elements of collegiate life, we can become far more democratic in our operational practice. We can deepen faculty and student involvement in decision-making, create deliberative bodies in which work is done in public, honour collective bargaining and representative processes.

6. Taking a stand matters. Not everyone in a college or university will agree on matters of public policy or current social life. But that does not mean the college or university is neutral. De Anza has a constitutional commitment to

social equity: we were founded to provide open access to all who seek to attend (the "top 100 per cent"). We are diverse and honour the multiplicity of our communities. We will speak out on issues of education, the budget, state policy. We will scrupulously obey the protocols of non-partisan advocacy but we will not be silent.

7. Coalitions matter. De Anza is one of 1 200 community colleges across the country, every single one of which is tied to universities where our students transfer and every single one of which is in communities where our graduates will work, raise families, vote, provide community leadership. We cannot do democratic work without formal coalitions and agreements between ourselves and local government, community-based non-profits, other colleges and universities.

Conclusions

More than half of the graduates of American comprehensive public state universities are transfer students from community colleges. In California, 55 per cent of the graduates at the 23 campuses of the California State University attended a community college; 28 per cent of all graduates of the eight undergraduate campuses of the University of California come from the community colleges – and 48 per cent of all their graduates in engineering and sciences. These numbers are replicated across the nation.[89] No movement for democratic engagement among American undergraduates can succeed without the community colleges.

This is true not only because of the traditional role played by community colleges – the social mobility provided by a system of open access to higher education – but because of the brutal social demographics of America's current passage. More and more of our people are marginalised, more and more alienated from a political process they cannot trust. Any movement for an American democratic renewal will depend on a much broader swath of Americans having the living experience of democratic practice, in their communities, their workplaces, their schools. This must include our colleges and universities, all of us.

---

89. The American Association of State Colleges and Universities (AASCU) monitors these statistics. See www.aascu.org.

23. Institutional change in a culture of democracy

Edward J. Ray

The challenge

The conference held in Oslo entitled Reimagining Democratic Societies: A New Era of Personal and Social Responsibility? was a remarkable event for me in a number of respects. Much of the formal programme dealt with efforts to introduce curriculum elements in higher education that would better prepare our graduates for greater civic engagement and commitment to democratic policies and practices in societies throughout the world. A good portion of the discussion engaged colleagues from both sides of the Atlantic on how best to instruct other institutions and our students in ways to advance the application of democratic policies and procedures to our various societies. My assessment is that most of us felt that no one could claim the moral high ground. That conversation was frustrating to me because we are each imperfect instruments for good and yet the need to prepare our students for greater civic engagement and a more democratic future is critical – and will not be done, if not by us.

The discussion groups dealt more directly with issues of implementing curriculum changes and here I was struck by the frustration of colleagues from central and eastern Europe and emerging democracies around the world. They did not talk about curriculum reform to promote a civil society, but rather the difficulty of creating a framework for any curricular changes within systems of higher education that are hierarchical, rigid and the legacy of command economies, totalitarian regimes and anti-democratic political systems.

Higher education throughout the world is challenged in its efforts to prepare the next generation of leaders in the face of declining public financial support, distrust of the political leanings of academia and traditional governance structures in higher education that resist all change – both faculty and administrators. The task facing our colleagues in new and emerging democracies seems much more daunting than for those of us from established democracies. Therefore, I want to recount the recent history of my university with respect to processes and policies that can facilitate institutional changes, including curricular changes, with an appreciation for the greater challenges facing many of our colleagues.

Let me begin by noting that our effectiveness in promoting civic engagement and democratisation across societies is not simply a product of the courses we teach, but also the behaviour we model. Because we are engaged in teaching adult students, we easily forget that students learn from what we do as well as what we say. The way we govern our universities and our ability to entertain, accept, implement and hold ourselves accountable for change in our curriculum and other aspects of the business of running our universities sends clear signals to our students about how they should conduct themselves as citizens and leaders of the future.

The challenges facing Oregon State University (OSU) in modelling democratic, collaborative, open and transparent transformational change in our university are common to many universities in the United States and somewhat familiar to colleagues in long-established democracies. But they pale compared to the challenges faced by those in emerging democracies. Hopefully, the practices we have followed to create change in governance, policies and procedures, administrative and support services and the curriculum will be illustrative and encouraging to some and suggestive for colleagues in emerging democracies.

The institution

Oregon State University was established in Corvallis, Oregon, in 1868, as one of the original land-grant universities in the United States under the terms of the Morrill Act of 1862, signed into law by President Abraham Lincoln. [90] At the time of the signing, President Lincoln referred to the land grants as the "people's colleges". When adopted, the Morrill Act was based on the revolutionary idea that higher education should be available to people from ordinary social and economic circumstances and the land-grant universities were instructed to prepare their graduates in liberal studies, the mechanical arts and agriculture so that their communities could prosper. The mandate to serve others is still the fundamental mission of the land-grant universities. Many would argue that the dynamism of the US economy over the past 150 years is directly related to the fact that through public higher education people from ordinary circumstances were given the opportunity to accomplish extraordinary things and their successes energised others to take risks, think big and promote economic development and social progress.

Today, Oregon State University has just under 25 000 students: over 19 000 undergraduates and 4 300 in graduate and professional programmes. Of its 7 300 employees, 4 400 are regular staff and nearly 1 700 are teaching faculty, 1 033 of whom are tenured or tenure-track faculty. Classified staff and graduate students are represented by unions. The university's education and general budget exceeds US$316 million and annual expenditure is over US$800 million.

The changes described below span the entire university and include changes in business practices, academic administrative structures, community culture and the

---

90. These public universities are called land-grant universities because the federal government gave each state a grant of federal land to use and/or sell to start a state university.

curriculum. The facts just cited and the documents and elements of change discussed in the following sections can be found at the following university websites:

- − Strategic Plan: http://oregonstate.edu/leadership/strategic-plan
- − organisational charts: http://oregonstate.edu/admin/aa/ir/org-charts
- − academics and community culture: http://oregonstate.edu/main/academics.

The context

Change began at Oregon State University in 2003, but it had its roots in conversations across campus that included more than 2 000 participants in the previous two years, on the future of the university. In fact, a document entitled "Vision 2007" had been developed in draft form by spring 2003. Public funding was continuing to decline in Oregon as in most states at that time. Fundraising at Oregon State was averaging US$25 to 35 million per year, without much of an organised fundraising effort; annual research grants and contracts expenditures were US$133 million and annual awards totalled US$156 million for 2002/03. In-state tuition had just increased by 10 per cent for the 2003/04 academic year in response to state budget cuts in support of public higher education. [91] A salary freeze was implemented by the state for the next two years and cuts in the university operating budgets were in order.

The draft strategic plan contained many excellent ideas to change and improve the university, but it lacked any vision and primarily called for programme consolidations or elimination, and cuts in services. Moreover, despite the many conversations and extensive individual engagement in the process, no one seemed to own the strategic plan and many claimed they simply could not make sense of it.

The process and product of democratisation of governance

In mid-2003 it became clear that despite the best of intentions the effort to create a blueprint for the future of the university had failed to generate support or enthusiasm; it failed to set a simple and understandable course for the future. Rather than start all over again, we revisited the thousands of comments and suggestions that had been collected over the previous two years and rewrote the strategic plan with five major themes for programme activity and a clear goal to become one of the nation's top ten land-grant universities over the next 20-30 years as measured by rankings such as *U.S. News and World Report*. A draft of the plan was distributed

---

91. In-state tuition is the tuition rate charged to students who are legal residents of the state. Tuition rates for in-state students are often set by the state legislature, and in-state undergraduate enrolment receives funding from the state. Tuition for non-resident students from other states and abroad is often two or three times higher.

across campus for comment during the autumn term of 2003 and a final plan was released in February 2004.

The plan included statements of values and principles, and an honest (in some places, brutal) assessment of the strengths and weaknesses of the university. Specific actions and metrics were identified to be tracked annually over the next five years at which time the strategic plan would be updated. It is worth noting that the strategic plan has always been viewed less as a blueprint for success than as a surface map across time to help us navigate towards our ultimate goal of being a top ten land-grant university. As we learn more about the terrain ahead of us over time and see beyond the initial horizon, the plan is to be adapted to capture opportunities and avoid pitfalls that simply could not be seen when the journey began. The goal of "top ten" is shorthand for aspiring to be excellent in all of our programmes. The land-grant universities were created to serve the educational and economic development needs of the people they serve in their state and nation. The more excellent our programmes are, the more positively and profoundly we will benefit those we serve.

While the adoption of the strategic plan was a good step in participatory governance and community-building, we recognised the need to take additional steps to signal the fact that change would occur through collaborative efforts from that point forward. Consequently, we determined that all financial transactions of the university should be published online so that anyone could review them. This was one of our most significant steps in assuring all of our colleagues that the business of the university would be open and transparent.

During the first five years of executing the strategic plan, the financial challenges facing the university continued as enrolment remained fairly steady. Tuition increases were kept in single digits through state legislative oversight and university efforts to continue to provide students with affordable access to higher education. Efforts to grow our research portfolio and increase philanthropy were dramatically restructured. And, after a brief respite, state budget cuts for higher education continued.

With the help of the OSU Foundation, we built a highly professional and experienced fund-raising team and launched the first university-wide fundraising campaign with a goal of raising US$625 million by June 2011. In 2003 fundraising totalled US$29.3 million. We created an office of research and recruited an experienced research scientist to lead an effort to improve the effectiveness of that office. We created a public–private partnership with INTO, a British firm which specialises in recruiting international students to campuses and providing them with language and other training to prepare them for college. Our aim was to double our international student enrolment over a five-year period and enhance establishment of a diverse and inclusive university community. And, we challenged ourselves to conceptualise how we could restructure the business side of the university to improve services and cut costs.

The creation of an updated strategic plan in 2009 was the next major step in re-organising our business and academic governance structures, and we created an Advisory Council on Budget and Strategic Priorities. While the original strategic plan reflected our determination to make hard choices in how we directed scarce resources, the updated plan provided us with much greater focus for the future. We asked ourselves what are our current or potential areas of excellence in which we could make major contributions to knowledge and provide solutions to problems that would be of increasing importance to human beings over the next 20-30 years. The provost, deans and other academic leaders worked with their colleagues, including the faculty senate, to identify three signature areas, and the arts and sciences to be our common focus for excellence. The three signature areas are: Advancing the Science of Sustainable Earth Ecosystems, Improving Human Health and Wellness, and Promoting Economic Growth and Social Progress. The Advisory Council on Budget and Strategic Priorities developed a series of recommendations to address budget problems, flatten our administrative structure and reduce the scope of our course offerings in alignment with the strategic plan, which were adopted.

Our academic leaders next took a remarkable step. The 11 colleges of the university were clustered into divisions corresponding to the three signature areas, and arts and sciences colleagues throughout the university were encouraged to reinvent the academic structure and curriculum based on conversations among themselves, as well as in and across their respective clusters. Executive deans were identified for the clusters to facilitate conversations, but no new administrative positions were created.

The creation of the academic divisions paralleled a conversation about reorganising the business side of academic programmes through consolidation of such functions as personnel management and fiscal operations that historically had resided within each college, school and department. We then created seven regional campus business centres for both academic and university business activities, with four of them associated with the academic divisions. As a consequence we were able to upgrade and speed up business services for academic programmes and reduce the associated staffing by 35 positions over several years despite an increase of more than 4 000 enrolled students and a budget growth of US$108 million.

Within and across clusters, colleagues considered changes in academic programmes and the curriculum, all of which have now been submitted to the faculty senate for review and recommendation to the president. While this process will continue throughout 2012, if all the proposals advanced by faculty are adopted, the number of colleges, schools and departments in the university will decrease from 63 to 38. Moreover, even though the foundations for all of higher education, the arts and sciences, are often viewed as resistant to change, our own College of Liberal Arts has proposed to combine 13 departments and two programmes into five schools and one programme. One school that has been approved is the School of Public Policy, which includes economics, sociology and political science.

Existing undergraduate degree programmes in the disciplines as well as the Master of Public Policy are being maintained and there is a proposal to add a PhD programme in public policy, which would be unique in the state.

Numerous other combinations are being created and curricular changes will accompany many of them. Our department of fashion and design will transfer to our College of Business and our department of geosciences has shifted to the College of Oceanic and Atmospheric Sciences, now the College of Earth, Oceanic, and Atmospheric Sciences. A newly completed research agenda is guiding the growth of our research portfolio. The realignment of three departments into two schools in the College of Public Health and Human Sciences has positioned the university to seek accreditation for the first school of public health in the state of Oregon. Overall, the magnitude and speed of change in the academic structure of Oregon State University may well be unprecedented in American higher education.

The financial foundations of sustainable change

As noted earlier, it was apparent to us by 2003 that state funding for public higher education would continue to decline over time and that we could not hope to realise our aspirations for Oregon State University unless we grew and diversified our sources of revenue, managed our costs effectively and made tough decisions to reallocate existing resources to where they could have the greatest effect in implementing the strategic plan. With respect to revenue, we have increased our annual research grants and contracts funding from US$156 million in 2002/03 to a high of US$275 million in 2009/10. Licensing revenue from university-developed intellectual property has increased more than 60 per cent in the last three years. The university-wide fundraising campaign, expected to raise US$625 million by the end of June 2011, actually reached US$738 million by that date and US$783 million by the end of 2011. The campaign goal was raised to US$850 million by 2013 and that has been increased again to US$1 billion by 2014. Efforts to increase enrolment, particularly international and non-resident enrolment, have been very successful and overall university enrolment increased from just under 19 000 in 2003 to 25 000 in 2011/12. At the same time, enrolment of US minority students at the university has increased from 13.7 per cent to 18.9 per cent and international student enrolment has nearly doubled. We are working hard to create a just and inclusive campus community because we believe that excellence is achieved through diversity.

Our efforts to plan strategically and engage our entire university campus in considering and implementing changes has produced many worthwhile results. The creation of the regional campus business centres and information system upgrades across the university helped us to contain costs. Using the focus on signature and foundation disciplines established by the updated strategic plan we redirected existing resources to high-enrolment-demand areas and the four focus areas in general. The overall growth in revenue to the university despite continued cuts in state funding allowed us to fund new tenure-track faculty positions in each of the four focus areas in 2011, including 15 positions in arts and sciences and five positions in each of the signature areas. We are funding a total of 50 new tenure-track faculty positions in and across the four focus areas and in high-enrolment-demand programmes for the up-coming academic year. The university's revenue growth, especially through philanthropy and a state programme to match private funds to build academic facilities, has resulted in more than two dozen capital improvement projects valued at more than US$500 million that are either completed or in process.

Conclusions

The formal presentations at the Oslo conference focused primarily on the need for higher education throughout the world to prepare our graduates to be leaders in building a more democratic and civil society in the future. Much of the accompanying conversation dwelled on whether or not any of us can define the curricular changes necessary to achieve that. The informal discussions focused more generally on the difficulty of implementing governance, structural and curricular changes of any kind. We spent little time discussing the curricular changes required to advance the democracy and civil society agenda.

Our own experiences at Oregon State University demonstrate that the adoption of an open, transparent and inclusive process to develop a statement of vision, values and principles drove the creation of new academic and support structures, embraced shared governance and dramatically changed the curriculum. We created a Shared Governance Task Force to provide feedback on the change process we initiated and that group provided a set of 15 recommendations that we adopted to position us for greater success in the future. Civility and democratic methods have been used to great effect to achieve those ends. The Morrill Act of 1862 was a major step in democratising access to higher education in the United States. Community connections were fostered through efforts by the land-grant universities to go to communities throughout their states and ask people what their problems were and how the universities could meet their needs. Given that legacy, we were comfortable going to our colleagues throughout the university and to external stakeholders for creative ideas to reimagine our university. Civil discourse and democratic practices were at the heart of our transformation.

While each of us must be attentive to designing our curriculum to prepare graduates to advance civil discourse and democratic practices as future leaders, we must also recognise that our students are not simply listening to our declarations. They are watching whether or not we actually model change in democratic and civil ways. The approach we took to address the challenge of change at Oregon State

University has made a great difference, contributing to our success. The behaviour we have mode lled promotes civility and democratic change that we hope our students will embrace.

This year our students, through their elected governing organisation, agreed to raise their current activity fees to build a student experience centre to house student activity organisations in the future. In effect, current students are taxing themselves willingly to benefit future generations of students. This is a wonderful example of civic responsibility.

24. The Anchor Institutions Task Force: promoting democratic engagement

David J. Maurrasse

Leaders, residents and policy makers search for strategies to improve conditions in neighbourhoods, cities and metropolitan regions faced by instability and economic insecurity. What have become known as "anchor institutions" remain generally stable – they do not tend to drift away. These enduring entities are rooted in their surroundings, and are usually among the most significant local employers and purchasers. They maintain substantial landholdings and services, and bring knowledge and human capital. Universities and hospitals are among the more visible anchor institutions. However, many other organisations, from corporations and museums to convention centres, libraries and churches, can be local sources of stability.

Recognition of the significance of anchor institutions has increased in the face of persistent socioeconomic challenges in neighbourhoods, cities and metropolitan regions – but increased awareness is only the beginning. The potential to harness enduring local institutions to transform communities has simply not been fully tapped. In a number of cases, institutional partnerships have combined with local stakeholders to address critical common concerns. [92] There is still much to learn about the best ways to leverage resources to improve communities through genuine collaboration. The University of Pennsylvania's experience shows the depth of thinking and effort required in forging local partnerships (Netter Center 2008).

The Anchor Institutions Task Force (AITF) [93] was created in this context. The AITF emerged in 2010 on the heels of a collaborative writing project. Dr Ira Harkavy of the University of Pennsylvania was asked to assemble a team to compose a chapter on anchor institutions in a report for the United States Department of Housing and Urban Development, *Retooling HUD* (Harkavy et al. 2009). The team comprised distinguished academics, university presidents and leading practitioners, and it identified the need for an ongoing association. The new effort would bring together those who have been directly leveraging the resources of anchor institutions to solve local problems to strengthen the effectiveness of local partnerships. Additionally, this group would constitute a collective voice that could influence policy makers.

---

92. The University of Pennsylvania is well known for having transformed its role as an anchor institution to work with others on issues facing the community. The Cleveland Clinic is an example of a hospital engaging locally.

93. More information on the Anchor Institutions Task Force online at www.margainc.com/initiatives/aitf/.

The AITF is driven by the need to improve the ways in which anchor institutions engage in their localities, and is guided by four core values: collaboration and partnership; equity and social justice; democracy and democratic practice; and commitment to place and community. By creating a space in which various leaders and relevant partners can coalesce around these values, the AITF can shape the kinds of practices that can truly improve communities.

The rationale for the AITF

A commitment to place is one of the core values of the Anchor Institutions Task Force. Anchor institutions are enduring in their local neighbourhoods, municipalities and regions. It is easier for anchor institutions to remain where they are based than go elsewhere. The health and well-being of these locally-grounded entities and their surroundings are interdependent. They are economic engines, providing jobs and bringing human, knowledge, social, cultural and physical capital as well. As the nature of local communities evolves and shifts, these institutions are consistent, stable sources of existing resources but also beacons of innovation and opportunity. With challenges confronting local communities, such as high unemployment and vast educational or health disparities, it is hard to imagine progress without their active engagement.

The AITF shares strategies among its growing membership, to improve communities and refine a common advocacy voice to influence policy and funding. It is important to work on both of these levels, given the need to improve how anchor institutions engage in their communities through peer exchange and raise awareness among policy makers about the valuable emerging strategies to address critical social and economic problems.

Local partnerships take many forms, even just among higher education partnerships. One subset of this diverse field addresses the civic purpose of higher education, emphasising the benefits of student voluntarism, service learning and democratic participation. Another highlights the economic impact of colleges and universities. Yet other critical categories are the involvement of higher education in schools and community health. Furthermore, higher education is quite diverse, ranging from community colleges and small private colleges to major research universities and public universities. The leading role that higher education has played in forging a movement based on long-standing commitment to place is at the foundation of the AITF, which is building from this strength.

The AITF is structured to encompass colleges and universities of all types, as well as many other anchors, from hospitals to convention centres to museums to sports franchises, and so on. Institutions of higher education are natural anchors because they tend to stay where they are. Their vast local investments ground universities and colleges almost uniquely. In the case of some other types of enduring entity, circumstances determine the degree of local commitment. Corporate locations shift rapidly in the constant pursuit of lower overheads, but some corporations remain and act as anchors.

Components of the AITF

AITF structure

The University of Pennsylvania continues to be intimately involved in advancing the AITF's comprehensive agenda. The AITF is co-ordinated by Marga Incorporated, a consulting firm providing strategic advice and research to philanthropic initiatives and community partnerships, in collaboration with the Netter Center for Community Partnerships. [94]

The AITF is governed by a Steering Committee, chaired by Dr Ira Harkavy, Director of the Netter Center at the University of Pennsylvania. Steering Committee members include Genie Birch of the University of Pennsylvania; Nancy Cantor, President of Syracuse University; Henry Cisneros, Executive Chairman of CityView and former Secretary of the US Department of Housing and Urban Development; David Cox of the University of Memphis; Richard Guarasci, President of Wagner College; Jim Harris, President of Widener University; Eduardo Padrón, President of Miami Dade College; David Perry of the University of Illinois at Chicago; Beverly Tatum, President of Spelman College; Henry Taylor of the University at Buffalo; and Nancy Zimpher, President of State University of New York.

The AITF also includes two core standing committees – Policy and Research. A Media Committee was recently created to connect a communications strategy to emerging policy and research approaches. The AITF initiated a new emphasis on the civic mission of schools in collaboration with the Campaign for the Civic Mission of Schools (CCMS). Since one of the most prevalent and significant ways in which anchors engage in communities is through partnerships with primary and secondary schools, it is important to develop programming in this area. Thematic opportunities are catalysed through events. The civic mission of schools was the AITF's 2011 conference theme. A subgroup emerged at the conference that agreed to continue refining the AITF's partnership with CCMS. Healthy communities and local economic development are two other thematic areas in development.

Membership

The Anchor Institutions Task Force is an individual membership organisation with about 170 members. The growth of this membership has been steady; by the end of 2012, membership is likely to exceed 200. While the long-term vision is to reflect the range of types of anchor and the different manifestations of partnership, current membership reflects the tremendous energy in higher education around local engagement. As it stands, the composition of this membership is unprecedented, reflecting the diversity of public and private colleges and universities,

---

94. For the Netter Center for Community Partnerships, see www.upenn.edu/ccp/index.php.

with significant community college participation. Those individuals committed to the AITF's values may join. This structure, individual versus institutional membership, has been appealing to numerous university presidents, among others. Barriers to joining are minimal, as the AITF does not charge dues.

Overall, this membership approach unites individual leaders representing varying environments, engaged in different types of anchor partnerships, in one association with a common belief in the potential of anchors to transform communities. Individual (versus institutional) membership was the chosen path to enable those believing in the values to join. Entire institutions may or may not support the values. Consequently, an individual interest in joining cannot be hindered by institutional constraints.

Publications and research

Advances in research and publication are already evident. The AITF's Research Committee has been editing an issue of the *Journal of Higher Education Outreach and Engagement*. This issue,[95] devoted to anchor institutions, is to include several articles by members. These articles, many of which are authored by university presidents, provide first-person accounts of local institutional partnerships in action.

The AITF, via the University at Buffalo, is conducting an extensive literature review of recent writing on anchor institutions, which will include recommendations for future research. Initiated in late 2011, this process has already identified over 200 publications. Overall, the research agenda will continue to identify promising practices to enhance the quality of the engagement of anchors in localities. The literature review will help the AITF continue to become a central clearing house for information on this topic.

Field engagement and policy

As the AITF is open to various representatives across a diverse field, it complements a range of associations. The Coalition of Urban and Metropolitan Universities (CUMU), the Coalition of Urban Serving Universities (CUSU), the Association of Public and Land-grant Universities (APLU), and other associations addressing the role of anchor institutions, have collaborated from the beginning. The AITF, realising that the dynamics of anchor institutions in broader societies have global implications, was well represented at the June 2011 conference in Oslo

---

95. This issue does not yet have a title or volume number, but should be published in 2013, edited by David Perry of the University of Illinois at Chicago, Henry Taylor of the University at Buffalo and Genie Birch of the University of Pennsylvania.

on Reimagining Democratic Societies, co-sponsored by the Council of Europe, the International Association of Universities, the International Consortium for Higher Education, Civic Responsibility and Democracy, the University of Oslo and Norwegian governmental authorities.

The AITF has collaborated with the Association of American Colleges and Universities (AAC&U) around an important new effort sponsored by the US Department of Higher Education designed to strengthen the civic role of higher education. This effort, the Civic Learning and Democratic Engagement Project, along with the American Commonwealth Project, is instrumental in facilitating high-level dialogue in the Federal Administration.

The AITF's policy strategy must be collaborative in order to be effective. Additionally, the AITF will engage various other associations of anchors representing different government agencies. The idea of harnessing the assets of anchor institutions to transform communities is not specific to one federal agency. In fact, just about all federal agencies could benefit from an anchor institutions strategy. At this point, the AITF will continue to be engaged in important policy discussions at the Department of Housing and Urban Development and the Department of Education. But the AITF must engage other federal agencies, like the Department of Labor, Health and Human Services and the Department of Commerce. State and municipal policy will become an important future emphasis as well.

Communications

The AITF has been building its communications infrastructure. Its website, an important mode of communication with members, will undergo continuous enhancement, particularly to improve learning exchange between members. The formation of the media committee was partly informed by the AITF's experiences with the *Chronicle of Higher Education.* This periodical published an article criticising Syracuse University's local partnership (Wilson 2011). The *Chronicle* published AITF's response to this article, which highlighted the value of community partnerships to the mission of higher education. Ongoing media strategies will include developing a database of relevant media outlets and placing Op Eds.[96]

Philanthropic engagement

Given that private philanthropy has invested in strategies to strengthen local communities, it is important to align the collective effort of philanthropy and that of anchor institutions. The AITF represents a space in which philanthropic institutions

---

96. Signed articles in newspapers, opposite the editorial page.

and the membership can plan and co-ordinate strategies. Membership is open to foundation representatives.

The AITF was launched without collecting membership dues or conference registration fees, because of grants from private philanthropy. The Annie E. Casey Foundation, the Surdna Foundation and the Carnegie Corporation provided initial philanthropic support. The incentive to join is only greater without dues and fees. With reduced barriers to joining, those who believe in the AITF's values have become involved.

Events

Events have been critical to building the membership. The AITF's first conference in 2010 generally addressed the progress, challenges and potential of the public engagement of anchor institutions. This initial attempt to convene the field truly illustrated the appetite for information and collegiality around these matters. Originally designed for 30 participants, this first event drew over 70. The 2011 conference attracted almost 100 participants.

The AITF is considering a mini-conference on economic development. In accordance with the AITF's overall approach, this event would provide a space in which representatives of anchor institutions engaged in local economic development, practitioners in the field partnering with anchor institutions on issues such as purchasing and workforce development, and funders of economic development activities could collaboratively share ideas and practices. The role of anchor institutions in reducing health disparities is another important theme under consideration.

Analysis, challenges, conclusions

Creating an association in a burgeoning, somewhat undefined, field is compelling and challenging. The rationale for the AITF is based on future opportunity, grounded in the belief that many of today's most pressing social challenges can be effectively addressed when anchor institutions are engaged. It is based on the idea that localities will be healthier, better educated and more economically stable when anchor institutions are leveraged to participate more directly in their neighbourhoods, cities and regions. The basis for the AITF suggests that localities will not advance to their highest potential unless anchor institutions are adequately involved as partners with local governments, schools and civil society.

Many examples of anchor partnerships demonstrate the potential to live up to these ideals. However, in reality, so much has not yet been pursued or accomplished. Many anchor partnerships represent the involvement of individuals in institutions, not necessarily the overall commitment of institutions. True institutional commitment to being engaged locally requires buy-in from leadership and a range of constituents. In this internal alignment, local democratic engagement is a priority – an extension of the core mission (Maurasse 2001).

Institutions of higher education are naturally rooted locally. The AITF's membership reflects this, as over 90 per cent of members represent some segment of higher education. The AITF is organising the "champions" – those who already believe that anchor institutions should be engaged in local problem-solving. Those who originally came to the table mostly represent higher education. But the AITF hopes to reflect the broader range of anchor institutions. In reality, associations often do not bring people together across industries. That the AITF has brought public and private universities under the same tent is a monumental accomplishment in itself.

Challenges

The AITF's programming will have to attract representatives from other sectors. Events addressing health could help bring hospitals to the table. Content addressing issues of universal interest to anchors, such as how to hire and purchase locally, could bring others to the table. Moreover, to achieve global relevance, expanded international communication is required. The AITF should strengthen dialogue with its membership's counterparts in various countries. The need to leverage stable resources in insecure environments is not only a consideration for the US. Universities, for example, are anchor institutions in Europe and various parts of the world.

In the developing world, and in some extremely impoverished rural environments, anchor institutions (as defined in the AITF's context) are generally not present. However, all nations include local assets. There is not one panacea to meeting the most pressing needs in local, especially vulnerable, communities. However, the approach to creatively seeking solutions by leveraging existing resources is useful across borders. Policy makers, NGOs, donors, international agencies and others are all challenged to build from institutions and their capital in addressing pressing concerns. The AITF can be a voice with resonance in myriad global contexts. Practically, this will mean greater international engagement, and ultimately a membership reflecting greater global diversity.

Around the world, cross-sector partnerships, which combine the resources and expertise of representatives of the public, private and non-governmental sectors, reflect the spirit of the AITF's intentions. These efforts tend to broaden the range of resources that can be tapped in order to address pressing social matters.[97] For example, the UK's Strategic Partnerships encouraged and funded local collaborative

---

97. The forthcoming book by David Maurrasse, *Strategic Public–Private Partnerships: innovation and development* (Cheltenham: Edward Elgar, 2013), captures a range of examples of cross-sector partnerships in the US, UK, Europe, Africa, Asia and Latin America that join government, business, anchor institutions and non-governmental organisations in collective problem-solving around matters ranging from economic development to global health concerns, hunger, the environment and others.

initiatives across the United Kingdom in areas with substantial vulnerable populations. These efforts helped local governments engage business, institutions of higher education, medical centres, non-governmental organisations and others to design comprehensive strategic plans to address priority needs.

In general, the idea that multiple sectors and industries must collaborate to meet contemporary complex needs is a global trend. In many rapidly emerging economies, such as China's, industrial clusters that link business and universities have been critical to the substantial expansion of cities and the growth of their local economies. Higher education is essential to developing industries and stimulating employment globally. The need to tap anchor institutions in this respect is internationally relevant. The development of a new government in South Africa, for example, routinely relied upon engagement across government, business, higher education and non-governmental organisations. And the globalisation of many US universities, establishing sites in the Middle East and elsewhere, is helping to create new anchors that facilitate local development as well as democratic thinking. And the future of relatively devastated nations, such as Haiti, can substantially improve with stronger anchor institutions.

The AITF can add value in all of these contexts, because no one has perfected a universal way to leverage local institutions and create the processes that can maximise the combination of resources in new partnerships. We expect the AITF's efforts to become increasingly instructive to nations hoping to build, strengthen and/or harness anchor institutions. This value will become clearer when the AITF expands its membership in different nations and disseminates its learning widely.

Overall, the AITF has created a unique structure, flexible enough to bring a range of leaders to one table to define a transformative agenda. Its approach is an organising model reminiscent of a movement, as it convenes those who are already convinced to collectively encourage change. Sustainability will be a long-term challenge for the AITF, as it relies on substantial volunteer time and modest philanthropic support. However, if enough constituents recognise the AITF's significance, sustainability will not be a problem. Anchor institutions simply have not been harnessed enough in meeting public needs. Once enough policy makers arrive at the same conclusion, the AITF should be at the centre of a major shift in approaches to addressing persistent social and economic challenges.

Conclusions

First of all, anchor institutions can be an important means to many ends. Whether the goal is to improve literacy, strengthen schools, enhance economic opportunity, reduce health disparities, clean up air quality or beyond, anchor institutions – especially universities – can play a valuable role. Policy makers would be wise to strategically integrate these entities into their overall efforts. This is not exclusive to any particular issue; it is true across the board.

Secondly, much work is required to improve the way anchor institutions currently engage in communities. Many previous attempts have failed or faced numerous obstacles. Indeed, some places have not converted to the idea because of their unpleasant experiences in relying on anchors to meet local needs. Some of the sceptics are justifiably wary. Acknowledging the work to be done to improve practice can turn the corner towards improved implementation of anchor partnerships.

The AITF is critical in both of these areas. It is poised to co-ordinate the common voice that can encourage policy makers to incorporate anchor institutions into their strategies. Additionally, it can improve practice through refining knowledge on what it takes to create and maintain effective anchor partnerships.

References

Harkavy I. et al. (2009), "Anchor Institutions as partners in building communities and local economies" in *Retooling HUD for a Catalytic Federal Government: a report to secretary Shaun Donovan, project directors, Paul Brophy and Rachel Godsil*, Philadelphia: Penn Institute for Urban Research and Rockefeller Foundation, pp. 147-68.

Maurrasse D. (2001), *Beyond the campus: how colleges and universities form partnerships with their communities*, New York: Routledge.

Netter Center for Community Partnerships (2008), *Anchor Institutions Toolkit: a guide for neighborhood revitalization*, Philadelphia: Netter Center for Community Partnerships at the University of Pennsylvania.

Wilson R. (2011), "Syracuse's slide: as chancellor focuses on the 'public good', Syracuse's reputation slides", *Chronicle of Higher Education* (2 October).

25. Student–community engagement at Queen's University, Belfast

Tony Gallagher

Throughout its long history, a commitment to Northern Ireland has been part of the DNA of Queen's University. In recent times Queen's has been a key centre of discussion and debate throughout the Northern Ireland conflict and an important centre for engagement and debate in the ongoing conflict-transformation process. During the period of violence in Northern Ireland from the late 1960s to the 1990s, Queen's was a space in which debate and dialogue around possible solutions and ways forward could take place. The university was actively engaged in reaching out to its various communities (political and civil society) to draw them into these debates. A constitutional settlement for Northern Ireland was reached through negotiation in 1998 and is enshrined in the Belfast Agreement of that year.

Queen's researchers were then, and are now, involved in public and private, community and policy-driven debate and discussion of important policy initiatives, including the transformation of policing and prisons in Northern Ireland, the enhancement of equality legislation and the development of a "good relations" dimension to public policy generally (see, for example, Dickson 2010; Guelke 2010, McEvoy and Shirlow 2008; O'Dowd and Coakley 2010; Taylor 2011; Wilford and Wilson 2006; Wilson 2010; Wispeleare, McBride and O'Neill 2007).

History

Queen's University Belfast (QUB) was founded in 1845 as part of a federal system of Queen's Colleges across Ireland. The main barrier to educational advance at the time on the island was that the religion established by law was not that followed by the majority of its people (Moody and Beckett 1959). In the National School system this was addressed by setting religious instruction apart from the normal school day (Akenson 1970). A similar approach was taken in the Queen's Colleges, which were not allowed to operate religious tests on entry or provide a Faculty of Theology. Queen's University Belfast became an independent degree-awarding body in its own right in 1908 and currently has over 17 500 students (full-time equivalent) and 3 600 staff. Belfast is the main urban centre in Northern Ireland, a region with a population of approximately 1.5 million. Although the number of students attending Queen's from outside Northern Ireland has risen in recent years, it still draws the vast majority of its students from its local region, and many of its alumni play key roles in the social, cultural, political and business life of the region.

Civic and social engagement

The university has a strong record in public engagement, which was embodied in the first Queen's in the Community Strategy developed in 2002. This strategy was designed to support the work of staff within the university's administrative structures, particularly arts and culture, personnel and the university's Science Shop,[98] who have significant outreach responsibilities and act as valuable contacts for collaborative research between QUB students and organisations in the community. The breadth of the Science Shop's engagement with the statutory, voluntary and community sectors in Northern Ireland makes its role a vital and important building block for development.

The Science Shop offers students across the university an opportunity to work with a wide range of community organisations through the curriculum and enables students to apply their skills and experience to issues identified by civil society organisations as important. This exposure to real-life issues can both motivate and educate students. Understanding the problems facing disadvantaged groups in our society in an applied context often has a maturing effect on students and helps to inform the development of their own world view. It also helps them to make an informed decision about whether they are interested in a career in research – for some it clarifies that this is not their goal, while for others it inspires them. This model is seen as a way of both satisfying the demands of students and community groups and demonstrating the wider social value of higher education to political leaders.

Since its establishment, the Queen's Science Shop has worked with 650 community groups. Queen's students complete over 60 projects each year for these organisations, involving more than 150 students. The demand for this work continues to increase with over 100 new projects being submitted by community and voluntary organisations each year. The Science Shop has continued to develop from being a resource principally for social science students to involving students across a range of disciplines. In particular, a strong partnership with the School of Management has emerged, partly in response to increased demand from social economy agencies in the non-profit/community sector.

There are other forms of engagement, particularly with schools, many of which provide opportunities for students. Queen's runs access programmes aimed at schools that traditionally have not sent students to higher education. These programmes are underpinned by a range of outreach activities aimed at raising aspirations among young people. Among these are Medics in Primary Schools,[99] an accredited module which places medical students in primary schools on a weekly

---

98. See www.qub.ac.uk/sites/ScienceShop/ (accessed 14 February 2012).
99. See www.qub.ac.uk/home/QueensintheCommunity/OutreachDirectory/ProjectDetails/?proj_cd= MEDIPS (accessed on 14 February 2012).

basis in order to raise health and lifestyle issues with pupils; Soundlive[100] is a project in collaboration with the Princes Trust, and involves 35 young people, enhancing their social and employability skills, while highlighting the merits of higher education. Participating youths are taken on a week-long residential where mentors and musical tutors bring them on a journey of musical and personal development. They then showcase this at a celebration concert in the Whitla Hall, Queen's University.

Queen's Film Theatre[101] (QFT) is the only dedicated art-house cinema in Northern Ireland (NI) and a wide range of screenings and associated events have been developed in association with university departments and many external organisations, such as Northern Ireland Screen Education, Film Education, the Cinemagic International Film and Television Festival, AGE NI and the Polish Association NI. QFT has also delivered an award-winning community-outreach project in partnership with Belfast City and the Community Relations Council entitled "Bridging the Divide", which delivered film projects for young people in partnership with local community groups living in interface areas, that is, areas often marked by violence because they represent demarcation lines between rival communities.

The Naughton Gallery[102] at Queen's has an ongoing engagement programme for schools and community groups across Northern Ireland, enabling over 3 000 participants of all ages and abilities to work with professional artists and curators each year. Over 15 000 visitors come to Queen's via this gallery each year and an outreach project has accompanied each of the 20 exhibitions organised since 2006, among them Mechanical Doodles: Art and Technology in Motion, where the gallery joined with the School of Mechanical and Aerospace Engineering at Queen's and students from 15 schools across Northern Ireland, which each created their own kinetic sculpture or mechanical doodle. Supported by the Equality Commission for Northern Ireland, the Community Alphabets project was created with schools and communities across the region. Each letter illustrates something that is unique, peculiar or important to each of the groups, identifying local stories, revealing touchstones and talismans in the landscape, exploring shared emotions and illuminating hidden histories. The groups debated and discussed their individual and shared experiences in collaboration with their assigned artist and came to a consensus on the objects and experiences that best defined their community.

Some of this activity is reflected in the online Community Directory.[103] This holds details of almost 400 outreach projects across the university and provides a basis for the community-outreach element in the promotion criteria for academic

100. See www.qub.ac.uk/home/QueensintheCommunity/OutreachDirectory/ProjectDetails/index.html? proj_cd=SOUNDL (accessed on 14 February 2012).

101. www.queensfilmtheatre.com/ (accessed on 14 February 2012).

102. See www.naughtongallery.org/ (accessed on 14 February 2012).

103. See www.qub.ac.uk/home/QueensintheCommunity/OutreachDirectory/ (accessed on 14 February 2012).

staff. The Queen's Community Network, co-ordinated by Science Shop staff, brings together staff with responsibilities for community outreach, to ensure a joined-up approach to this work. Over 50 staff across the university are more directly involved in a range of activities under the Queen's in the Community banner, including academic-related staff whose primary responsibilities lie in this area, as well as academic staff involved both through their own work and through supporting and encouraging students to engage with community needs and issues.

Promoting the civic engagement of students

The Students' Union [104] is the representative body for students at Queen's. It is led by seven elected sabbatical officers [105] who are accountable to a 100-strong Student Council, elected from across the faculties and schools of the university. Students can participate in over 170 clubs and societies. One of the most successful societies in recent years has been the Queen's Chapter of SIFE [106] (Students in Free Enterprise). SIFE is a global non-profit organisation, active in 42 countries, in which student teams work together with university and business advisers to develop projects that focus on teaching others the skills needed to bring economic opportunity to all. The Queen's SIFE team was established in 2008. Led by Lisa Collins, former SIFE chairperson and founder of Share Uganda, Queen's SIFE won awards as UK Rookie Champions of the Year and QUB New Society of the Year. The following year they developed a broader portfolio of projects to include Share Uganda, Ethical-Me, Money+ and Musical Fusion. They competed at the UK national competition at Canary Wharf and won Best Ethics Project as well as QUB Society of the Year and QUB Community Contribution Award.

Examples of the projects run by Queen's SIFE include:

- Rebycle, a project that generates funds by finding old, broken and unwanted bicycles locally. SIFE has a team who repair the bikes and a final design team who give the bikes a unique re-spray. They team up with some unemployed people from Belfast and train them in practical work experience and skills. The refurbished, custom-designed bikes are then resold at a very reasonable price around Queen's.

- Musical Fusion is a cross-community project that brings together young people from both sides of the community in Northern Ireland and helps them gain an insight into working in the music industry. The young people form

---

104. See www.qubsu.org/ (accessed on 14 February 2012).
105. The sabbatical officers take a year off their studies to work full-time as Students' Union officials and receive a grant to cover their living costs.
106. www.qub.ac.uk/sites/sife/ (accessed on 14 February 2012).

bands, are given music coaching, attend song-writing classes and then compose, write and record their own songs. They are also given an insight into the music industry by professionals, and learn about products, sales and marketing so they can sell their CDs. Finally the bands give public performances in a battle of the bands.

- Share Uganda works to provide a Ugandan community with a sustainable income by providing women with the tools to start their own pig-farming businesses. Ugandan children are given scholarships and linked directly with primary schools in Northern Ireland. SIFE fundraises in Queen's and the University of Nottingham to build schools and medical centres. A group of students go to Uganda each year to develop the project, paying for their own flights, visas and medical expenses.

- Money+ is a student-led project that aims to help students in higher education become financially competent, encouraging them to confront debt and take control of their finances before they get into difficulties. The project provides practical financial skills to students as they embark on university life, allowing for a more enjoyable university experience and increased financial confidence, which is carried forward beyond graduation. Money+ also takes its work out to post-primary schools throughout Northern Ireland in order to give 16- to 18-year-olds an insight into university life and advice on managing money on a student budget.

In recent years the Students' Union has also welcomed a variety of NGOs, giving them an opportunity to recruit student volunteers, but this was taken to a new level by current Vice President, Community, Aidan Hughes, who wanted to facilitate more student-led community volunteering. Having brought together students who were interested in a volunteering role, he organised discussion groups on potential areas of work and allowed the students to vote on the activities they wanted to support. Up to 149 students are now involved in these projects, which include:

- working with the elderly in nursing homes and residential areas in the university area;

- working with families who have come to visit family members in prison and helping build up a support network: they particularly want to understand problems and concerns felt by families and plan to bring these to the attention of the Minister for Justice;

- developing a student-led project working with homeless people, which will involve helping create homeless football teams across Belfast, and encouraging and aiding participation in the homeless world cup.

In addition, the Students' Union is establishing and staffing an after-school homework club for local schoolchildren, and a range of clubs in the Union raise significant amounts of money for various charities each year.

The Education Strategy for the University (Queen's University 2011) includes a commitment to support active citizenship among our students. The formal statements in the policy include the following:

> The University's graduates should emerge as informed, active, responsible global citizens, sensitive to issues of social justice, sustainability and cultural diversity. They should also have an appreciation of the implications of globalisation for their lifetime's employment. The emphasis on globalisation subsumes the University's support for both the implementation of the Bologna Process and the achievement of the aims of the European Higher Education Area (EHEA); the aims include facilitating the mobility of students and graduates, and preparing them for their future careers and for life as active citizens in democratic societies.

The strategy's vision for the curriculum commits the university to:

> develop curricula which promote and value diverse international perspectives and prepare students to become informed, active, responsible global citizens, sensitive to issues of social justice, sustainability and cultural diversity.

The intention is to build on the decade of work already established in Queen's and to gain further synergies through collaboration with the Students' Union, to promote greater civic awareness among students and challenge any sense of insularity that may arise from living in a society that is still largely inward-looking. In 2008 the university established Degree Plus [107] as a means of providing official recognition of extra-curricular activities and achievements. The initial impetus behind Degree Plus was to enhance the employability of graduates, and the range of activities supported includes many aspects of volunteering, activities in the community and representative roles undertaken by students.

Challenges

Clearly there are significant economic challenges facing most countries. In many places this has led to budget cuts and increases in the personal cost of higher education. Youth unemployment generally is rising, and there is evidence that many young graduates are finding increased difficulties in achieving employment commensurate with their qualifications. In such a context it is entirely understandable that students ask about the worth of their university experience and their employment prospects. It is equally understandable why universities feel it appropriate to enhance the employability of students by increasing their engagement with employers, ensuring their curricula align with the requirements of the marketplace and providing experience of the wider set of attributes and experiences that will help graduates get good-quality jobs when they complete their studies.

In such a context, however, it is important not to lose sight of the wider purpose of higher education. It is about providing individuals with the qualifications, skills and

---

107. See www.qub.ac.uk/directorates/degreeplus/Whatsitallabout/#d.en.179359 (accessed 14 February 2012).

attributes that will allow them to gain meaningful and worthwhile employment, but it is also about the development of the whole person. In particular, higher education should produce graduates with a sense of the wider social responsibility they will carry not only as citizens but, in large part, as leaders in society. Throughout its history, Queen's University has played a key role in its city and region, and it has educated many of the leaders of business, politics, culture and the arts, and communities. A decade ago this was acknowledged in a community-outreach strategy that tried to underpin and encourage public engagement by staff and students. Since then, this work and contribution has evolved and developed in a range of different ways, evidenced notably in work supported by the Students' Union. With the establishment of a new Education Strategy for the period 2011-16, we are attempting to underpin and extend this work still further and add to the quality of the graduates who will go on to lead our society.

References

Akenson D. H. (1970), *The Irish education experiment: the national system of education in the nineteenth century*, London: Routledge & Kegan Paul.

Dickson B. (2010), *The European Convention on Human Rights and the conflict in Northern Ireland*, Oxford: Oxford University Press.

Guelke A. (ed.) (2010), *The challenges of ethno-nationalism: case studies in identity politics*, London: Palgrave Macmillan.

McEvoy K. and Shirlow P. (2008), *Beyond the wire: ex-prisoners and conflict transformation in Northern Ireland*, London: Pluto.

Moody T. W. and Beckett J. C. (1959), *Queen's Belfast, 1845-1949: the history of a university*, London: Faber & Faber.

O'Dowd L. and Coakley J. (eds) (2010), *Crossing the border: new relationships between Northern Ireland and the Republic of Ireland*, Dublin: Irish Academic Press.

Queen's University (2011), *Education strategy, 2011-2016*, Belfast: Queen's University.

Taylor R. (ed.) (2011), *Consociational theory: McGarry and O'Leary and the Northern Ireland conflict*, Routledge Research in Comparative Politics, London: Routledge.

Wilford R. and Wilson R. (2006), *The trouble with Northern Ireland: the Belfast Agreement and democratic governance*, Dublin: New Island Books.

Wilson R. (2010), *The Northern Ireland experience of conflict and agreement: a model for export?* Manchester: Manchester University Press.

Wispeleare J. de, McBride C. and O'Neill S. (eds) (2007), "Recognition, equality and democracy: normative perspectives on Irish politics", *Irish Political Studies* (special issue).

Ways forward

26. Reimagining democratic societies: personal reflections on a multi-faceted debate

Gwen Dungy

As higher education leaders and representatives of public authorities from the United States and Europe and participants from other parts of the world, as well as NGOs, met for the global forum on Reimagining Democratic Societies: A New Era of Personal and Social Responsibility? in June 2011 in Oslo, it became clear to me that some very fundamental assumptions would have to be examined. I applaud the forum planners for their sensitivity to the history of "democracy" throughout the world by using the term "reimagining", suggesting that there is an opportunity for a collective, contemporary vision of democracy, rather than language implying the notion of "reclaiming", "reviving" or "restoring" a previous legacy that had been allowed to wither (Musil 2011: 247).

The conference was part of the co-operation between partners committed to promoting democracy, human rights and the rule of law, as well as intercultural dialogue to promote social harmony and justice. Participants held a shared belief that education plays a key role in furthering these goals. Through discussion and careful consideration, participants were challenged as to whether all of these goals were even necessarily congruent. As a participant, I took notes on the panellists' presentations and I attempted to take notes verbatim of the comments and questions from participants following the presentations. Caryn McTighe Musil, senior vice-president at the Association of American Colleges and Universities, also took notes throughout the conference, which she graciously shared with me.

Together, these notes provide a sense of the robust exchanges that took place throughout the conference. To provide context for the rich discussion, I have formed questions around common threads that provoked considerable discussion by participants and presenters, all of which were varying perspectives on the overarching theme of the conference.

- What is a democracy?
- What is the role of higher education in democratic societies?
- What is the purpose of higher education, and how will students and educators collaborate for student-centred learning in order to realise the aspiration of democracy?

What is a democracy?

First, the very nature of the term democracy needed to be further defined. Each speaker during the opening session commented on some characteristic of democracy to set the stage for the ensuing discussions:

- Ole Petter Ottersen, Rector of the University of Oslo, suggested that democracy has been in decline since 2008, with complacency marking the beginning of the decline.
- Tora Aasland, Minister of Higher Education and Research of Norway, spoke about the Bologna Process aspiring to be a borderless academic community and how academic freedom should include political freedom as well.
- Sjur Bergan, Head of the Education Department, Council of Europe, responded to the question "Why reimagine democratic societies?" He declared that civil society demands and cannot live without democracy, which is about participating in the lives of society, daily.
- Ira Harkavy, Netter Center for Community Partnerships, University of Pennsylvania and Chair of the U.S. Steering Committee of the International Consortium for Higher Education, Civic Responsibility and Democracy, raised questions such as "What kind of education do we need? What kind of society do we want?" He claimed: "No democratic school, no democratic society".
- Carola Bjørklund, Ambassador, Ministry of Foreign Affairs of Norway, asserted that education is a fundamental human right.
- Aksel Braanen Sterri, President of the Student Parliament at the University of Oslo, wondered why scholars are not online engaging in discussions with students about policy-making.
- Ana Perona-Fjeldstad, Executive Director of the European Wergeland Centre, asked a series of provocative questions, which included the following:

    - How will higher education organise to reimagine?
    - What are the good practices?
    - What has not been tried?
    - What partnerships may promote change?
    - How can higher education contribute to and act on imagination?

One would assume that among college and university participants, there would be a prolonged and serious academic discussion about the definition of democracy, given the theme and title of the conference. Interestingly and refreshingly, from the comments following the panel presentations, the emphases of the discussion were less on the freedoms and rights afforded by a democratic government and more on the personal and social responsibilities of citizens in a democratic society.

With all that occurred in the world in 2011 – from the Arab Spring and student protests, including the Occupy Movement, to changes to the fee/tuition structure of United Kingdom universities and continued state funding cuts for higher education across most of the United States, and the high unemployment or under-employment of college and university graduates – in the following comments from participants, it is notable how many of them mentioned the actions and responsibilities of citizenship.

Student panellist: "Democracy is not only about having institutions in place and having fair procedures and elections, but it's about the daily participation of citizens in a society, and apathy, lack of interest is the biggest threat to our democratic development."

Participant: "Places where people can take time to come together to learn, listen, reflect, to think and talk."

Participant: "Lack of active citizenship weakens democracy; we need a paradigmatic shift in education to give incentives to students to have time to be active out of class, and work toward urgent social problems."

Participant: "Activism and reflection individually and collectively."

Participant: "At the core of democracy, there must be a fight to transform the reality of the people at the bottom of society."

As these comments might suggest, democracy and democratic societies ideally are created by active citizens working together to solve societal problems. In addition to action, it is critical that citizens take responsibility for their civic education, such as learning how their government works and how they can become actively involved citizens.

What is the role of higher education and democratic societies?

For more in-depth discussions, conference participants were assigned to one of the facilitated working groups focusing on the following specific questions:

- What does a democratic college or university look like?
- What are particularly effective ways to deepen students' education for globally responsible democratic citizenship?
- What kind of partnerships between higher education institutions and local, national, and/or global communities promote democratic commitments and cultures?

I was in the working group that addressed the question "What does a democratic college or university look like?" This was a particularly challenging assignment given the fact that the very structures of higher education in many ways are antithetical to the promotion of democracy, judging by the way some members of our working group described the hierarchy of their administration and how decisions are made at their institutions. The incongruence is most apparent in governance structure and the challenges of access. A lack of access for qualified candidates and competition among institutions to be part of the elite and selective of their student body serves to reinforce social stratification. Traditional teaching styles and examinations further reflect a power differential between teacher and learner. Based on our group's discussion, it seems that this question needs an entire conference of its own to discuss the roles of students, professors, non-academic staff, governance and accountability.

With the many different types of institutions globally and their unique missions, processes and governance structures, it was difficult to come to a consensus on how "academic institutions might be reimagined to foster civic knowledge and skills and a sense of agency in students and staff". If our group could have seen the report, *A Crucible Moment*, [108] prior to our discussion, we might have talked about the idea of a "civic ethos governing campus life" that includes infusing "democratic values into the customs and habits of everyday practices, structures, and interactions" (National Task Force 2012: 15). As it happened, in our group it was difficult to think beyond the structures and practices currently in place. We needed to create a new model, rather than begin with what we have and make adjustments around the edges.

The question that more directly addressed the overarching theme of the conference was "What is the role of higher education in democratic societies?"

I noted that Hilligje van't Land, Director of Membership and Programme Development, International Association of Universities, stated early in her presentation that "higher education is key in creating democratic societies". On the panel with van't Land were Jan Egeland, Director of the Norwegian Institute of International Affairs, and Eduardo Padrón, President of Miami Dade College and Chair of the American Council on Education. Egeland talked about socio-economic discrepancies and Padrón talked about an inclusive approach or access to education. In the open discussion following this panel, participants' comments focused on the themes of access, affordability and jobs, and did not directly address the assertion that higher education was key in creating democratic societies.

It was not until the open discussion following the panel with Srbijanka Turajlić, former Deputy Minister for Higher Education of Serbia and former Chair of the Alternative Academic Education Network, Bert Vandenkendelaere, Chair of the European Students' Union, and Maria Helena Nazaré, President-elect of the European University Association, that the participants tackled the question about the role of higher education in democratic societies. As can be seen from the

---

108. *A Crucible Moment* was prepared at the invitation of the US Department of Education under the leadership of the Global Perspective Institute and the Association of American Colleges and Universities. The publication used input from a series of national roundtables involving leaders from all parts of the higher education and civic renewal communities. The report calls on the nation to reclaim higher education's civic mission, challenging a prevailing national dialogue that limits the mission of higher education to workforce preparation and training while marginalising disciplines basic to democracy. The report calls on educators and public leaders to advance a 21st-century vision of college learning for all students – a vision with civic learning and democratic engagement an expected part of every student's college education.

comments, there was no agreement on the role of higher education and whether or not it is "key in creating democratic societies".

Participant following panel: "Teachers say that teaching democracy is not our mission; we have to publish. We have to live and not just teach democracy."

Response from student panellist: "Reduce the emphasis on publishing. Students could evaluate teaching quality and have peer learning assessments."

Participant: "We're under the illusion that universities have a central function in society. We're not a lighthouse in the complex and post-modern society."

Response from panellist: "Universities have the responsibility of being role models. They should be watchers and inform public policy. The mission today is broader than it was 50 years ago."

Response from student panellist: "The university is teaching society's leaders. They play an important role in generating and steering public opinion. Universities should function as much as possible as a lighthouse in its small area."

The role of higher education in creating democratic societies is different from its purpose. The role has more to do with the place of higher education in the larger political scheme of things, whereas the purpose has to do with the actual work done towards the goal of achieving the desired democratic society – the most highly educated people bringing their knowledge to bear in taking a stand and working to bring about the desired outcome.

Caryn McTighe Musil, discussing important concepts like "citizenship" and "democracy", provides, in my judgment, a cogent and succinct explanation of a contemporary role of higher education:

> Flowing from democracy are the twin terms "social responsibility" and "social justice," which are emergent crosscutting terms that suggest both agency and public policy action. Both concepts also help move civic engagement from purely service to also advocacy, and from a cautiously apolitical stance to an unabashedly political but not doctrinaire one. (Musil 2011: 253)

In carrying out the role of higher education, members of the academic community take stands based on their unique mission and collective values of higher education and become what Musil refers to as "civic practitioners" in pursuing the ends of social justice.

What are the purposes of higher education and how will students and educators collaborate in student-centred learning to realise the aspiration of democracy?

Purposes of higher education

I must confess that the question I've written (in the heading above) about the purposes of higher education did not start out like that; it evolved as I read and re-read my notes from the forum's discussion. The first iterations of the question about purpose placed educators in a position of power, ignoring the important role of students as agents and partners in their own learning. For example, my original question, "What is the purpose of higher education and how should we educate students to be active citizens in a democratic society?" undermines the notion of creating democratic colleges and universities, robs students of their opportunity to exhibit personal responsibility and denies them a forum in which they can practise active citizenship within an academic community.

Beginning with the idea that educators will work with students, there will be different views about the purposes of higher education in democratic societies. However, there may be consensus that education is critical in democratic societies and, as Sjur Bergan noted on the importance of education, "democracy cannot be built on empty minds".

I agree with Caryn Musil that the purpose or central mission of higher education is to advance knowledge. In addition to the advancement of knowledge, Musil notes the responsibility of higher education "to ask new questions about how knowledge is applied, who is benefiting from it, and how it addresses enduring questions and urgent social problems that affect our shared futures and the planet's sustainability" (Musil 2011: 257).

Panellists and participants shared their thoughts on the purposes of higher education, ranging from the abstract to the concrete and from the ideal to the practical.

Panellist: "The goal is to learn and honour community with fair and democratic processes."

Panellist: "The goal is to help students understand the beliefs and cultures of others."

Panellist: "This generation of students is more focused on learning outcomes and they have a greater sensitivity to others."

Panellist: "Education is a transaction [109] for a degree as opposed to a transformation in creating learning and citizens."

Panellist: "Is higher education an individual or social good? We need to say to society that higher education has a social advantage."

Panellist: "Graduates often work in different fields than their major. What is the value we offer them then? We need to give them something they can use for their life, not as a job but to live with others."

Panellist: "Norwegians choose their studies based on what they want to be, not only on what they learn. Businesses say they want independent people trained to think critically."

---

109. Here "transaction" refers to the somewhat impersonal investment of tuition in exchange for the accumulation of credits leading to a degree.

Panellist: "Students say they want to be rich, famous, movie stars."

Panellist: "What competences do we want in graduates?"

Panellist: "Is education for democracy something that we can't afford during a financial crisis?"

Panellist: "Education is not a luxury, it is a necessity."

Participant: "One of the most provocative things is an assumption that there is an antithetical relationship between students' desire to make money and civic engagement. Those who make money can be philanthropic. The question is how do we prepare them to reach their instrumental goals and teach them to develop values to contribute to society?"

Participant: "Bring research and learning together by getting students involved in research projects."

Participant: "Engage students in the self-conscious evaluation of the context in which they function."

Participant: "We must produce citizens who are unwilling to tolerate conditions of poverty and injustice."

Participant: "Raising political consciousness should be at the heart of the curriculum."

Panellist: "Research should have roots in functional justice; we need to work with communities in partnership to effect change."

Panellist: "Students have to meet relevant dilemmas and study the history of politics and religion in order to produce the counter-arguments."

Panellist: "Higher education should facilitate public debate and promote internationalisation."

Given the international focus of the forum and increasing globalisation, immigration and the blurring of borders, I was surprised that there were not more references to the purposes of higher education for students who will be citizens of the world, particularly through the use of technology. It is imperative that not only students, but also those who have roles as educators, be interculturally competent. In *The Sage Handbook of Intercultural Competence,* Derek Bok asserts that "intercultural experience alone is not enough … mere contact is not sufficient to develop intercultural competence. … Building authentic relationships, however, is key in this cultural learning process … we must be intentional about developing learners' intercultural competence" (Bok 2009: xiii). Today, an important purpose of education is to ensure intercultural competence.

Both panellists and participants acknowledged the transactional nature of higher education today in a globally competitive job market. In *A Crucible Moment,* under the subheading "Higher education: more than workforce training", the report clarifies that "educating students for purposeful work in a dynamic, complex economy is more than ever an essential goal of higher education" (National Task Force 2012: 10). The case is then made for shared capacities and correspondences between workforce expectations and civic learning.

While the majority of panellists and conference participants understandably spoke to the civic learning capacities, given the theme of the conference, there was recognition that higher education also has an obligation to prepare students for careers.

Caryn Musil brought forward a question from her working group: "What are concrete examples of how to foster the development of democratic capacities in students?" The responses from panellists tended to describe the outcome for students rather than "how" to foster the development of democratic practices, with responses such as:

> [Students will] identify problems and engage with others to tackle the problems. We want students to be reflective, creative and have a voice as well as be good listeners. We want students to have the ability to mediate, negotiate, collaborate and therefore demonstrate the arts of democracy. We want students to bring people together to achieve good things for common purposes.

> We want students to be able to use their education anywhere. They should be competent to think and find solutions to complicated things.

Musil raised the issue of whether it was effective to engage students in the thick of a debate when there may be clashes of values, as well as moral and other irreconcilable differences – what one presenter termed "moral disturbance". Interestingly, there was little response to this important question, but it seems essential that we take advantage of such "teachable moments". Higher education then becomes the laboratory in which students learn to work across differences, defend positions respectfully and determine when it is best to compromise in working towards a common goal. In this way, students have an opportunity to practise active and engaged citizenship.

Several participants near the end of the discussion became impassioned about what they saw as the key or core challenges of democracy. The running theme from these comments might be summed up by the participant who referred to Egeland's comments from the previous day's panel about how the impact of socio-economic discrepancies today is more powerful and may have a more devastating effect because, as Egeland noted, "poor people can now see how the wealthy live because of the Internet". The participant saw the core issue and challenge as rising inequality. Whether the issue is rising inequality or the increased awareness of this inequality, we must ask what the role of higher education is in addressing this issue. Who has access and who is marginalised? Is the Occupy Movement an example of the success of higher education in achieving a goal of individuals thinking about and taking action around social justice, or is it an example of its abdication of a meaningful civic role, leaving others to bring attention to the important issues of our time?

Collaboration between students and educators to realise the aspiration of democracy

While there has been much talk of student-centred learning over the years, very little of it has actually involved the input of students. It is critical that institutions of higher education meaningfully involve different stakeholders – academic, administration, student and local communities – in governance, curriculum design and delivery of education. If we in higher education are willing to examine how we educate students, we must also be willing to examine our capacities to listen, to question, to analyse, to care and to work across differences in looking at fundamental methods of pedagogy. If one important result of education is critical thinking skills and critical consciousness, there must be effort and intention to create spaces that allow students to engage others in a civil manner that fosters further development of values for democratic engagement.

Student participant in small group: "I would not like to see students only as consumers of higher education but as full partners in the decision-making process throughout the university."

Student panellist: "The demand for student-centred learning is very legitimate and even in times of mass higher education, the European Students' Union believes student-centred learning is paramount for students to fully develop their potential, for universities to skill the future workforce and to create the leaders for tomorrow."

Student panellist: "The new way of learning should be independent and problem-based, going out into the field to collect data, digest this and transform it into academic knowledge."

Panellist: "We need to work with communities in partnership to effect change."

The student panellist referred to the "new way of learning". Deep and transformative learning "always occurs in the active context of students' lives" (Keeling 2004: 13). What will be new is the realisation that "students learn what they need to know to accomplish a particular task" (ibid.). Student-centred learning is one way of democratising higher education by moving away from the traditional model of how teaching is done to how learning is achieved. In addition to democratising higher education, student-centred learning is, in my opinion, an effective and efficient way to bring the most innovative thinking from students and educators to complex societal challenges.

As indicated in a commissioned report on the results of a study of 14-year-olds in the United States in 1999 (the cohort that is 27 years of age in 2012) "students who experience interactive discussion-based civic education (either by itself or in combination with lecture-based civic education) score the highest on "21st-century competencies", including working with others (especially in diverse groups) and knowledge of economic and political processes. Students who experience neither interactive nor lecture-based civic education have the lowest scores on all of the 21st-century competencies examined (Torney-Purta and Wilkenfeld 2009).

Partnerships should, in my judgment, begin with university faculty and staff to provide an integrated and interactive approach to working with students as they develop the competences of critical thinking and personal and social responsibility.

Educators can invite students as collaborators in teaching and learning, or they can be spectators as students use their power to create the academy that they will "reimagine". Students are coming to realise that the structures of institutions in higher education, the corporate world and political and legal systems, do not prevent them from having their voices and opinions heard.

Conclusion

From these conversations, it seems to me that there are at least three goals that warrant further discussion.

Making the structures of higher education institutions more democratic

If our goal is to reimagine higher education as democratic institutions, we must create new models based on how best to advance knowledge in purposeful ways for the common good. New models would make the borders between institutions and within institutions as permeable as necessary to accomplish common goals. This would require a willingness to tackle the difficult questions that lie at the intersection of access and privilege in the competition for "elite" status. For example, in the USA, students should not have to risk losing credit hours when they transfer from community colleges to four-year colleges and universities.

Central to this democratisation of higher education is the meaningful engagement of students in institutional decision-making. Permeable borders within institutions would mean there was no culturally imposed hierarchy among educators, whether they are faculty, student affairs counsellors, librarians or other staff. Working towards the same goal, all within the academic community would strive to understand one another's contributions to the mission of the institution and give due respect to all roles. To accomplish such respect and permeability of borders in an academic community, there would need to be commitment by the top leadership in the institution to encourage relational understanding across all departments and units.

Leadership would need to set the example by establishing relationships across institutions to address common challenges related to fulfilling the purposes of higher education. For example, knowledge cannot be advanced if students are not healthy and safe. Recent publicity about the pernicious problem of hazing among college students in the United States is one of those challenges for which there are no proven solutions. It is this kind of common challenge that all within the academic community and across institutions might begin to address, to see how borders can become permeable in order to create democratic institutions.

Acting as a beacon or lighthouse in reimagining democratic societies

If we are serious about the role of higher education in reimagining democratic societies, then colleges and universities can no longer sit on the sidelines; they must be active in the societies they seek to influence. They must play a visible role in their society through concrete, tangible actions. Encouraging active citizenship means that higher education must set an example in being more engaged. It is not enough for colleges and universities to require service from their students. They must make civic inquiry and literacy integral to the curriculum, both inside and outside the classroom, so that students understand the economic, political and social context in which they are doing service. Working in concert with students eager to serve, higher education can become a beacon or lighthouse to influence change, stand up for social justice and contribute to solutions for pressing social problems.

Infusing civic learning and democratic engagement into the curriculum and measuring long-term effectiveness

We must go beyond simple service learning and identify measures of student learning related to deeper levels of civic engagement and sustained commitment to a cause. Possible measures might include voter participation; service on a community board or committee; active engagement around a political issue through lobbying, letter writing, organising, educating neighbours, publishing an opinion piece; or volunteering.

We need to know how hours of service in college relate to civic engagement after college, and we need to attempt to determine the impact of our alumni on the communities in which they live and work, and their engagement in political processes of their country. Intentional efforts to infuse civic learning and democratic engagement throughout the college or university can change the culture. However, we learn from the report *A Crucible Moment* that the current programmes on citizenship development in the United States are typically "not deliberately orchestrated in a developmental arc; are not pervasive across students' experiences, and are not expected of every graduate" (National Task Force 2012: 42). As *A Crucible Moment* concludes, "correcting these omissions would transform higher education into a far more powerful national resource for strengthening democracy, communities, and lifelong citizen engagement" (ibid.).

Educating for democratic citizenship involves reflection and activism, individually and collectively. Higher education must become more than a transaction where the value is primarily in the accumulation of credits – it must be transformative. It must be about more than helping students attain skills to secure a job – it must empower students to create and sustain democracy.

Some think the status quo is preserved through higher education. If this is the case, there can be no reimagining of democratic societies. In a reimagined democratic society, higher education will disrupt received and normative thinking and values by fostering critical thinking and civic engagement for all within reach of the academic community. The Oslo Conference raised the questions. The next step, as I see it, is to work together to create international democratic models of higher education that will help realise the vision of reimagined democratic societies.

References

Bok D. (2009), "Preface" in D. K. Deardorff (ed.), *The Sage handbook of intercultural competence*, Thousand Oaks CA: Sage.

Keeling R. P. (ed.) (2004), *Learning reconsidered*, Washington DC: ACPA/ NASPA.

Musil C. M. (2011), "Remapping education for social responsibility: civic, global, and U.S. diversity" in J. Saltmarsh and M. Hartley (eds), *To serve a larger purpose: engagement for democracy and the transformation of higher education*, Philadelphia: Temple University Press.

National Task Force on Civic Learning and Democratic Engagement (2012), *A crucible moment: college learning and democracy's future*, Washington DC: AAC&U.

Torney-Purta J. and Wilkenfeld B. S. (2009), *Paths to 21st century competencies through civic education classrooms – an analysis of survey results from ninth graders*, Technical Assistance Bulletin, Chicago: American Bar Association Division for Public Education.

27. Reimagining democratic societies: analysing a new era of personal and social responsibility

Martina Vukasović[110]

The conference "Reimagining Democratic Societies: A New Era of Personal and Social Responsibility?" took place in Oslo in June 2011. The University of Oslo, celebrating its 200th anniversary, hosted the conference and also co-organised it with the Council of Europe, the US Steering Committee of the International Consortium for Higher Education, Civic Responsibility and Democracy, the European Wergeland Centre and the International Association of Universities, with the support of the Norwegian Ministry of Education. Less than a month after the conference, Oslo and the whole world were shaken by the events of 22 July 2011: the bombs in the government quarter of Oslo and shooting at the participants of the Labour party youth camp at Utøya. The aftermath of this tragedy, the debates and discussions, the practice, inside the university as well as in the rest of the society, has been an important test for democracy in Norway. While it is certain that our discussions would have been much different had the conference happened after 22 July 2011, it seems important to emphasise that the challenges to democracy and the implications for individuals and society that were identified during the conference are only highlighted by the July events and not overshadowed by them.

This chapter does not present verbatim the conference speeches and discussions. Rather, these are used as the basis for an analysis furthering the questions about the basic characteristics of democracy, the potential contextuality of this concept, the relationship between (higher) education and democracy, and the responsibilities of individuals and institutions for further democratisation of our societies.

---

110. The author wishes to thank the European Wergeland Centre, the Council of Europe, the International Association of Universities, the University of Oslo and the US Steering Committee of the International Consortium for Higher Education, Civic Responsibility and Democracy for organising the conference on which this chapter is based. The author is particularly indebted to those who acted as working group chairs and rapporteurs; without their help, writing this report would not have been possible. The author would like to thank Jens Jungblut for his valuable help in discussing the concept of democracy, and also Sjur Bergan, Ira Harkavy, Ana Perona-Fjeldstad and Hilligje van't Land for their comments on earlier versions of this report. The opinions expressed are those of the author and, where indicated, those expressed by participants in the conference. They do not necessarily reflect the opinion of the co-organisers of the conference.

A dose of realism

In discussing the concept of democracy and how it can be introduced and consolidated, one needs to strike a fine balance between idealism and realism. Idealism is necessary for progress. It is often the striving for unattainable goals that drives individuals and societies to test the boundaries of their institutions, to think beyond the taken-for-granted-rules and outside the box, to demand more from themselves and their fellow human beings. Sure, the ideals are often not noble and often not shared but contended, but they nevertheless challenge the status quo.

Realism, however, is also essential. Realism here includes in-depth knowledge about the contexts and dynamics of certain processes, about different actors and their vested interests and sometimes conflicting ideals. While we have been witnesses to transformative changes around the world, it is often the slow, incremental change that goes unnoticed and whose significant impact becomes evident only after a long period of time. This is in particular true for complex societal institutions like democracy or the university (Musselin 2005; Thelen and Mahoney 2010). Institutions do not change easily, and realism is necessary to evaluate the potential for change and the course of action that is most likely to result in change (although often the result is not exactly what was envisaged at the outset). While one could argue that "reimagining democratic societies" is necessarily an idealistic activity, it is the "personal and social responsibility" which requires a bit of a realistic approach as well.

Therefore, this report takes some of the perspectives and ideas that were presented during the conference and puts the following questions: are these ideas realistic, is it possible to implement them, are we not expecting too much (or too little) of higher education in general and from us as members of the academic community in particular, are we having too great expectations, and are we painting a too rosy picture? As demonstrated by Srbijanka Turajlić (Chapter 9, above), great expectations coupled with too rosy a picture and insufficient understanding of what works and what does not work in higher education, and why, seem like a rather sure recipe for failure in democratisation. Put differently, tree hugging may save the tree that is being hugged, but it fails to save the forest.

My report starts by discussing the concept of democracy and how democratic our societies actually are at this moment. I then focus on the university and put forward questions designed to provoke critical consideration of, among other things, whether a university is inherently (un)democratic and what, if anything, should and can be done to strengthen its democratic character. The next section discusses pedagogy for democracy and university functions, and how they relate to democratisation. The concluding section offers some tentative suggestions for further discussion and action.

What is democracy?

Jan Egeland, (then) Director of the Norwegian Institute of International Affairs, suggested that one could argue that we have never been better off as a species in terms of average poverty or the decline in armed conflicts and wars (at least until 2003). He also emphasised that this progress had happened in the context of a population explosion, and that inequalities between but also within countries are increasing. [111] While it is easy to get access to virtually any type of food in Norway, shortages of food are still an insurmountable problem in some parts of the world, Africa in particular. Furthermore, "new" global challenges had emerged: climate change, resource sustainability, terrorist threats, increasing numbers of refugees and internally displaced persons and so on.

The state of humanity as a species can also be seen in more quantifiable terms – for example, how much of the world's population lives in democratic countries. From that perspective, it is interesting to note that the Economist Democracy Index (EDI) [112] decreased between 2008 and 2010 in all regions of the world. Only 12 3% of the world's population live in so-called full democracies. What is perhaps more disturbing is that, according to the EDI, almost three quarters of the world's population live in flawed democracies or authoritarian regimes, and these include several EU countries: Bulgaria, Cyprus, Estonia, France, Greece, Hungary, Italy, Lithuania, Poland, Romania, the Slovak Republic and Slovenia. Of South American countries, only Uruguay is considered a full democracy. In Africa, only Mauritius is labelled a full democracy. In the Index, none of the BRIC [113] countries is considered a full democracy. Kazakhstan, which recently joined the Bologna Process, is considered to be an authoritarian regime, similar to Belarus which is, however, not taking part in the construction of the European Higher Education Area and is not a member of the Council of Europe (though it is a party to the European Cultural Convention).

On the other hand, the United States is labelled a full democracy although, according to some US citizens (and not only them) who took part in the conference, it has too often failed to live up to a higher standard and sacrificed integrity and values to fear since 9/11. Belgium is also considered in the index as a full democracy despite breaking the world record for the number of days without a government. The Netherlands is referred to as a full democracy even though in late June several people were injured (and some arrested) for peacefully protesting against budget cuts for arts and culture. In the United Kingdom one of the parties in the current government broke its election campaign promise not to raise tuition fees in higher education.

A cynic would say that the European Union generally suffers from a democratic deficit, that international relations and diplomacy have very little to do with ideas and principles but more with interests, that small states such as Mauritius do not

---

111. UN Human Development Report for 2010 at http://hdr.undp.org/en/reports/global/hdr2010/ (accessed on 14 September 2011).
112. See http://graphics.eiu.com/PDF/Democracy_Index_2010_web.pdf (accessed on 14 September 2011).
113. Brazil, Russia, India and China.

count, that the big players are shaping the game, that a country can function (and indeed it does!) without a government and that it is extremely naive to expect politicians to hold to the promises they make during campaigns.

However, these questions and the democracy index results resonate with challenges that we encountered during the conference when trying to clarify what we actually mean by "democracy". How do we know what is a democratic society? Is democracy an absolute or a contextualised concept, that is, are we referring to multiple democracies, as highlighted in one of the group discussions, where the ingredients of democracy need to be evaluated with respect to the context? What should we do in situations in which democratic processes result in undemocratic outcomes or rather: what if undemocratic forces come to power democratically?

Although this was not discussed extensively during the conference, it might be helpful to distinguish whether we refer to democracy in terms of procedures, contents or results, and to break down the concept into five dimensions (Croissant and Merkel 2004; Merkel 2004):

- electoral regime;
- political participation rights;
- civic liberties;
- horizontal division of power; and
- effective power of government (in particular the relationship between military and politics).

Five similar dimensions were used in the development of the Economist Democracy Index. They also enable the gradation of democracy in terms of its quality: from the fully fledged embedded democracies via different types of deficit democracies[114] to authoritarian regimes. The next question thus comes to the fore: is the university democratic, and what is its role in "reimagining democratic societies"?

Is the university democratic?

The issue of the democratic character of the university was discussed during the conference mainly in terms of its conceptualisation and operationalisation. Some suggestions on how to assess the democratic character of a university were to assess how representative of the overall population the student population is; to measure the university's contribution to the democratisation of society and

---

114. Depending on the dimensions in which there is a deficit, the following deficit democracies are possible: (a) exclusive democracy (deficits in electoral regime and political participation rights, e.g. a specific part of the population is excluded); (b) illiberal democracy (not all civil liberties are guaranteed for everyone); (c) delegative democracy (horizontal division of power is not adequate, executive power is stronger than it is supposed to be) and (d) enclave democracy (the military is not under civic democratic control).

evaluate its relationship to the community; to assess the democracy of its internal procedures and overall governance.

The first suggestion is about representativeness, which is connected to equity in access and, not less important, equity in completing higher education. However, even if there is full equity in terms of access and completion, mere representativeness may not be sufficient if these students cannot participate in the governance of higher education at departmental, institutional and system level. Put differently, it is possible to have full equity in higher education but that does not automatically prevent students being seen as mere customers, either by the university itself or by other stakeholders.

The second suggestion runs into problems of measurement. How can one adequately measure the contribution of the university to the democratisation of society? What are the indicators for this? What time frame should be used? How does one separate the impact of the university from the potential impact of other levels of education or other institutions? The link between democracy and university seems obvious if one focuses on the attempts of dictators to put the university under their control or on the student movements around the world that have tried to challenge dictators and their regimes, and sometimes succeeded. However, the direction of the causal link is less obvious, because it could also be argued that in order to democratise higher education one needs to spark the democratisation of society in general first.

Is "practising what you teach" the only way to "prepare for life as active citizens" as one of the four purposes of higher education as defined by the Council of Europe states (Council of Europe 2007)? In some of the group discussions this was particularly highlighted as being different from the internal democratic practice of the university, which means the democratic character of decision-making processes related to curriculum, teaching and assessment criteria and procedures, budgetary priorities, selection of students, appointment of staff and election of leadership.

Here the problem of contextuality and the difference between cultures and structures becomes evident, especially in comparison between the United States and Europe. The top leadership of US institutions is almost always appointed through a competitive process, which may of course involve academic and non-academic politics. At least according to the US conference participants, regardless of the presidential selection process, at the department level there tends to be significant autonomy in terms of key decisions on education and research. However, a European perspective on structures such as boards of trustees is much less supportive and in many instances the recent changes in system- and institution-level governance arrangements are seen as a move towards less democracy, which implies that the previous situation of collegial decision-making where the major decisions are made by essentially only one constituency was seen as more democratic.

Four visions of the ideal university

Maassen and Olsen (2007), on the basis of two dimensions – whether actors share norms and objectives or not, and how autonomous the university is with respect to external pressures – have identified four idealised visions of a university: 1. a rule-governed community of scholars (shared norms and high autonomy), 2. an instrument of national political agendas (shared norms but limited autonomy), 3. an internally representative democracy (high autonomy but conflict about norms) and 4. an enterprise embedded in competitive markets (low autonomy and conflict). To some extent these different (even competing) visions can be seen in every higher education system or institution, since higher education is characterised by goal ambiguity and potential for internal conflicts (Clark 1983). In this sense, none of the visions can be considered a complete assessment of US or European higher education.

The first vision – a rule-governed community of scholars – grants legitimacy to only one group of actors: academic staff. The legitimacy of academic staff within this vision is seen to arise from its expertise and rooting in particular disciplines and their related cultures, the expertise in two key missions of the university (education and research) and belonging to an academic profession (Clark 1983). The same arguments are used to legitimise significant institutional autonomy and individual academic freedom. Thus, it is seen as natural that the rules that govern this community of scholars are also established by scholars themselves and do not include other internal actors (students or administrative staff) nor external stakeholders (societal and government representatives, employers, etc.). While this vision is probably seen as democratic by academic staff, some other actors (in particular, students) do not agree, as evidenced in continual demands for more participation of student representatives in decision-making around the world. The lack of democratic character here can be seen as mainly an issue of process (who is involved in decision-making) and content (what is being decided).

In the second vision, a university that is predominantly an instrument of national political agendas is essentially governed "from the outside", by "predetermined political objectives" (Maassen and Olsen 2007: 30). Although these political objectives might be the result of a democratic process, it could be argued that the chain of events starting with elections, going through government formation and ending with policy development is too long to guarantee the democratic nature of the final policy decision, essentially implying problems with the outcome of a supposedly democratic process. Furthermore, the question is also whether the fact that none of the internal actors (not even those who possess the necessary expertise in refinement, transmission and development of knowledge) are involved in decision-making about their own operations may be sufficient to assess the university governance as undemocratic, if democracy is understood as participation of internal stakeholders. Naturally, being an instrument for national political agendas does not necessarily mean that the other actors make no decisions themselves but it does imply that their decisions will be heavily constrained by the aforementioned predetermined political objectives, and therefore both the potential lack of democracy in the process and content of decision-making leads to the conclusion that this vision of a university is also undemocratic.

A university that is envisaged as a representative democracy at first glance seems democratic in process and content. The relevant internal actors are involved in the decision-making processes and they negotiate and vote on a number of issues relevant to university functions (including decisions on what the primary functions are and how they can be fulfilled). However, as usual, the devil is in the details because a number of new questions arise. Who are the relevant internal actors? Is it just academic staff (essentially being equal to the first vision of the university) or is it also the students or administrative staff? Is it just tenured professors or also postdocs? Is representation organised in terms of one person, one vote or is the academic staff vote "worth" substantially more than the student vote, as is the case in many countries that allow participation of students in (for example) elections of the rector, supposedly because of differences in competence in key missions of the university? What about external actors who may have an interest in the university, given its expected contribution to consolidation of democracy and strengthening of the economy? Furthermore, the representative democracy vision refers only to those who are in higher education and thus might not be a guarantee of equity in access and completion or representativeness with respect to the overall population. Therefore, though it may seem the most democratic so far, this vision might not be assessed as absolutely democratic either.

Finally, a university that is seen as a service enterprise may imply a clear hierarchical structure internally and a focus on economy, efficiency and survival. In that sense it puts most focus on outcomes and the needs of its "sovereign customers" (Maassen and Olsen 2007: 30). The lack of focus on process and content could be sufficient to label this vision as undemocratic, but there are problems in the focus on outcomes as well. Who are the key customers that the university should focus on? Is it the students or the employers? Is it the local community? Is it the entire society? And how are their needs identified and assessed? More fundamentally, is the reference to "customers" in the first place essentially undemocratic? To include the issues of process and content again, in cases of contradictions between or need to prioritise some constituencies over the others, who makes the final decision? This vision of the university is often seen as particularly undemocratic, both by academic staff and students, as evidenced in some statements of their representative organisations on national or international level[115] and in the literature (e.g. Kladis 2011).

That said, do democracy and one of the basic principles in higher education – academic freedom – go hand in hand? Or do they also contradict each other? If we agree that knowledge is the main building block of higher education and that disciplinary cultures will also shape how access to, production of and transmission of knowledge are organised (Clark 1983), and given that these disciplinary cultures

---

115. Such as the European University Association, European Students' Union or Education International.

are not in essence democratic (participation is not open to all), do we not come to the conclusion that higher education is inherently undemocratic (and perhaps does not need to be democratic)?

Universities and democratisation

The conference identified a number of good practices in pedagogy for democratisation. It was suggested that competences to be acquired in higher education should include not only skills and knowledge but also attitudes, dispositions and values. Specific structures that foster community focus and education for democracy should be developed, in particular shifting the curriculum towards more problem-based, experiential learning, improving the opportunities for students to work in their communities and/or developing countries or participate in mobility programmes with an expectation that this could raise awareness and understanding between different cultures. The principle of student-centred learning should therefore embrace both the needs of the labour market and the values and principles of an open and democratic society, thus essentially contributing to an "education of the whole citizen" (as one of the participants in the conference put it). This should be reflected in curricula by focusing on societal change and challenges of multi-culturality and demographic changes; in teaching and assessment methods favouring peer learning and self- and peer-assessment as well as internal governance (i.e. decision-making about curriculum and teaching and assessment processes). It was noted by some that while the USA has institutions that particularly foster this approach (liberal arts colleges), this is still a novel and not widely accepted practice in European higher education systems and institutions.

Roles and functions of higher education

The differences between the United States and Europe, coupled with the four visions of the university discussed above, lead us to consider the roles or functions of higher education. The Council of Europe sees four key tasks of higher education: (a) to provide a broad and advanced knowledge base, (b) to prepare for sustainable employment, (c) to prepare for life as active citizens in a democratic society, and (d) to offer opportunities for personal development (Council of Europe 2007). On these issues, what higher education should do, there is agreement amongst stakeholders in general and participants in the conference in particular.

On the other hand, Manuel Castells (2001), adopting a more instrumentalist approach, identifies the following four functions for higher education, that is, what it actually does:

- generation and transmission of ideology;
- selection and formation of dominant elites;

- production and application of new knowledge; and
- training of bureaucracy and the skilled labour force.

Ideology here should be in terms of values, ethical principles and so on, and does not have a negative connotation. A focus on elites does not necessarily preclude broad and equitable access to higher education, but it does indicate clearly (and this was shared by a number of contributors to the conference) that elites, in the sense of "leadership", should be and most often are (s)elected from those who have higher education. Development and application of new knowledge is about both basic and applied research and how this is applied to innovation, including innovation aimed at contributing to further development of immediate communities of higher education institutions.

It is interesting to observe that Castells does not include one of the purposes that the Council of Europe highlighted, namely opportunity for personal development. As indicated earlier, Castells' functions of higher education are not about what should be, but what is. Furthermore, they correspond to the macro-level, for society as a whole. Castells' message is also that not all higher education necessarily provides these opportunities. Part of this is a consequence of massification of higher education in the sense that higher education institutions are expected to do more with less. While massification plays a key role in democratisation of higher education, in the sense of opening it up to previously excluded parts of society, the stratification in prestige and (perceived) quality that may come after massification may in essence diminish its democratisation potential. On that note, the expectation sometimes voiced in national strategies that it is possible to 1. increase access while 2. maintaining or even enhancing quality with 3. decreasing resources while 4. sticking to traditional pedagogical approaches, and current promotion and reward mechanisms for academic staff, is unrealistic to say the least (or rather a testimony to a disturbing lack of knowledge of higher education dynamics). Quality needs to be measured in relation to purposes and a distinction needs to be made between quality of the system as a whole and quality of its individual higher education institutions.

Castells is also rather reserved when it comes to "preparing for life as active citizens" since he phrased it as "generation and transmission of ideology". He therefore recognises that higher education institutions can be and indeed are home to the most democratic, open and progressive groups in society, but also a place where many nationalistic and inherently undemocratic groups find their intellectual legitimisation – as was and unfortunately still is the case in many countries (my home country of Serbia being one of them) or, on a different scale, as was the case with universities and scientists in Nazi Germany or the USSR and other Communist countries. The existence of such positions is often considered as a side effect of academic freedom, and moreover as the key ingredient of democracy, but in many cases one may find oneself tempted to limit this freedom. Such temptations therefore immediately raise the question where to draw the line (if the line indeed must be drawn, especially in relation to hate speech and discriminatory utterances) and then who should do this.

277

On that note one should also focus a bit more on the often-heard claim that today's students are not as engaged in society and are mostly focused on getting a job. This formulation can imply that there is something wrong with today's students and that in the good old days students were more engaged. This line of reasoning is flawed on several counts, including the failure to consider change in external conditions (not only in terms of job security as such but also the decrease in relative value and thus competitiveness of those with a degree). The other flaw is in what some may call "reproducing the myth of 1968" as the heyday of higher education engagement in democratisation.

If the aim is to understand the conditions conducive to such high engagement and whether any of these conditions exist today (and if we apply the same analytical rigour we demand from historians, sociologists or political scientists), we need to ask the following question: which subcultures (Clark 1983) in the university were involved in the transatlantic phenomenon of 1968; or more concretely what was the relative participation of students and academic staff? Was a majority of these subcultures involved? That is, were all students involved, regardless of their background, or was it mostly the more privileged ones? Did the movement spread to all fields and all types of higher education institutions, or was it the more elite or the more liberal arts-orientated institutions that were the focus of the 1968 student rebellion? Finally, what were the immediate as well as long-term outcomes of this? The discussion of these questions goes beyond the scope of this report and indeed was not the central topic of the conference, but a number of scholarly works (Altbach 1989; Boren 2001; DeGroot 2009) have been published on the issue.

More importantly for the present day, it is necessary to avoid too much backward looking and not base the "university as the beacon of democracy" position on something that happened more than 40 years ago in very different circumstances. Or, to be more provocative – can we drop 1968 finally and stop using it as an excuse, and rather ask ourselves – since 1990, or even since 2000 – has higher education lived up to the higher standard of democracy? Has it held others to these higher standards? How many public debates were held in higher education institutions around the world about the Ghadaffi regime and bombing of Libya or the famine in East Africa? Do we keep reminding ourselves and the general public about processes and events when they stop being the top media news? How visible in academia and in public are the scholars who point our attention to interesting additions to our language – sometimes labelled as doublespeak but strangely resonating like something from a George Orwell book, perhaps 20 years too late – such as "friendly fire" or "collateral damage"? Are we capable of having open scholarly debates about sensitive issues, not succumbing to the negative aspects of being "politically correct" (something that Hilligje van't Land and Caryn McTighe Musil also addressed during the conference[116]), maintaining academic standards and being sufficiently detached and neutral but also sufficiently connected to the

---

116. See also Cynthia Fleury (2010), *La Fin du courage* [The end of courage], Fayard, Paris.

problem at hand and capable of not "academising" too much? And is the lack of debate only the fault of apathetic students who are no longer willing to be "moral disturbances" (as Inga Bostad stated they should be in the panel debate)? Would it perhaps be more appropriate to test the democratic nature of universities by the quality of life and learning in society (as Henry Taylor, David Maurrasse, Richard Gaurasci and others suggested), especially for the poor and marginalised?

A number of conference participants also noted that, though universities are some-times "beacons of democracy", they have failed to take responsibility and be more critical of their own core actors. These internal contradictions within a university were also reflected in a statement from one of the working groups that "our worst enemy is often our elected representatives". This should also motivate the question – is higher education, and in particular its academic staff, often its own worst enemy? How often are academic staff protesting against the rules of the game but at the same time thinking up new ways to get around them or use them to their own advantage, an issue that was also highlighted in the panel debate during the conference? The existence of such internal contradictions is actually quite natural according to Castells (2001): a single higher education institution cannot effec-tively cater equally to all four functions. Moreover, institutions may themselves (although often, if not always, in response to different external incentives) opt to prioritise one over the other. The question then becomes, which of the functions that Castells offered is most relevant for the social responsibility of the university in "reimagining democratic societies"?

It could be argued that "the production and application of new knowledge" seems to come closest to what is one of the key elements of social responsibility of higher education – to try to provide effective solutions to contemporary societal prob-lems. In this, it is essential to strike the right balance between academic interests and furthering our knowledge on the one hand, and responsiveness and as deep an understanding as possible of the context on the other. An interesting example of what this may entail was presented at the University of Oslo recently.

On a Saturday in mid-June 2011 the University of Oslo campus was the venue of the second "diversity" festival. Oslo and Norway are becoming more and more culturally diverse and there are a number of policies to facilitate the integration of immigrants of different generations. At the same time, though it may not seem so obvious at the first glance, Oslo is a segregated city (not as segregated as some, but still segregated). Immigrants and the working class live predominantly east of the Akerselva river. In some of these areas, life expectancy is reported to be 10 years lower than in some parts of Oslo West. (For sure, life expectancy may be higher than in the countries where some of the immigrants came from, but such relative improvement should not be used as an excuse for lack of action.) During the festi-val a number of public debates, lectures, concerts and exhibitions took place. One exhibition included the work of several multidisciplinary teams of students, who were asked to envisage Oslo in 2100 and to address a number of important and rather practical issues, for example:

- the consequences of climate change in terms of rising water levels, where a dam will be built, how the dam as such can be used as a power plant, how much new land may be gained by building the dam and what new crops may be grown due to climate change;

- how to ensure access to key resources, how to decrease energy consumption per capita, how to develop new ways of producing and distributing food, using old infrastructure (e.g., abandoned metro tunnels for living quarters);

- how to solve transport problems given the rise in population (the estimate was that Oslo will have 10 million inhabitants), moving the centre of Oslo to the south and completely reorganising the public transport network.

All the above are predictable topics to some extent. Some of the solutions were rather innovative and also sensitive to cultural differences (in ways of living, size of families, wider community relations in different cultures, etc.). They were also refreshingly not utopian. Oslo 2100 is likely to be a city where quality of life will not be the same for all, although one can hope that the differences will decrease.

Concluding remarks

As discussed in previous sections, the conference did not necessarily provide a definite proposal on how (if at all) democratic societies could be reimagined and what specific steps a university must take to contribute to this reimagination. Yet, a number of important points about social and personal responsibilities for (further) democratisation of societies around the world can be made.

To start on a realistic note, it is important to do justice to what is already known about higher education, society or humans as a species. It is important to do justice to their complexities. It is important to recognise that humanity does not always live up to its own higher standards. Higher education tends to be more change-resistant and less responsive than one would prefer. Surely, it is somewhat of a paradox: the university is rather resistant to "deep" change but at the same time it is also rather adaptive, given that it has survived significant changes in societies over the centuries in a form that resembles its origins to a large extent (Kerr 2001), or, as some would argue, initiated and influenced the changes in society as well. In addition, humanity is often more selfish or more irrational than one might want it to be.

This brings forward the issue of personal responsibility. It is essential to realise that – apart from requiring changes in collective terms, of institutions, procedures and organisational cultures – democratisation also requires changes in personal attitudes and behaviour. In some cases this requires changes in voting preferences and accepting one's own share of involvement in solutions to major policy problems. If, for example, some of the suggestions for improving the university's capacity to contribute to democratisation included increased funding, which might not be possible without increases in taxes on personal income, then one would have to be prepared to increase one's own taxes for the greater good.

Moving further towards idealism, Neil Postman, author of a number of books on education, in his *Teaching as a subversive activity* (a book from late 1960s) said that education should help us develop two basic skills. The first one is the skill of asking the right questions. Therefore, higher education should not be afraid to ask the difficult, sensitive, even disturbing questions, if they are the right ones. We should observe (and promote) the basic societal norms and values when asking these questions, but not be constrained by existing frames of thinking. The second skill is the skill of "crap detecting" (Postman and Weingartner 1969: 6). In the context of social and personal responsibility for democratisation it could be translated as "holding ourselves to higher standards" as well. This entails detecting crap from (financially or intellectually) corrupt colleagues, detecting and not accepting crap from politicians and the media. It also involves not accepting too-rosy pictures of ourselves and especially not of the good old days, observing the same methodological and critical rigour when analysing ourselves as we observe when analysing others.

Finally, but not least important, conferences or publications on the university and its role in democratisation should not be used as an alibi for lack of continuous effort and pressure on ourselves and other colleagues, staff and students alike, to further democratic principles, the rule of law and respect for human rights. While the conference and the publication may be an excellent opportunity for debates and are certainly important milestones and signals to the public, the day-to-day practice of individuals in the university and the university itself as an organisation must be geared to consolidation of democracy and continual "moral disturbance".

References

Altbach P. G. (1989), *Student political activism: an international reference handbook*, Westport CT: Greenwood Press.

Boren M. E. (2001), *Student resistance: a history of the unruly subject*, London: Routledge.

Castells M. (2001), "Universities as dynamic systems of contradictory functions" in J. Muller, N. Cloete and S. Badat (eds), *Challenges of globalisation: South African debates with Manuel Castells*, Cape Town: Maskew Miller Longman, pp. 206-23.

Clark B. R. (1983), *The higher education system: academic organization in cross-national perspective*, Berkeley: University of California Press.

Council of Europe (2007), Recommendation Rec(2007)6 of the Committee of Ministers to member states on the public responsibility for higher education and research.

Croissant A. and Merkel W. (2004), "Introduction: democratization in the early twenty-first century", *Democratization*, 11 (5): 1-9. doi: 10.1080/13510340412331304570.

DeGroot G. (2009), *The sixties unplugged: a kaleidoscopic history of a disorderly decade*, London: Pan.

Kerr C. (2001), *The uses of the university*, Cambridge MA: Harvard University Press.

Kladis D. (2011), "Democracy vs. efficiency in higher education governance" in S. Bergan, E. Egron-Polak, J. Kohler and L. Purser (eds), *Leadership and governance in higher education*, basic edn, Berlin: Raabe Verlag.

Maassen P. A. M. and Olsen J. P. (2007), *University dynamics and European integration*, Dordrecht: Springer.

Merkel W. (2004), "Embedded and defective democracies", *Democratization*, 11 (5), 33-58. doi: 10.1080/13510340412331304598

Musselin C. (2005), "Change or continuity in higher education governance?", in Bleiklie I. and Henkel M. (eds) *Governing knowledge*, Higher Education Dynamics series 9 (1): 65-79, Dordrecht: Springer.

Postman N. and Weingartner C. (1969), *Teaching as a subversive activity*, New York: Delacorte Press.

Thelen K. A. and Mahoney J. (2010), *Explaining institutional change: ambiguity, agency, and power*, Cambridge: Cambridge University Press.

28. Reimagining democratic societies: thoughts for the road

Sjur Bergan, Ira Harkavy and Hilligje van't Land

This book examines the reasons why reimagining democratic societies is necessary and it identifies some paths that might take us forward towards reimagining and reinvigorating democracy in practice. It does both these things through theoretical and contextual essays as well as a diverse set of case studies. In this final, brief essay, we – as editors – would like to bring together some of the many interesting suggestions made throughout the book, look at some of the elements the highly varied essays have in common and take a final look at the various ways higher education might contribute to reimagined and strengthened democracies. We would like to emphasise our use of the plural. There is not a single way forward; there are several roads towards the kind of societies in which future generations could live meaningful and happy lives.

The essays in this book, we believe, make a strong case that higher education has an essential role to play. Higher education has several purposes, relating to individuals and to society, of which the economy is one and only one. The subtitle of the book, which highlights personal and societal responsibility, alludes to the roles and responsibilities higher education has for developing individuals as well as society.

As individuals, from early childhood, we undergo what are often called "formative experiences". They help decide not only what we know, understand and are able to do but who we are. We of course have many of our formative experiences outside formal education. In modern societies, highly developed competences are an essential requirement, but the view of what these essential competences should be is often dominated by a view of what is considered "immediately useful". This book argues that higher education needs to maintain a vision of its role as developing not only a strong knowledge base and specific skills but also competences, developing not only future participants in the labour market but also the personality of learners. Education should be a process through which new skills and competences are developed, but it should also be a formative, even transformational, experience.

This links to the second aspect of our subtitle focusing on social and societal responsibility. No man is an island unto himself;[117] human beings are social animals. Most of us need some time and space to ourselves, but few of us would be comfortable with solitary time filling our entire existence. Societies are obviously

---

117. The phrase is adapted from John Donne's *Meditation XVII* (1624).

more than the individuals who constitute them. For societies to function effectively, individuals cannot act in parallel, but in consort, in collaboration and at times in conflict. Higher education should play an essential role in providing individuals with the competences and the formative experiences that make them able and eager to work together. Higher education should also actively seek to influence the democratic development of society.

Higher education itself has many constituencies. Students, faculty and staff act as individuals or as collective bodies and can often exercise considerable influence. The European Higher Education Area would not have been what it is today without the strong contributions of students as part of the academic community and as participants in higher education governance at faculty and institutional level as well as in the governing bodies of the Bologna Process. Students, faculty and staff can take initiatives that lead to their institutions engaging democratically with their communities, as in the University of Pennsylvania's long-term partnership with its neighbours to develop and implement university-assisted community schools which serve as local centres of learning, services and engagement for school students, their parents and other community residents. As Jens Stoltenberg, Prime Minister of Norway, said in an interview to mark the first anniversary of the attacks in Oslo and on Utøya on 22 July 2011, which have been referred to in many chapters of this book: "democracy is not something that can be built from the top of the government building".[118] Democracy needs to be built with all higher education stakeholders. IAU's commitment to building a worldwide higher education community aims at furthering this broad goal by offering services and programmes that help build synergies, better understanding and closer co-operation between systems, institutions and people, and thus contributes to more respect and recognition of values and perspectives and also to democracy-building around the world.

Higher education institutions also act in at least two other capacities. They provide the institutional and physical framework within which most higher education is provided. They select and employ the faculty that provide courses and devise study programmes as well as the staff that manage the institution, one of whose tasks is to make students feel at home there. In many cases, the institution or the campus provides the setting for an important part of students' lives as well as their studies. Also, higher education institutions have the authority, within existing regulations, to grant or withhold the degrees towards which students study. For many, very possibly most, citizens, such institutions also provide the single image that is likely to come to mind whenever the words "higher education" are pronounced.

---

118. See www.aftenposten.no/webtv/--Jeg-er-mer-takknemlig-for-livet-6945696.html (accessed on 20 July 2012). The reference to "the government building" is particularly significant, as many Norwegian ministries were housed in a single high-rise building in downtown Oslo (and others nearby), which was the main target for the 22 July 2011 bomb attack.

Higher education institutions provide an institutional framework, but they work within a systems framework that makes them, for example, American, Dutch, Lebanese, Malaysian, Norwegian or Rwandan institutions. National higher education systems are established and governed by public authorities. Education systems provide a legal and regulatory framework so that issues like access, quality assurance and the degrees that institutions can grant are clearly regulated. Laws and regulations are, however, the codification of policies. If an important political and policy goal is to provide broad access to higher education, this should be reflected in legislation. Laws are neutral in the sense of providing equal treatment, but not in the sense that the goals they are intended to achieve are given and timeless. A democratic society needs democratic legislation and that can only be provided on a background of, as well as in support of, democratic policies and democratic practice. In our context, the higher education policies promoted by public authorities must contribute to reimagining democratic societies by establishing a framework within which higher education institutions, students, faculty and staff can do so.

Higher education also powerfully influences the school system at all levels since it educates the teachers and the teachers' teachers. Higher education institutions serve as a model, a reference point, for teaching, learning and knowledge development and acquisition for other educational institutions, particularly "earlier" schooling. Whether or not colleges and universities teach democratically – and for democracy – will significantly shape how far schools function as sites of democracy and how far societies reach their democratic potential.

The essays in this book provide many ideas and examples of policies and practices that the academic community can pursue to promote and reimagine democracy. The examples are varied but there are some common denominators.

One is that they recognise the importance of democratic institutions and laws. Giedrius Viliūnas' description of Mykolas Romeris University in Vilnius may provide the clearest case, but Gilbert Rochon and Thierno Thiam's description of Tuskegee, as well as the chapters by Tora Aasland and Ole Peter Ottersen, are also among those providing examples.

A second common denominator is that frameworks must be filled with policy. Institutions must be used, structures must be filled with life and opportunities must be grasped. Sev Ozdowski's description of the University of Western Sydney, Tony Gallagher's piece on Queen's University Belfast and Brian Murphy's account of De Anza College are among the examples that show how institutions can establish policies to make higher education more widely accessible as well as to give it a profile and content that serve a broader purpose. The proposition that democracy is promoted through policies and actions within the framework of democratic institutions is something like a main theme in this book.

The term "democratic institutions" is telling. In many contexts, it is used to refer to the institutions that form the backbone of democracy: elected parliaments and governments, independent courts and a public administration operating under the guidance of elected public authorities. We do use the term in this sense but in addition, throughout the book, the term "democratic institutions" also refers to higher education itself. Higher education institutions must not "only" be training institutions for future leader and citizens. They must also practise democracy and participation on campus. They must, as an earlier joint project of the Council of Europe and the International Consortium for Higher Education, Civic Responsibility and Democracy stated, be sites of democratic citizenship (Plantan 2004). Institutions must educate as well as train. As shown by the co-operation between the International Association of Universities and the Council of Europe on intercultural dialogue, the will and ability to communicate across cultures is also fundamental (Bergan and van't Land 2010).

A third common denominator is the need not only to work for, but also with, society. This is another main thread throughout the book. In an age of globalisation, it is important to emphasise that society is local as well as national and global, and several chapters provide examples of how higher education institutions engage with the local community. These include Henry Taylor's description of the University at Buffalo and Paul Pribbenow's account of how Augsburg College met a potential crisis in its relationship with the local community when a student of immigrant background was murdered. In his article about the Anchor Institutions Task Force, David Maurrasse shows how institutions can come together to strengthen democratic co-operation between higher education and local communities.

A fourth common denominator is leadership. Higher education institutions and systems, as well as faculty, staff and students, need organisations and leaders who can bring committed individuals and members of the academic community together for a common purpose. Leaders must motivate and also demonstrate the ability to define goals as well as to devise policies to reach those goals. It is essential that higher education leaders, whether in public authorities (illustrated by Tora Aasland and Srbijanka Turajlić), higher education institutions (illustrated by Ole Petter Ottersen, Eduardo Padrón and others) or organisations (illustrated by Caryn McTighe Musil, Muriel Howard and Jennifer Domagal-Goldman and Bert Vandenkendelaere) define goals and policies that serve democracy.

The task at hand is an eminently educational one. We need to change attitudes as well as develop skills and competences and put these skills and competences into practice. Reimagining democratic societies is about judging whether our current institutional arrangements are still fit for purpose and, if they are not, about imagining alternative structures that better serve democracy. Reimagining democratic societies requires developing competences that serve this purpose. We need not only to know more but also to think and do differently and innovatively. We may need to rethink the structures of democracy, but maybe also to look at our own understanding of democracy. This is not an entirely new undertaking: societies which excluded women from voting or active participation in political life, which instituted tests designed to keep an important part of the population, most easily identified by the colour of their skin, away from the polls or which did not pay elected representatives a salary because it considered only those financially independent fit to serve the public purpose were once considered acceptable. Fortunately, our understanding of democracy has evolved.

Higher education must help its students develop competences that have a solid academic foundation and that also span across the boundaries of academic disciplines. Intercultural dialogue is also needed between the "two cultures"[119] that make up the academic world. There are frequent calls for higher education to improve its ability to teach its students entrepreneurship. Why should the calls for higher education to improve its ability to stimulate the democratic imagination not be equally frequent?

In reimagining democratic societies, educating the whole person and educating for all of society come together. Our societies need citizens committed to the common good and who define "common" as applying to local, national and global levels. We need people with advanced knowledge and competence in specific areas as well as the ability to put this competence into a broader context. We need a public opinion – which is to say all of us – that is able and willing to weigh long-term gain against short-term loss. We also need a public opinion that recognises the value of those whose backgrounds and convictions differ from our own and one that is committed to upholding human dignity.

Reimagining democratic societies requires policy and practice, grassroots action and democratic leadership. It needs commitment to the proposition that leading by example is more effective than merely leading by decree. Not least, reimagining democratic societies requires public and institutional policies and leadership that recognise that higher education is essential to the development and even the survival of our societies. It needs leadership and policies that act on the conviction that higher education, in order to be of true service to our societies, needs to serve a larger purpose (Saltmarsh and Hartley 2011).

We hope this book will provide examples of how higher education can serve that larger purpose, inspiring policy makers and practitioners, faculty and students, communities and institutions. Solutions cannot be dictated or imposed. They must be developed by each institution and each education system through a process of broad thought and consideration, critical thinking and creative solutions.

Ambrose Bierce famously defined education as "that which discloses to the wise and disguises from the foolish their lack of understanding" (Bierce 1911: 105). That is a good starting point but, in order to reimagine democratic societies, the higher education community must take an important step further: it must take the lead in helping to remedy our lack of understanding, our lack of imagination and also our lack of commitment, by developing ideas and creating paths with its community and societal partners that will not only reimagine, but also revitalise and sustain inclusive and just democratic societies.

---

119. The concept of two cultures was coined by C. P. Snow in his 1959 Rede Lecture at the University of Cambridge to describe the gulf he perceived between the humanities and natural sciences.

References

Bergan S. and van't Land H. (2010), *Speaking across borders: the role of higher education in furthering intercultural dialogue*, Higher education series No. 16, Strasbourg: Council of Europe Publishing.

Bierce A. (1911/1983), *The enlarged Devil's dictionary*, ed. E. J. Hopkins, London: Penguin American Library.

Plantan F. (2004), "The university as a site of citizenship" in S. Bergan (ed.), *The university as* res publica *– Higher education governance, student participation and the university as a site of citizenship*, Higher education series No. 1, Strasbourg; Council of Europe Publishing, pp. 83-128.

Saltmarsh J. and Hartley M. (eds) (2011), *To serve a larger purpose: engagement for democracy and the transformation of higher education*, Philadelphia: Temple University Press.

Appendix I: About the editors and authors

Editors

Sjur Bergan is Head of the Council of Europe's Education Department. From an initial focus on higher education, he has gradually expanded his work to various areas of education policy. He represents the Council of Europe on the Bologna Follow-Up Group and Board and chairs the Bologna Working Group on Qualifications Frameworks. In the latter capacity, he is also an active member of the EQF Advisory Group. He was a member of the editorial group for the Council of Europe's White Paper on Intercultural Dialogue and a main author of the Council of Europe/UNESCO Recognition Convention. Sjur Bergan is series editor of the Council of Europe higher education series and the author of *Qualifications: Introduction to a Concept* as well as of numerous articles on various aspects of higher education policies. His latest publications are *Speaking across Borders: the Role of Higher Education*, co-edited with Hilligje van't Land, and *Not by Bread Alone*, a collection of essays on higher education.

Ira Harkavy is Associate Vice President and Director of the Barbara and Edward Netter Center for Community Partnerships, University of Pennsylvania. As Director of the Netter Center since 1992, Dr Harkavy has helped to develop service-learning courses as well as participatory action research projects that involve creating university-assisted community schools in Penn's local community of West Philadelphia. Dr Harkavy chairs the Anchor Institutions Task Force and the US Steering Committee of the International Consortium for Higher Education, Civic Responsibility and Democracy. He is a Senior Fellow of the Leonard Davis Institute of Health Economics and a member of the National Science Foundation's Advisory Committee on Equal Opportunities in Science and Engineering (CEOSE). Dr Harkavy's publications include *Dewey's Dream* (with Lee Benson and John Puckett), *The Obesity Culture* (with Francis Johnston) and *Higher Education and Democratic Culture* (co-edited with Josef Huber in the Council of Europe Higher Education Series).

Hilligje van't Land is Director of Membership and Programme Development at the International Association of Universities (IAU). She was educated in France, the Netherlands and Canada and obtained her doctorate in contemporary literature from Groningen University. Dr van't Land started her academic career working in the humanities and taught comparative francophone literatures at universities in the Netherlands, Canada and France while heading the Institute for American Universities in Avignon, before joining the IAU at UNESCO headquarters in

Paris. She has worked for IAU for 16 years and is in charge of IAU member-ship development and of its thematic priorities on the role of higher education in promoting sustainable development and intercultural dialogue (special projects, thematic webpages, publications). She is Editor of *IAU Horizons*, the association's magazine, works with the IAU secretary general and IAU team on co-ordinating the association's annual and general conferences, and runs several projects, for example on the changing nature of doctoral programmes in sub-Saharan Africa and the role of higher education in promoting sustainable development in sub-Saharan Africa. She co-edited the book *Speaking across Borders: the Role of Higher Education* with Sjur Bergan of the Council of Europe.

Authors

Tora Aasland was the minister responsible for all post-secondary education and research in Norway in 2007-12. From 1985 to 1993, she was Member of the Storting, the Norwegian Parliament, for Akershus County and also Vice-President of the Odelsting (the former first chamber for matters regarding legislation) from 1989 to 1993, when she became County Governor in Rogaland. Ms Aasland has a higher degree in sociology from the University of Oslo. Ms Aasland has worked as a researcher, and also as head, of the Institute for Social Research. She has also been Secretary General of the Norwegian Non-fiction Writers' and Translators' Association (NFF), an organisation working to secure and protect the professional and economic interests of authors and translators of non-fiction. Ms Aasland has held key positions in the Socialist Left Party at local, regional and national levels. She has also been elected or appointed member of numerous government and roy-al committees and commissions, particularly in the areas of education and culture.

Inga Bostad is Pro-Rector at the University of Oslo and was Vice-Rector from 2006 until 2009. She has been an Associate Professor in philosophy since 2004 in the Department of Philosophy, Classics, History of Art and Ideas at the University of Oslo. Dr Bostad specialises in language philosophy, scepticism and pedagogical philosophy, especially philosophy as a method in school. Her publications include *Tenkepauser – filosofi og vitenskapsteori* [Breaks for thinking – philosophy and the-ory of science], co-authored with Hilde Bondevik (2003), *Tvil eller tro – en rekon-struksjon av skeptisisme* [Doubt or belief – a reconstruction of scepticism] (2005), *Dialog og danning. Det filosofiske grunnlaget for læring* [Dialogue and general education: the philosophical basis for learning], with Tove Pettersen (2006) and *Søk!* [Search!] (2006). Her book *Existential Education and the Quest for a Moral Disturbance* is forthcoming.

Gwen Dungy, an accomplished speaker, leader and educator, served as execu-tive director of NASPA – Student Affairs Administrators in Higher Education from 1995 until 2012, when she was named Executive Director emeritus. In her capacity as an advocate for students, she draws on more than 40 years of experience in higher education. In the international arena, Dr Dungy has increased alliances and collaborations between NASPA and associations and non-profit groups around the world. A licensed psychologist and a nationally certified professional counsellor and career counsellor, Dr Dungy earned BS and MS degrees from Eastern Illinois University, an MA degree from Drew University in New Jersey and a PhD from Washington University in St Louis.

Tony Gallagher is Professor of Education and Pro-Vice-Chancellor at Queen's University Belfast. He was Head of the School of Education from 2005 to 2010. As Pro-Vice-Chancellor he is responsible for academic planning, staffing and external relations. His main research interest relates to the role of education in divided societies, a theme on which he has worked in South East Europe, the Middle East and Northern Ireland. He is currently leading the Sharing Education Programme, a project encouraging school collaboration to promote higher standards and reconciliation (www.schoolsworkingtogether.co.uk).

Jennifer M. Domagal-Goldman is the National Manager of the American Democracy Project at the American Association of State Colleges and Universities (AASCU). She earned her doctorate in higher education from Pennsylvania State University. She received her master's degree in higher education and student affairs administration from the University of Vermont and a bachelor's degree in English from the University of Rochester. Dr Domagal-Goldman's dissertation research focused on how faculty participation in a multidisciplinary community of practice affected their undergraduate teaching practices with regard to teaching for civic purposes and with community-engaged pedagogies in their disciplines. The study has practical and theoretical implications for advancing student learning outcomes and civic engagement, and for understanding and enhancing faculty development initiatives. Jennifer is an editorial board member of the *eJournal of Public Affairs* and a member of the National Conference on Citizenship's Conference Advisory Council.

Vidar L. Haanes is Professor of Church History and President of MF Norwegian School of Theology, Oslo. He chairs the Association of Private Universities and Colleges in Norway, and is a member of the board of the Oslo Knowledge Alliance, the Transatlantic Forum, the National Council of Theology and Religious Studies and committees of the Norwegian Association of Higher Education Institutions. He is also a member of the working group on Higher Education and Research of the European Federation of Education Employers and of the Co-ordinating Committee of the Forum of Theological Higher Education and Research in Europe.

Muriel Howard has been president of the American Association of State Colleges and Universities since 2009. Dr Howard was the president of Buffalo State College, State University of New York from 1996 to 2009 and served in a number of leadership positions at the University at Buffalo, State University of New York, over a 23-year career. Her professional and scholarly interests include educational leadership, women and minorities in the academy and a long-standing personal commitment to community service and outreach.

Helene Lund is Associate Professor at MF Norwegian School of Theology. Dr Lund completed her PhD in Systematic Theology in 2010 and graduated (Cand. Theol.) in 1998. Her research interests are in the area of religion and conflicts, human rights, ecumenism and ecclesiology.

Lars Løvlie is Professor Emeritus of the Philosophy of Education at the Institute for Educational Research at the University of Oslo. He has directed research groups supported by the Research Council of Norway and has been Visiting Professor at various departments of education and social studies, most recently at the Department of Education at Örebro University. He is co-editor of *Educating Humanity: Bildung in Postmodernity* (2003), *Dannelsens forvandlinger* [Transformations of education] (2003), and *Pedagogikkens mange ansikter* [The many faces of education] (2004).

David J. Maurrasse is the President and Founder of Marga Incorporated, a consulting firm providing advice and research to strengthen philanthropy and innovative cross-sector partnerships. Dr Maurrasse is Director of the Anchor Institutions Task Force, which Marga co-ordinates along with the Netter Center for Community Partnerships at the University of Pennsylvania. Affiliated with Columbia University since 2000, Dr Maurrasse is Director of the Program on Strategic Partnerships and Innovation at the university's Earth Institute. He was an Assistant Professor at Yale University and a Senior Program Advisor at the Rockefeller Foundation. He is a Trustee at Bucknell University and the author of several books.

Brian Murphy is the President of De Anza College in Cupertino, California. He is one of the founders of The Democracy Commitment, a national coalition of American community colleges committed to the democratic engagement of their students. Prior to his current position, Dr Murphy served as the Executive Director of the San Francisco Urban Institute at San Francisco State University, after serving as the chief policy consultant on the Master Plan for Higher Education in the California State Legislature. Dr Murphy holds a bachelor's degree from Williams College and a master's and doctorate from the University of California at Berkeley, all in political science. He has taught political theory, urban politics and American government at the University of California, Santa Cruz, Santa Clara University, and San Francisco State University.

Caryn McTighe Musil is Senior Vice President of the Association of American Colleges and Universities, where she oversees the Office of Diversity, Equity, and Global Initiatives. At AAC&U she has directed more than two dozen externally funded national projects with colleges and universities seeking to reform the curriculum, improve teaching, promote civic engagement and create more inclusive academic institutions. Her most recent publication on behalf of the National Task Force on Civic Learning and Democratic Engagement is *A Crucible Moment: college learning and democracy's future*, released at the White House in Washington DC in January 2012. Dr McTighe Musil received her BA from Duke University and her MA and PhD in English from Northwestern University. She has served as a member of the Steering Committee of the International Consortium for Higher Education, Civic Responsibility and Democracy since its inception.

Sondra Myers is Senior Fellow for International, Civic and Cultural Projects at the University of Scranton, Pennsylvania. Dr Myers' work focuses on strengthening democracy and the culture of interdependence, with particular emphasis on the central role that citizens play in making democracy work. She has conducted international roundtable discussions in Paris, Berlin, Washington, Prague and Kigali, and has published several handbooks on the subject. The first two, the *Democracy is a Discussion* handbooks, have been translated into over 20 languages and the most recent, *The New Rwanda: prosperity and the public good*, has been serialised in the *New Times*, the English-language newspaper in Kigali.

Sev Ozdowski OAM is Director of Equity and Diversity at the University of Western Sydney and Honorary Professor in the Centre of Peace and Conflict Studies at Sydney University. Dr Ozdowski is also President of the Australian Council for Human Rights Education. As the Australian Human Rights Commissioner (2000-05) he conducted the ground-breaking *National Inquiry into Children in Immigration Detention – "A last resort?"* and the *National Inquiry into Mental Health Services –"Not for Service"*. Dr Ozdowski has an LLM and MA in Sociology from Poland and a PhD from the University of New England. Dr Ozdowski's lifelong commitment to multiculturalism and human rights was recognised by an Order of Australia Medal and an honorary doctorate from the Royal Melbourne Institute of Technology.

Ole Petter Ottersen is Professor of Medicine and has been Rector of the University of Oslo since August 2009. He has received several international prizes and is included in the Institute of Scientific Information list of Highly Cited Scientists. From 2002 to 2009 he was Director of the Centre for Molecular Biology and Neuroscience, a Centre of Excellence sponsored by the Research Council of Norway. Since 2008 he has been panel chairman (Advanced Grants) in the European Research Council. He is currently chairing the Lancet–University of Oslo Commission on Global Governance for Health, in collaboration with Harvard University.

Eduardo J. Padrón has served as President of Miami Dade College (MDC) since 1995. MDC is recognised as a national model of student achievement and is the largest institution of higher education in the United States, with more than 174 000 students. In 2009, *Time* magazine included President Padrón among its 10 Best College Presidents in the USA. In 2010, *Florida Trend* magazine named him Floridian of the Year. In 2011, the *Washington Post* identified him as one of the eight most influential US college presidents, and the Carnegie Corporation of New York granted him the prestigious Centennial Academic Leadership Award. He is a past Board chair of the Association of American Colleges and Universities and the immediate past Board chair of the American Council on Education. He has been selected to serve on posts of national prominence by six American presidents. Most recently, President Obama named him chairman of the White House Commission on Educational Excellence for Hispanic Americans. He serves on the boards of the Council on Foreign Relations, the College Board Advocacy and Policy Center, the White House Fellows Selection Panel (chair) and the International Association of University Presidents, among others.

Paul C. Pribbenow is President of Augsburg College, a private liberal arts college of the Evangelical Lutheran Church in America located in Minneapolis, Minnesota. He holds a BA from Luther College and an MA and PhD in social ethics from the University of Chicago. Dr Pribbenow is the author of numerous articles on the professions, ethics, and not-for-profit management, and publishes a bi-monthly e-newsletter, "Notes for the Reflective Practitioner."

Edward J. Ray became president of Oregon State University in July 2003. Under his leadership, OSU has completed and updated a visionary campus-wide strategic plan that is guiding the university's development in profound and historic ways. Annual research awards and contracts have increased substantially and totalled US$261.7 million in fiscal year 2011. Dr Ray partnered with the OSU Foundation to launch the university's first comprehensive fundraising campaign. The public phase launched in autumn 2007 with a goal of US$625 million. By June 2012, the campaign total had reached US$842 million and it recently has been extended to 2014 with a goal of US$1 billion. Dr Ray was a member of the economics faculty at Ohio State University from 1970 until 2003, serving as economics department chair from 1976 to 1992. He later served as an associate provost; senior Vice-Provost and, from 1998 to 2003, as executive Vice-President and Provost. Dr Ray received his undergraduate degree from Queens College. He earned his master's and doctorate degrees in economics from Stanford University.

Gilbert L. Rochon is President of Tuskegee University and chairs the Council of 1890 Universities. Dr Rochon received his PhD from Massachusetts Institute of Technology in urban and regional planning, an MPH in health services administration from Yale University School of Medicine, and a bachelor's degree from Xavier University of Louisiana. He directs a NATO Science for Peace Project for real-time remote sensing for disaster early warning in Morocco and is an Adjunct Professor of Natural Resources/Environmental Management at Mae Fah Luang University in Thailand. He also serves on the Technology Advisory Committee for South Africa's Centre for High Performance Computing in Cape Town. Previously, Dr Rochon served as Director of Purdue Terrestrial Observatory, Senior Research Scientist at the Rosen Center for Advanced Computing and Associate Vice-President Collaborative Research & Engagement at Purdue University. He has held a Conrad Hilton endowed Chair at Dillard University and several national and international fellowships.

Henry Louis Taylor, Jr, a historian/urban planner, is a full professor in the University at Buffalo Department of Urban and Regional Planning and is founding director of the UB Center for Urban Studies. Professor Taylor is one of the leading authorities on distressed urban neighbourhoods in the United States. Professor Taylor's resource focuses on urban studies, anchor institutions and the rebuilding of neighbourhoods in a metropolitan context. He has written and/or edited five books and published more than 90 articles, book reviews, commentaries and technical reports. Professor Taylor is also the planning co-ordinator for the Buffalo Municipal Housing Perry Choice neighbourhood revitalisation project, funded by the US Department of Housing and Urban Development.

Thierno Thiam is Special Assistant to the President for Global Initiatives and Assistant Professor of Political Science at Tuskegee University. Dr Thiam joined Tuskegee University in December 2010 from the Institute for State Effectiveness (ISE) based in Washington DC. The ISE blends conceptual thought, analysis and direct experience to rethink relations between citizen, state and market in the globalised world. Dr Thiam's academic activities span across several major universities including Howard University, where he taught the Graduate Seminar in Comparative Politics, the University of Maryland – College Park, where he taught the Politics of Africa, and Purdue University where he taught courses in International Relations. Dr Thiam holds a PhD in Political Science with a focus on International Relations and Comparative Politics from Purdue University.

Srbijanka Turajlić was born in Belgrade and obtained all her degrees (Dip.Ing, MSc and PhD) from the School of Electrical Engineering at the University of Belgrade. She spent her professional life lecturing control theory at the University of Belgrade, with occasional visiting professorships in the region and the USA. In the mid-1990s she focused her interest on the area of higher education. In March 2003 Dr Turajlić was appointed the holder of the UNESCO Chair for the Development of Education. From March 2001 till March 2004 she served as the Deputy Minister for Education of the Republic of Serbia, and was in charge of steering the higher education reform process.

Bert Vandenkendelaere was the Chairperson of the European Students' Union (www.esu-online.org) for the academic year 2010/11. He graduated as Master of Law at the Catholic University of Leuven and did a part of his studies at the Università degli Studi di Firenze. He was vice-chair of the Leuven Student Council, treasurer of VVS (the National Union of Students in Flanders) and member of ESU's Executive Committee before starting his mandate as chair. He is currently employed as Business Development Manager at a Belgian multinational.

Giedrius Viliūnas has been Vice-Rector for Education at Mykolas Romeris University in Vilnius since 2010. Between 2006 and 2010 he was head of the Department of Research Policy at the Research Council of Lithuania, and adviser to the Minister Secretary of the Ministry of Education and Science of Lithuania. From 1989 to 2007 he taught Lithuanian literature at Vilnius University. He graduated from Vilnius University in 1986 and presented his doctoral dissertation at the same university in 1990. Giedrius Viliūnas has published and edited 10 books and about 30 scholarly papers in literary scholarship, research and higher education policy.

Martina Vukasović is a doctoral student at the Department of Educational Research, Faculty of Education, University of Oslo and NATED – the Norwegian Graduate School in Education. She is also a member of the Higher Education: Institutional Dynamic and Knowledge Cultures research group at the Faculty of Education. In her dissertation she focuses on change in the education function of flagship universities in three countries of the former Yugoslavia in the context of European integration. Prior to starting her PhD, she worked as director and researcher at the Centre for Education Policy. She was Chair of ESIB – the European Students Union in 2001.

Piotr Wilczek is Professor of Comparative Literature and Intellectual History at the Artes Liberales Institute for Interdisciplinary Studies, University of Warsaw. He is also Head of the Collegium Artes Liberales – a liberal arts college at the University of Warsaw. He has been a visiting professor and guest lecturer at numerous British and American universities, including Oxford, Harvard, Boston College, Brown University, Rice University and the University of Chicago. He is an elected member of the Committee for Literary Studies of the Polish Academy of Arts and Sciences and a member of editorial boards of several international academic journals. He has published 10 books and numerous journal articles.

Appendix II: Publications in the Council of Europe higher education series

Series Editor: Sjur Bergan

No. 1: *The university as* res publica – *higher education governance, student participation and the university as a site of citizenship* (2004) Sjur Bergan, Annika Persson, Frank Plantan, Sergiu Musteaţă and Angela Garabagiu
ISBN 978-92-871-5515-1

No. 2: *The public responsibility for higher education and research* (2005) Luc Weber and Sjur Bergan (eds)
ISBN 978-92-871-5679-4

No. 3: *Standards for recognition: the Lisbon Recognition Convention and its subsidiary texts* (2005) Sjur Bergan and Andrejs Rauhvargers (eds)
ISBN 978-92-871-5903-3 (ISBN 978-92-871-5902-1 French version)

No. 4: *Recognition in the Bologna Process: policy development and the road to good practice* (2006) Sjur Bergan and Andrejs Rauhvargers (eds)
ISBN 978-92-871-6007-4

No. 5: *Higher education governance: between democratic culture, academic aspirations and market forces* (2006) Jürgen Kohler, Josef Huber and Sjur Bergan (eds)
ISBN 978-92-871-5957-2

No. 6: *Qualifications: introduction to a concept* (2007) Sjur Bergan
ISBN 978-92-871-6125-3

No. 7: *The heritage of European universities*, 2nd edn (2007) Nuria Sanz and Sjur Bergan (eds)
ISBN 978-92-871-6121-5 (ISBN 978-92-871-6120-8 French version)

No. 8: *Higher education and democratic culture: citizenship, human rights and civic responsibility* (2008) Josef Huber and Ira Harkavy (eds)
ISBN 978-92-871-6274-8

No. 9: *The legitimacy of quality assurance in higher education* (2008) Luc Weber and Katia Dolgova-Dreyer (eds)
ISBN 978- 92-871-6237-3

No. 10: *New challenges in recognition* (2008) Andrejs Rauhvargers and Sjur Bergan (eds)
ISBN 978-92-871-6331-8

No. 11: *Intercultural dialogue on Campus* (2009) Sjur Bergan and Jean-Philippe Restoueix (eds)
ISBN 978-92-871-6503-9 (ISBN 978-92-871-6502-2 French version)

No. 12: *Improving recognition in the European Higher Education Area: an analysis of national action plans* (2010) Andrejs Rauhvargers and Agnese Rusakova
ISBN 978-92-871-6648-7

No. 13: *Developing attitudes to recognition: substantial differences in an age of globalisation* (2010) E. Stephen Hunt and Sjur Bergan (eds)
ISBN 978-92-871-6697-5

No. 14: *Advancing democratic practice: a self-assessment guide for higher education* (2010) Douglas Barrera and Virgílio Meira Soares
ISBN 978-92-871-6663-0

No. 15: *Higher education for modern societies: competences and values* (2010) Sjur Bergan and Radu Damian (eds)
ISBN 978-92-871-6777-4

No. 16: *Speaking across borders: the role of higher education in furthering intercultural dialogue* (2010) Sjur Bergan and Hilligje van't Land (eds)
ISBN 978-92-871-6941-9

No. 17: *Not by bread alone* (2011) Sjur Bergan
ISBN 978-92-871-6971-6

No. 18: *Reimagining democratic societies – A new era of personal and social responsibility* (2012) Sjur Bergan, Ira Harkavy and Hilligje van't Land (eds)
ISBN 978-92-871-7537-3